naked economics

naked economics

Undressing the Dismal Science

CHARLES WHEELAN

Foreword by Burton G. Malkiel

W. W. Norton & Company
New York • London

The text of this book is composed in Janson with the display set in Helvetica
Composition by Julia Druskin
Manufacturing by Courier Westford
Book design by BTDnyc
Production manager: Julia Druskin

Library of Congress Cataloging-in-Publication Data
Wheelan, Charles J.
   Naked economics : undressing the dismal science / Charles Wheelan ;
   foreword by Burton G. Malkiel.
     p. cm.
   Includes bibliographical references and index.
   ISBN 0-393-04982-5
   1. Economics. I. Title.

HB171 .W54 2002
330—dc21   2002023580

W. W. Norton & Company, Inc., 500 Fifth Avenue, New York, N.Y. 10110
www.wwnorton.com

W. W. Norton & Company Ltd., Castle House, 75/76 Wells Street,
London W1T 3QT

1 2 3 4 5 6 7 8 9 0

For Leah

Contents

Foreword
by Burton G. Malkiel

t is widely believed that Scotsman Thomas Carlyle labeled economics the "dismal science" well over one hundred years ago because it seemed boring, uninteresting, unclear, and full of "on the one hand, on the other hand." Indeed, Harry Truman is reported to have said that to avoid ambiguity, he wanted to have "one-armed economists." In fact, Carlyle had something very different in mind. What Carlyle reminded us was that scarcity was pervasive—that we have to make choices between competing satisfactions, between jam today and jam tomorrow, and between conflicting values and goals. Above all, the dour Scot emphasized that everything has a cost and nothing can be produced without work and sacrifice.

To be sure, many people do believe that economics and economists are dismal in the popular sense, that is, extraordinarily dull. As one definition goes: "An economist is someone who is good with numbers but does not have the personality to be an accountant." The tarnished image of economists is in large part earned by their tendency to opaque writing, their use of often inscrutable diagrams, and their excessive use of mathematics. Moreover, they often fail to admit what they don't know.

Why is economics the butt of so many jokes, and why do students often become glassy-eyed when confronted with the study of economics as a discipline? The reasons, I think, are that economists generally do not write well and that most economics texts rely far too much on algebraic manipulation and complex diagrams. Moreover, few economists are able to transmit the considerable excitement of economic analysis or to show its relevance to everyday life. This book by Charles Wheelan changes all that. Wheelan has an anti-Midas touch. If he touched gold he would turn it to life.

This is a truly unique book. It contains no equations, no inaccessible jargon, and no inscrutable diagrams. While equations and diagrams may well be behind many of the ideas in economics, Wheelan shows that they can be reduced to plain English. He boils economics down to its essentials. He demonstrates that the term "lucid economist" is not an oxymoron.

In these pages, we see how many of the criticisms of economists are undeserved. Economic analysis is a hard and complex subject—in many cases far more complex than analysis in the physical sciences. Physics can elegantly explain simple contained systems such as the planets revolving around the sun or electrons in orbit around an atom. But even the physical sciences have difficulty understanding phenomena in nature. Weather forecasting is a case in point. Despite complex satellite observations and intricate weather forecasting models, meteorologists often cannot improve on very naive forecasting models such as "The weather tomorrow will be exactly like it is today." To be sure, the inertia model misses all the turning points but retains an excellent overall record. And when forecasters are asked to make longer-run projections on such subjects as global warming, their range of forecasts makes economic forecasts appear precise by comparison.

Economics is more difficult than the physical sciences because we cannot usually run controlled laboratory experiments and because people do not always behave predictably. A whole new branch of behavioral economics has attracted considerable attention by combining the insights of psychologists and economists, but we still are unable to predict individual behavior with any precision. But that we are far from understanding everything does not mean that we understand nothing. We do know that individual behavior is strongly influenced by incentives. We do know that there are many logical regularities, and we have enjoyed a steady accumulation of knowledge. We do know that every sale involves a purchase and that obvious opportunities for profit are rarely over-looked—the basic idea behind the theory that our securities markets are remarkably efficient.

And as inexact as economic science may be, it has a direct impact on our lives and it has a critical role to play in government policymaking. Economists influence all branches of government. The tasks of promoting economic growth and high employment while avoiding inflation have long been recognized as the domain of government economists. Remember Bill Clinton's most successful campaign slogan during the 1992 election? "It's the economy, stupid!" Promoting competition and restraining monopolies (Justice Department), limiting pollution (Environmental Protection Agency), and providing medical care (Health and Human Services) are examples of major activities within different cabinet departments that have crucially important economic components. Indeed, it is hard to think of any political decisions, be they on social, tax and expenditure, international, agricultural, or national security issues, that do not have economic consequences. And however skeptical politicians may be about the ability of economists to solve these problems, the economists' advice is not ignored. Indeed, as John Maynard Keynes once wrote, "Practical men, who believe themselves to be quite exempt from any intellectual influence, are usually the slaves of some defunct economist. Madmen in authority, who hear voices in the air, are distilling their frenzy from some academic scribbler of a few years back."

The influence of economists is also increasingly pervasive in the business and financial communities. Peter Lynch, the former manager of Fidelity's Magellan mutual fund, once opined that if you spent fourteen minutes talking to an economist you would have wasted twelve minutes. Perhaps it is ironic that the investment performance of professional mutual fund managers is now regularly evaluated based on techniques developed by financial economists. Moreover, economists influence countless other business decisions. They project product demand for companies as diverse as General Motors and Procter & Gamble. They are employed in large numbers by consulting firms engaged in business tasks from strategic planning to inventory control. They help investment firms fashion portfolios of securities by analyzing the trade-offs between expected return and risk. They advise chief financial officers of corporations on dividend policy and on the effect of debt on the price of the firm's common stock. In our financial markets, option traders on the floors of the major options exchanges carry hand-held computers programmed with an economic model to tell them the prices at which they should trade put and call options. The fact is that economic analysis is incredibly useful for investors and producers as well as for government policymakers.

Ordinary consumers will also find that economics can illuminate many perplexing everyday issues. Why is it so hard for individuals to buy health insurance? Why do we stop at McDonald's along a highway even though many other establishments may make better hamburgers? Why do so many people apply to "prestige" colleges even though many other institutions offer just as good an education at far lower prices? Have you ever wondered what such common terms as "adverse selection," "public goods," and "the prisoner's dilemma" have to do with everyday life? These are among the subjects treated in this delightful book.

It's often said that if you ask ten economists the same question you will get ten different answers. But I'll wager that if you asked ten economists why there is a shortage of cabs and apartments in New York City, all ten would tell you that limitations on the number of taxi medallions and rent control are what restrict the supply of these goods and services. There are certainly many areas where economists are in virtual unanimous agreement. Economists overwhelmingly agree that free international trade can improve the standard of living of the trading countries and that tariffs and import quotas reduce general welfare. Economists generally agree that rent controls reduce the volume and quality of housing. Economists were virtually unanimous in their forecast that the horrific tragedy of September 11, 2001, would lead to a contraction of economic activity. My own experience in government suggests that there is far less difference in the views of economists (be they conservative Republicans or liberal Democrats) than there is between economists and those who come from different disciplines. Economists of contrasting political views agree among themselves on most issues. A bipartisan majority of economists is quite likely to unite on the opposite side of a bipartisan coalition of politicians.

The reason, I believe, is that economists have a unique way of viewing the world and thinking about how to solve problems. Thinking like an economist involves chains of deductive reasoning in conjunction with simplified models such as supply and demand. It involves identifying tradeoffs in the context of constraints. It measures the cost of one choice in terms of the foregone benefits of another. It involves the goal of efficiency—that is, getting the most out of limited resources. It takes a marginalist or incremental approach. It asks how much extra benefit can be achieved by incurring some extra cost. It recognizes that resources have many diverse uses and that substitutions can be made among different resources to achieve desired results. Finally, the economist has a predilection to believe that welfare is increased by allowing individuals to make their own choices and to argue that competitive markets are a particularly efficient mechanism for giving expression to individual choices. And while all economic problems involve normative issues (views about what should be), thinking like an economist involves an analytical approach that usually abstracts from or at least downplays "value" issues.

This gem of a book is both well balanced and extremely comprehensive. It recognizes the benefits of the free market in making our lives better and shows why centrally controlled economies ultimately fail to increase the living standards of their citizens. At the same time it recognizes the crucial role of government in creating the legal framework that makes markets possible and in providing public goods. It also understands the role of government in correcting situations when the free market creates undesirable externalities such as environmental pollution or where private markets will fail to produce some of the goods the country's citizens desire.

Did you ever wonder why mohair farmers earned a subsidy from the federal government for decades? Wheelan explains how politics and economics can lead to such results. Do you really understand why Alan Greenspan is often referred to as the second most powerful person in the United States? Wheelan demystifies the effect of monetary policy on economic activity. Did you ever consider that you never fully understood the final scene from the movie *Trading Places* when the bad guys were wiped out in the commodities futures market? Wheelan makes the theory of supply and demand completely accessible. Have you ever wondered if the people who protest against globalization have a good point and whether either the developed or developing nations would be better off with less economic integration? Wheelan will make the issues crystal-clear. When you read the newspapers about disputes concerning current economic issues, are you often perplexed and dismayed at the cacophony of competing arguments? Wheelan parses the jargon and pierces the politics to lay bare the essential issues. In so doing, he successfully transforms the dismal science into a lively weaving of economics and politics into the fabric of national discourse and policy.

Wheelan has produced a delightfully readable guide to economic literacy. By boiling economics down to its essentials, he makes the reader a more informed citizen who can better understand the major economic issues of the day. He shows that economics can be explained without graphs, charts, and equations. He demonstrates that economic analysis can be intensely interesting. The book should provide a useful supplement for the college and high school basic course on the economy. More important, it can stand on its own as an introduction to the field that will change the views of those people who have rejected the study of economics as incredibly tedious and terminally boring. I have often considered writing a basic introduction to economics myself, but competing projects always intervened. Had I done so, this is the book I would have wanted to write.

BURTON G. MALKIEL
Princeton, New Jersey
December 2001

Introduction

The scene is strikingly familiar. At a large American university, a graduate student stands at the front of a grand lecture hall drawing graphs and equations on a chalkboard. He may speak proficient English; he may not. The material is dry and mathematical. Come exam time, students may be asked to derive a demand curve or differentiate a total cost function. This is Economics 101.

Students are rarely asked, as they might be, why basic economics made the collapse of the Soviet Union inevitable (allocating resources without a price system is overwhelmingly difficult in the long run), what economic benefit smokers provide for nonsmokers (they die earlier, leaving more Social Security and pension benefits for the rest of us), or why mandating more generous maternity leave benefits may actually be detrimental to women (employers may discriminate against young women when hiring).

Some students will stick with the discipline long enough to appreciate "the big picture." The vast majority will not. Indeed, most bright, intellectually curious college students suffer through Econ 101, are happy to pass, and then wave goodbye to the subject forever. Economics is filed away with calculus and chemistry—rigorous subjects that required a lot of memorization and have little to do with anything that will come later in life. And, of course, a lot of bright students avoid the course in the first place. This is a shame on two levels.

First, many intellectually curious people are missing a subject that is provocative, powerful, and highly relevant to almost every aspect of our lives. Economics offers insight into policy problems ranging from organ donation to affirmative action. The discipline is intuitive at times and delightfully counterintuitive at others. It is peppered with great thinkers. Some, such as Adam Smith and Milton Friedman, have captured mainstream attention. But others, such as Gary Becker and George Akerlof, have not gotten the recognition outside of academe that they deserve. Too many people who would gladly curl up with a book on the Civil War or a biography of Samuel Johnson have been scared away from a subject that should be accessible and fascinating.

Second, many of our brightest citizens are economically illiterate. The media are full of references to the powerful Alan Greenspan. But how many people can explain what exactly he does? Even many of our political leaders could use a dose of Econ 101. When Ross Perot asserted in the 1992 presidential debates that the North American Free Trade Agreement would lead to a "giant sucking sound" as jobs moved from the United States to Mexico, he was wrong. In fact, he was laughably wrong. His statement was the economic equivalent of warning that the U.S. Navy was at risk of sailing over the edge of the world. The problem was, not many Americans were laughing (at least not at his economic policies).

The Perot campaign was, as he might have put it, "a dog that didn't hunt." But that does not mean that those world leaders who do get themselves elected have a solid grasp of basic economics. The French government has undertaken a program to tackle chronic double-digit unemployment with a policy that is the economic equivalent of fool's gold. The Socialist-led government has lowered the maximum workweek from thirty-nine hours to thirty-five hours; the supposed logic is that if all people with jobs work fewer hours, then there will be work left over for the unemployed to do. The policy does have a certain intuitive appeal; then again, so does using leeches to suck toxins out of the body. Sadly, neither leeches nor a shorter workweek will cause anything but harm in the long run.

The French policy is based on the fallacy that there are a fixed number of jobs in the economy, which must therefore be rationed. It's utter nonsense. The American economy has created millions of new jobs over the last decade—all without the government trying to divvy up work hours.

Which is not to say that America doesn't have its own economic issues to deal with. Antiglobalization protesters first took to the streets in Seattle in 1999, smashing windows and overturning cars to protest a meeting of the World Trade Organization. Were the protesters right? Will globalization and burgeoning world trade ruin the environment, exploit workers in the developing world, and put a McDonald's on every corner? Or was *New York Times* columnist Thomas Friedman closer to the mark when he called the protesters "a Noah's ark of flat-earth advocates, protectionist trade unions and yuppies looking for their 1960's fix"?[1] After Chapter 11, you can decide.

I offer only one promise in this book: There will be no graphs, no charts, and no equations. These tools have their place in economics. Indeed, mathematics can offer a simple, even elegant way of representing the world—not unlike telling someone that it is seventy-two degrees outside rather than having to describe how warm or cool it feels. But at bottom, the most important ideas in economics are intuitive. They derive their power from bringing logic and rigor to bear on everyday problems. Consider a thought exercise proposed by Glenn Loury, a theoretical economist at Boston University: Suppose that ten job applicants are vying for a single position. Nine of the job candidates are white and one is black. The hiring company has an affirmative action policy stipulating that when minority and nonminority candidates are of equal merit, the minority candidate will be hired.

Further suppose that there are two top candidates; one is white, the other is black. True to policy, the firm hires the black candidate. Loury (who is black) makes this subtle but simple point: Only one of the white candidates has suffered from affirmative action; the other eight wouldn't have gotten the job anyway. *Yet all nine white candidates go away angry, feeling that they have been discriminated against.* Loury is not necessarily a foe of affirmative action. He merely adds nuance to a discussion that usually has none. Affirmative action can harm the very race relations that it seeks to heal.

Or consider the recent legislative campaign to mandate that insurance companies cover the cost of two nights in the hospital for women who have delivered babies, rather than just one. President Clinton found this issue sufficiently important that he vowed in his 1998 State of the Union address to end "drive-by deliveries." But there is a cost to such a plan that should be made explicit. An extra night in the hospital is not medically necessary in most cases, but it is expensive, which is why new parents don't pay for it themselves and insurance companies don't want to pay for it either. If insurance companies are forced to offer this benefit (or any other new benefit mandated by law), then they will recover their extra costs by raising premiums. And when premiums go up, some people on the margin will no longer be able to afford any health insurance at all. So the real policy question is: Are we willing to pass a law that will make many women more comfortable if it means that a much smaller number of men and women will lose coverage for basic care?

Is economics one big advertisement for the Republican Party? Not exactly. Even Milton Friedman, a Nobel laureate in economics and the most articulate spokesman for free markets, would concede that unfettered markets can lead to deeply flawed outcomes. Consider the American lust for the automobile. The problem is not that we like cars; the problem is that we don't have to pay the full cost of driving them. Yes, we buy the car and then pay for maintenance, insurance, and gasoline. But we don't have to pay for some of the other significant costs of our driving: the emissions we leave behind, the congestion we cause, the wear and tear on public roads, the danger we pose to drivers in smaller cars. The effect is a bit like a night on the town with Dad's credit card: We do a lot of things that we wouldn't do if we had to pay the whole bill. We drive huge cars, we avoid public transportation, we move to far-flung suburbs and then commute long distances.

Individuals don't get the bill for this behavior, but society does—in the form of air pollution, global warming, and urban sprawl. The best way to deal with this growing problem is not the stuff that laissez-faire conservatives usually talk about. It is higher taxes on gasoline and cars.

Only with those kinds of measures, as we shall explore in Chapter 3, will the cost of climbing behind the wheel of a car (or a hulking SUV) reflect the real social cost of that activity. Similarly, larger subsidies for public transportation would properly reward those commuters who spare the rest of us by not getting into their cars.

Meanwhile, economists have done some of the most substantive work on social issues like discrimination. Have the world's symphony orchestras historically discriminated against women? Harvard economist Claudia Goldin and Princeton economist Cecilia Rouse came up with a novel way of finding out. In the 1950s, American orchestras began to use "blind" auditions, meaning that the aspiring orchestra member would perform behind screens. Judges did not know the identity or gender of the musician trying out. Did women do better under this blind system than they did when judges knew their gender? Yes, decidedly so. Once the auditions became anonymous, women were roughly 50 percent more likely to make it past the first round and several times more likely to make the final cut.[2]

Economics presents us with a powerful, and not necessarily complex, set of analytical tools that can be used to look back and explain why events unfolded the way they did; to look around and make sense of the world; and to look forward so that we can anticipate the effects of major policy changes. Economics is like gravity: Ignore it and you will be in for some rude surprises. Take the savings and loan crisis. For many years, America's savings and loans were heavily regulated institutions. They were restricted in terms of how much interest they could pay to depositors as well as what kind of investments they could make with their depositors' funds (very conservative). Meanwhile, depositors' funds were insured by the federal government. The industry was profitable, if not particularly exciting. In his excellent book *Liar's Poker*, Michael Lewis described S&L executives as members of the 3-6-3 club: Borrow money at 3 percent, lend it out at 6 percent, and be on the golf course every afternoon by three o'clock.

In the early 1980s, the industry was partially deregulated. Savings and loans were freed to invest in a broader—and far riskier—range of investments. Yet the government insurance on deposits stayed in place. The partial deregulation created a scenario best described as "heads I win, tails the government loses." S&L executives could take big gambles with their depositors' money. If they won big, they would keep most of the spoils, since they owed their depositors only a fixed rate of interest. If they lost, they could go bust and have the federal government pay off their depositors. Is this a combination likely to encourage responsible behavior? Of course not. Savings and loans became involved in bad real estate deals, junk bonds, mortgage-backed securities, and a host of other risky investments that left many of them bankrupt. In the end, the government shut down 747 institutions and reimbursed depositors $155 billion. The most amazing thing about the whole debacle was that it was so predictable.

This book walks through some of the most powerful concepts in economics while simplifying the building blocks or skipping them entirely. Each chapter covers subjects that could be made into an entire book. Indeed, there are minor points in every chapter that have launched and sustained entire academic careers. I have glossed over or skipped much of the technical structure that forms the backbone of the discipline. And that is exactly the point: One need not know where to place a load-bearing wall in order to appreciate the genius of Frank Lloyd Wright. This book is not economics for dummies; it is economics for smart people who never studied economics (or have only a vague recollection of doing so). Most of the great ideas in economics are intuitive when the dressings of complexity are peeled away. *That is naked economics.*

Economics should not be accessible only to the experts. The ideas are too important and too interesting. Indeed, naked economics can even be fun.

Acknowledgments

Many waves of people have helped to bring this project to fruition, almost like a relay race with fresh legs pushing me toward the finish line at every stage. In the beginning, Tifanny Richards was a strong believer that there would be a market for an accessible book on economics. Her wonderful encouragement moved this book off the starting line. Tabitha Griffin brought the project to W. W. Norton, something for which I will always be grateful.

Then came the second leg. When Tifanny and Tabitha went on to other opportunities, I was fortunate to end up in excellent hands once again. Tina Bennett is everything that one could hope for in an agent: smart, supportive, and always interested in new ideas. Meanwhile, I was lucky to have Drake McFeely take on the task of editing the book. Who knows how the man can find time to run the company, edit books, and cavort with Nobel Prize winners, but he does and I am a beneficiary of his experience and judgment. Of course, Eve Lazovitz is the one who makes Drake's trains run on time, albeit with a delicate touch. Without their support (and deadlines), this book would have been finished somewhere around 2008.

As the finish line became visible, Mary Ellen Moore offered excellent research assistance, finding the facts, figures, and anecdotes that had eluded me. Three accomplished economists were kind enough to take time from their busy schedules to read the manuscript and make helpful comments: Burton Malkiel, Robert Willis, and Kenneth Rogoff. These three men are giants of the profession, and each had many other things that they might have done with their time.

I owe a debt to my editors at *The Economist*. John Micklethwait was generous in allowing me to disappear for a stretch while I finished the book and was also willing to read and make comments on the finished product. I owe Ann Wroe credit for her clever subtitle. The fact that both John and Ann find time to edit one of the world's great publications while also raising families and writing books of their own continues to be an inspiration.

I also owe a different kind of debt. The vast majority of ideas I describe in this book are not my own. Rather, I am a translator whose work derives its value from the brilliance of the original, which in this case is centuries of work done by great thinkers. I hope this book reflects my enormous respect for that work.

Last, I would like to acknowledge those who inspired my interest in the subjects that make up this book. I've made the case that economics is often poorly taught. That is true. But it's also true that the discipline can come alive in the hands of the right person, and I was fortunate to work and study with many of them: Gary Becker, Bob Willis, Ken Rogoff, Robert Willig, Christina Paxson, Duncan Snidal, Alan Krueger, Paul Portney, Sam Peltzman, Don Coursey, Paul Volcker. My hope is that this book will help to transmit their knowledge and enthusiasm to many new readers and students.

naked economics

CHAPTER 1

The Power of Markets:
Who feeds Paris?

n 1989, as the Berlin Wall was toppling, Douglas Ivester, head of Coca-Cola Europe (and later CEO), made a snap decision. He sent his sales force to Berlin and told them to start passing out Coke. Free. In some cases, the Coca-Cola representatives were literally passing bottles of soda through holes in the Wall. He recalls walking around Alexanderplatz in East Berlin at the time of the upheaval, trying to gauge whether there was any recognition of the Coke brand. "Everywhere we went, we asked people what they were drinking, and whether they liked Coca-Cola. But we didn't even have to say the name! We just shaped our hands like the bottle, and people understood. We decided we would move as much Coca-Cola as we could, as fast as we could—even before we knew how we would get paid."[1]

Coca-Cola quickly set up business in East Germany, giving free coolers to merchants who began to stock the "real thing." It was a money-losing proposition in the short run; the East German currency was still worthless—scraps of paper to the rest of the world. But it was a brilliant business decision made faster than any government body could ever hope to act. By 1995, per capita consumption of Coca-Cola in the former East Germany had risen to the level in West Germany, which was already a strong market.

In a sense, it was Adam Smith's invisible hand passing Coca-Cola through the Berlin Wall. Coke representatives weren't undertaking any great humanitarian gesture as they passed beverages to the newly liberated East Germans. Nor were they making a bold statement about the future of communism. They were looking after business—expanding their global market, boosting profits, and making shareholders happy. And that is the punch line of capitalism: The market aligns incentives in such a way that individuals working for their own best interest—passing out Coca-Cola, spending years in graduate school, planting a field of soybeans, designing a radio that will work in the shower—leads to a thriving and ever-improving standard of living for most (though not all) members of society.

Economists sometimes ask, "Who feeds Paris?"—a rhetorical way of drawing attention to the mind-numbing array of things happening every moment of every day to make a modern economy work. Somehow the right amount of fresh tuna makes its way from a fishing fleet in the South Pacific to a restaurant on the Rue de Rivoli. A neighborhood fruit vendor has exactly what his customers want every morning—from coffee to fresh papayas—even though those products may come from ten or fifteen different countries. In short, a complex economy involves billions of transactions every day, the vast majority of which happen without any direct government involvement. And it is not just that things get done; our lives grow steadily better in the process. It is remarkable enough that we can now shop for a television twenty-four hours a day from the comfort of our own homes; it is equally amazing that in 1971 a twenty-five-inch color television set cost an average worker 174 hours of wages. Today, a twenty-five-inch color television set—one that is more dependable, gets more channels, and has better reception—costs the average worker about twenty-three hours of pay.[2]

If you think that a better, cheaper television set is not the best measure of social progress (a reasonable point, I concede), then perhaps you will be moved by the fact that during the twentieth century, American life expectancy climbed from forty-seven years to seventy-seven, infant mortality plunged by 93 percent, and we wiped out or gained control over diseases such as polio, tuberculosis, typhoid, and whooping cough.[3]

Our market economy deserves a lot of the credit for that progress.

There is an old pre–Cold War story about a Soviet official who visits an American pharmacy. The brightly lit aisles are lined with thousands of remedies for every problem from bad breath to toe fungus. "Very impressive," he says. "But how can you make sure that every store stocks all of these items?" The anecdote is interesting because it betrays a total lack of understanding of how a market economy works. In America, there is no central authority that tells stores what items to stock, as there was in the Soviet Union. Stores sell the products that people want to buy, and, in turn, companies produce items that stores want to stock. The Soviet economy failed in large part because government bureaucrats directed everything, from the number of bars of soap produced by a factory in Irktusk to the number of university students studying electrical engineering in Moscow. In the end, the task proved overwhelming.

Of course, those of us accustomed to market economies have an equally poor understanding of communist central planning. I was recently part of an Illinois delegation visiting Cuba. Because the visit was licensed by the U.S. government, each member of the delegation was allowed to bring back $100 worth of Cuban merchandise, including cigars. Having been raised in the era of discount stores, we all set out looking for the best price on Cohibas so that we could get the most bang for our $100 allowance. After several fruitless hours, we discovered the whole point of communism: The price of cigars was the same everywhere. There is no competition between stores because there is no profit as we know it. Every store sells cigars—and everything else for that matter—at whatever price Fidel tells them to. And every shopkeeper selling cigars is paid the government wage for selling cigars, which is unrelated to how many cigars he or she sells.

Gary Becker, a University of Chicago economist who won the Nobel Prize in 1992, has noted (borrowing from George Bernard Shaw) that "economy is the art of making the most of life." Economics is the study of how we do that. There is a finite supply of everything worth having: oil, coconut milk, perfect bodies, clean water, people who can fix jammed photocopy machines, etc. How do we allocate these things? Why is it that Bill Gates owns a private jet and you don't? He is rich, you might answer. But why is he rich? Why does he have a larger claim on the world's finite resources than everyone else? At the same time, how is it possible in a country as rich as the United States—a place where Alex Hernandez can be paid $250 million to play baseball—that one in five children is poor or that some adults are forced to rummage through garbage cans for food? Near my home in Chicago, the Three Dog Bakery sells cakes and pastries *only for dogs*. Wealthy professionals pay $16 for birthday cakes for their pets. Meanwhile, the Chicago Coalition for the Homeless estimates that fifteen thousand people are homeless on any given night in that same city.

These kinds of disparities grow even more pronounced as we look beyond the borders of the United States. Three-quarters of the people in Chad have no access to clean drinking water, let alone pastries for their pets. The World Bank estimates that half of the world's population survives on less than $2 a day. How does it all work—or, in some cases, not work?

Economics starts with one very important assumption: Individuals act to make themselves as well off as possible. To use the jargon of the profession, individuals seek to maximize their own utility, which is a similar concept to happiness, only broader. I derive utility from getting a typhoid immunization and paying taxes. Neither of these things makes me particularly happy, but they do keep me from dying of typhoid or going to jail. That, in the long run, makes me better off. Economists don't particularly care what gives us utility; they simply accept that each of us has his or her own "preferences." I like coffee, old houses, classic films, dogs, bicycling, and many other things. Everyone else in the world has preferences, which may or may not have anything in common with mine.

Indeed, this seemingly simple observation that different individuals have different preferences is sometimes lost on otherwise sophisticated policymakers. For example, rich people have different preferences than poor people do. Similarly, our individual preferences may change over the course of our life cycle as we (we hope) grow wealthier. The phrase "luxury good" actually has a technical meaning to economists; it is a good that we buy in increasing quantities as we grow richer—things like sports cars and French wines. Less obviously, concern for the environment is a luxury good. Wealthy Americans are willing to spend more money to protect the environment *as a fraction of their incomes* than are less wealthy Americans. The same relationship holds true across countries; wealthy nations devote a greater share of their resources to protecting the environment than do poor countries. The reason is simple enough: We care about the fate of the Bengal tiger *because we can*. We have homes and jobs and clean water and birthday cakes for our dogs.

Here is a nettlesome policy question: Is it fair for those of us who live comfortably to impose our preferences on individuals in the developing world? Economists argue that it is not, though we do it all the time. When I read a story in the Sunday *New York Times* about South American villagers cutting down virgin rain forest and destroying rare ecosystems, I nearly knock over my Starbucks latte in surprise and disgust. But I am not they. My children are not starving or at risk of dying from malaria. If they were, and if chopping down a valuable wildlife habitat enabled me to afford to feed my family and buy a mosquito net, then I would sharpen my ax and start chopping. I wouldn't care how many butterflies or spotted weasels I killed. This is not to suggest that the environment in the developing world does not matter. It does. In fact, there are many examples of environmental degradation that will make poor countries even poorer in the long run. And obviously if the developed world were more generous, then Brazilian villagers might not have to decide between destroying the rain forest and buying mosquito nets. The point here is more basic: It is simply bad economics to impose our preferences on individuals whose lives are much, much different. This will be an important point later in the book when we turn to globalization and world trade.

Let me make one other important point regarding our individual preferences: Maximizing utility is not synonymous with acting selfishly. In 1999, the *New York Times* published the obituary of Oseola McCarty, a woman who died at the age of ninety-one after spending her life working as a laundress in Hattiesburg, Mississippi. She had lived alone in a small, sparsely furnished house with a black-and-white television that received only one channel. What made Ms. McCarty exceptional is that she was by no means poor. In fact, four years before her death she gave away $150,000 to the University of Southern Mississippi—a school that she had never attended—to endow a scholarship for poor students.

Does Oseola McCarty's behavior turn the field of economics on its head? Are Nobel Prizes being recalled to Stockholm? No. She simply derived more utility from saving her money and eventually giving it away than she would have from spending it on a big-screen TV or a fancy apartment. We all routinely make decisions like that, albeit usually on a smaller scale. We may pay a few cents extra for dolphin-safe tuna or send money to a favorite charity. Both of these things can give us utility; neither would be considered selfish. Americans give over $200 billion to assorted charities every year. We hold doors open for strangers. We practice remarkable acts of altruism. None of this is incompatible with the basic assumption that individuals seek to make themselves as well off as possible, however they happen to define that. Nor does this assumption imply that we always make perfect—or even good—decisions. We don't. But each of us does try to make the best possible decision given whatever information is available at the time.

So, after only a few pages, we have an answer to a profound, age-old philosophical question: Why did the chicken cross the road? Because it maximized his utility.

Bear in mind that maximizing utility is no simple proposition. Life is complex and uncertain. There are an infinite number of things that we could be doing at any time. Indeed, every decision that we make involves some kind of trade-off. We may trade off utility now against utility in the future. For example, you may derive some satisfaction from whacking your boss on the head with a canoe paddle at the annual company picnic. But that momentary burst of utility would presumably be more than offset by the disutility of spending many years in a federal prison. (But those are just my preferences.) More seriously, many of our important decisions involve balancing the value of consumption now against consumption in the future. We may spend years in graduate school eating ramen noodles because it dramatically boosts our standard of living later in life. Or, conversely, we may use a credit card to purchase a big-screen television today even though the interest on that credit card debt will lessen the amount that we can consume in the future.

Similarly, we balance work and leisure. Grinding away ninety hours a week as an investment banker will generate a lot of income, but it will also leave less time to enjoy the goods that can be purchased with that income. My twenty-nine-year-old brother is a successful management consultant whose salary has at least one more digit than mine. On the other hand, he works long and sometimes inflexible hours. Last fall, we both excitedly signed up for an evening film class taught by Roger Ebert. My brother proceeded to miss *every single class for thirteen weeks.*

However large our paychecks, we can spend them on a staggering array of goods and services. When you bought this book, you implicitly decided not to spend that money somewhere else. (Even if you shoplifted the book, you could have stuffed a Scott Turow novel in your jacket instead, which is flattering in its own kind of way.) Meanwhile, time is one of our most scarce resources. At the moment, you are reading instead of working, playing with the dog, applying to law school, shopping for groceries, or having sex. Life is about trade-offs, and so is economics.

In short, getting out of bed in the morning and making breakfast involves more complex decisions than the average game of chess. (Will that fried egg kill me in twenty-eight years?) How do we manage? The answer is that each of us implicitly weighs the costs and benefits of everything he or she does. An economist would say that we attempt to maximize utility given the resources at our disposal; my dad would say that we try to get the most bang for our buck. Bear in mind that the things that give us utility do not have to be material goods. If you are comparing two jobs—teaching junior high school math or marketing Camel cigarettes—the latter job would almost certainly pay more while the former job would offer greater "psychic benefits," which is a fancy way of saying that at the end of the day you would feel better about what you do. That is a perfectly legitimate benefit to be compared against the cost of a smaller paycheck. In the end, some people choose to teach math and some people choose to market cigarettes.

Similarly, the concept of cost is far richer (pardon the pun) than the dollars and cents you hand over at the cash register. The real cost of something is what you must give up in order to get it, which is almost always more than just cash. There is nothing "free" about concert tickets if you have to stand in line in the rain for six hours in order to get them. Taking the bus for $1.50 may not be cheaper than taking a taxi for $7 if you are running late for a meeting with a peevish client who will pull a $50,000 account if you keep her waiting. Shopping at a discount store saves money but it usually costs time. I am a writer; I get paid based on what I produce. I could drive ninety miles to shop at an outlet in Kenosha, Wisconsin, to save $50 on a new pair of dress shoes. Or I could walk into Nordstrom on Michigan Avenue and buy the shoes while I am out for lunch. I generally choose the latter; the total cost is $225, fifteen minutes of my time, and some hectoring from my mother, who will invariably ask, "Why didn't you drive to Kenosha?"

Every aspect of human behavior reacts to cost in some way. When the cost of something falls, it becomes more attractive to us. You can learn that by deriving a demand curve, or you can learn it by shopping the day after Christmas, when people snap up things that they weren't willing to buy at full price several days earlier. Conversely, when the cost of something goes up, we use less of it. This is true of everything in life, even cigarettes and crack cocaine. Economists have calculated that a 10 percent decrease in the street price of cocaine eventually causes the number of adult cocaine users to grow by about 10 percent. Similarly, researchers estimated that the first proposed settlement between the tobacco industry and the states (rejected by the U.S. Senate in 1998) would have raised the price of a pack of cigarettes by 34 percent. In turn, that would have reduced the number of teenage smokers by a quarter, leading to 1.3 million fewer smoking-related premature deaths among the generation of Americans seventeen or younger at the time.[4] Of course, society has already raised the cost of smoking in ways that have nothing to do with the price of a pack of cigarettes. Standing outside an office building when it is seventeen degrees outside is now part of the cost of smoking at work.

This broad view of cost can explain some very important social phenomena, one of which is the plummeting birth rate in the industrialized world. Having a child is more expensive than it was fifty years ago. This is not because it is more expensive to feed and clothe another little urchin around the house. If anything, those kinds of costs have gone down, because we have become far more productive at making basic consumer goods like food and clothing. Rather, the primary cost of raising a child today is the cost of the earnings forgone when a parent, still usually the mother, quits or cuts back on work in order to look after the child at home. Because women have better professional opportunities than ever before, it has grown more costly for them to leave the workforce. My neighbor was a neurologist until her second child was born, at which point she decided to stay home. *It's expensive to quit being a neurologist.*

Meanwhile, most of the economic benefits of having a large family have disappeared in the industrialized world. Young children no longer help out on the farm or provide extra income for the family (though they can be taught at a young age to fetch a beer from the refrigerator). We no longer need to have many children in order to ensure that some of them live through childhood or that we have enough dependents to provide for us in retirement. Even the most dour of economists would concede that we derive great pleasure from having children. The point is that it is now more expensive to have eleven of them than it used to be. The data speak to that point: The average American woman had 3.77 children in 1905; she now has 2.07—a 45 percent drop.[5]

There is a second powerful assumption underpinning all of economics: Firms—which can be anything from one guy selling hot dogs to a multinational corporation—attempt to maximize profits (the revenue earned by selling stuff minus the cost of producing it). In short, firms try to make as much money as possible. Hence, we have an answer to another of life's burning questions: Why did the entrepreneur cross the road? Because he could make more money on the other side.

Firms take inputs—land, steel, knowledge, baseball stadiums, etc.—and combine them in a way that adds value. That process can be as simple as selling cheap umbrellas on a busy corner in New York City when it starts to rain (where do those guys come from?) or as complex as assembling an $80 million military helicopter. A profitable firm is like a chef who brings home $30 worth of groceries and creates an $80 meal. She has used her talents to create something that is worth far more than the cost of the inputs. That is not always an easy thing to do. Firms must decide what to produce, how and where to produce it, how much to produce, and at what price to sell what they produce—all in the face of the same kinds of uncertainties that consumers deal with.

How? These are massively complex decisions. One powerful feature of a market economy is that it directs resources to their most productive use. Why doesn't Tom Cruise sell automobile insurance? Because it would be an enormous waste of his unique talents. Yes, he is a charismatic guy who could probably sell more insurance policies than the average salesman. But he is also one of a handful of people in the world who can "open" a movie, meaning that millions of people around the world will go to see a film just because Tom Cruise is in it. That is money in the bank in the risky Hollywood movie business, so studios are willing to pay handsomely to put Tom Cruise in a starring role—about $20 million a film. Insurance agencies would also be willing to pay for the Cruise charisma—but more like $20,000. Tom Cruise will go where he is paid most. And he will be paid most in Hollywood because that is where he can add the most value.

Prices are like giant neon billboards that flash important information. At the beginning of the chapter, we asked how a restaurant on the Rue de Rivoli in Paris has just the right amount of tuna on most nights. It is all about prices. When patrons start ordering more of the sashimi appetizer, the restaurateur places a larger order with his fish wholesaler. If tuna is growing more popular at other restaurants, too, then the wholesale price will go up, meaning that fishermen somewhere in the Pacific will get paid more for their tuna catch than they used to. Some fishermen, recognizing that tuna now commands a premium over other kinds of fish, will start fishing for tuna instead of salmon. Meanwhile, some tuna fishermen will keep their boats in the water longer or switch to more expensive fishing methods that can now be justified by the higher price their catch will fetch. These guys don't care about upscale diners in Paris. They care about the wholesale price of fish.

Money talks. Why are the pharmaceutical companies scouring the rain forests looking for plants with rare healing properties? Because the blockbuster drugs they may uncover earn staggering amounts of money. Other kinds of entrepreneurial activity take place on a smaller scale but are equally impressive in their own way. For several summers I coached a Little League baseball team near Cabrini Green, which is one of Chicago's rougher neighborhoods. One of our team customs was to go out periodically for pizza, and one of our favorite spots was Chester's, a small shack at the corner of Division and Sedgewick that was a testimony to the resiliency and resourcefulness of entrepreneurs. (It has since been demolished to make way for a new park as part of an aggressive development of Cabrini Green.) Chester's made decent pizza and was always busy. Thus, it was basically an armed robbery waiting to happen. But that did not deter the management at Chester's. They merely installed the same kind of bulletproof glass that one would find at the drive-up window of a bank. The customers placed their money on a small carousel, which was then rotated through a gap in the bulletproof glass. The pizza came out the other direction on the same carousel.

Profit opportunities attract firms like sharks to blood, even when bulletproof glass is required. We look for bold new ways to make money (creating *Survivor*); failing that, we look to get into a business that is making huge profits for someone else (thereby creating *Temptation Island*). All the while, we are using prices to gauge what consumers want. Of course, not every market is easy to enter. When Michael Jordan signed a one-year $30 million contract with the Chicago Bulls, I thought to myself, "I need to play basketball for the Chicago Bulls." I would have gladly played for $28 million, or, if pressed, for $28,000. Several things precluded me from entering that market, however: (1) I'm five-ten; (2) I'm slow; and (3) when shooting under pressure, I have a tendency to miss the backboard. Why was Michael Jordan paid $30 million a year? Because nobody else could play like him. His unique talent created a barrier to entry for the rest of us. Michael Jordan is also the beneficiary of what University of Chicago labor economist Sherwin Rosen dubbed the "superstar" phenomenon. Small differences in talent tend to become magnified into huge differentials in pay as a market becomes very large, such as the audience for professional basketball. One need only be slightly better than the competition in order to gain a large (and profitable) share of that market. Katie Couric would be another example. NBC will pay her a reported $60 million over four and a half years to continue as the anchor of the Today Show. She need not be 10 or 20 times better than her competition in order to justify that salary; she need only be a little better, the result being that millions of viewers tune into NBC in the morning rather than a competing channel.

Many markets have barriers that prevent new firms from entering, no matter how profitable making widgets may be. Sometimes there are physical or natural barriers. Truffles cost $500 a pound because they cannot be cultivated; they grow only in the wild and must be dug up by truffle-hunting pigs or dogs. Sometimes there are legal barriers to entry. Don't try to sell sildenafil citrate on a street corner or you may end up in jail. This is not a drug that you snort or shoot up, nor is it illegal. It happens to be Viagra, and Pfizer holds the patent, which is a legal monopoly granted by the U.S. government. Economists may quibble over how long a patent should last or what kinds of innovations should be patentable, but most would agree that the entry barrier created by a patent is an important incentive for firms to make the kinds of investments that lead to new products. The political process creates entry barriers for dubious reasons, too. When the U.S. auto industry was facing intense competition from Japanese automakers in the 1980s, the American car companies had two basic options: (1) They could create better, cheaper, more fuel-efficient cars that consumers might want to buy; or (2) they could invest heavily in lobbyists who would persuade Congress to enact tariffs and quotas that would keep Japanese cars out of the market.

Some entry barriers are more subtle. The airline industry is far less competitive than it appears to be. You and some college friends could start a new airline relatively easily; the problem is that you wouldn't be able to land your planes anywhere. There are a limited number of gate spaces available at most airports, and they tend to be controlled by the big guys. At Chicago's O'Hare Airport, one of the world's biggest and busiest airports, American and United control some 80 percent of all the gates.[6] Or consider a different kind of entry barrier that has become highly relevant in the Internet age: network effects. The basic idea of a network effect is that the value of some goods rises with the number of other people using them. I don't think Microsoft Word is particularly impressive software, but I own it anyway because I spend my days e-mailing documents to people who do like Word (or at least they use it). It would be very difficult to introduce a rival word-processing package—no matter how good the features or how low the price—as long as most of the world is using MS Word.

Meanwhile, firms are not just choosing what goods or services to produce but also how to produce them. I will never forget stepping off a plane in Kathmandu; the first thing I saw was a team of men squatting on their haunches as they cut the airport grass by hand with sickles. Labor is cheap in Nepal; lawn mowers are very expensive. The opposite is true in the United States, which is why we don't see many teams of laborers using sickles. It is also why we have ATMs and self-service gas stations and those terribly annoying phone trees ("If you are now frustrated to the point of violence, please press the pound key"). All are cases where firms have automated jobs that used to be done by living beings. After all, one way to raise profits is by lowering the cost of production. That may mean laying off twenty thousand workers or building a plant in Vietnam instead of Colorado.

Firms, like consumers, face a staggering array of complex choices. Again, the guiding principle is relatively simple: What is going to make the firm the most money in the long run?

All of which brings us to the point where producers meet consumers. How much are you going to pay for that doggie in the window? Introductory economics has a very simple answer: the market price. This is that whole supply and demand thing. The price will settle at the point where the number of dogs for sale exactly matches the number of dogs that consumers want to buy. If there are more potential pet owners than dogs available, then the price of dogs will go up. Some consumers will then decide to buy ferrets instead and some pet shops will offer more dogs for sale. Eventually the supply of dogs will match the demand. Remarkably, some markets actually work this way. If I choose to sell a hundred shares of Microsoft on the NASDAQ, I have no choice but to accept the "market price," which is simply the share price at which the number of Microsoft sellers on the exchange exactly equals the number of buyers.

Most markets do not look quite so much like the textbooks. There is not a "market price" for Gap sweatshirts that changes by the minute depending on the supply and demand of reasonably priced outerwear. Instead, the Gap, like most other firms, has some degree of market power, which means very simply that the Gap has some control over what it can charge. The Gap could sell sweatshirts for $9.99, eking out a razor-thin profit on each. Or it could sell far fewer sweatshirts for $29.99, but make a hefty profit on each. If you were in the mood to do calculus at the moment, or I had any interest in writing about it, then we would find the profit-maximizing price right now. I'm pretty sure I had to do it on a final exam once. The basic point is that the Gap will attempt to pick a price that leads to the quantity of sales that earn the company the most money. The marketing executives may err either way: They may underprice the items, in which case they will sell out; or they may overprice the items, in which case they will have a warehouse full of sweatshirts.

Actually, there is another option. A firm can attempt to sell the same item to different people at different prices. (The fancy name is "price discrimination.") The next time you are on an airplane, try this experiment: Ask the person next to you how much he or she paid for the ticket. It's probably not what you paid; it may not even be close. You are sitting on the same plane, traveling to the same destination, eating the same bad food—yet the prices you and your row mate paid for your tickets may not even have the same number of digits.

The basic challenge for the airline industry is to separate business travelers, who are willing to pay a great deal for a ticket, from pleasure travelers, who are on tighter budgets. If an airline sells every ticket at the same price, the company will leave money on the table no matter what price it chooses. A business traveler may be willing to pay $1,800 to fly round trip from Chicago to San Francisco; someone flying to cousin Irv's wedding will shell out no more than $250. If the airline charges the high fare, it will lose all of its pleasure travelers. If it charges the low fare, it will lose all the profits that business travelers would have been willing to pay. What to do? Learn to distinguish business travelers from pleasure travelers and then charge each of them a different fare.

The airlines are pretty good at this. Why will your fare drop sharply if you stay over a Saturday night? Because Saturday night is when you are going to be dancing at cousin Irv's wedding. Pleasure travelers usually spend the weekend at their destination, while business travelers almost never do. Buying the ticket two weeks ahead of time will be much, much cheaper than buying it eleven minutes before the flight leaves. Vacationers plan ahead while business travelers tend to buy tickets at the last minute. Airlines are the most obvious example of price discrimination, but look around and you will start to see it everywhere. Al Gore complained during the 2000 presidential campaign that his mother and his dog were taking the same arthritis medication but that his mother paid much more for her prescription. Never mind that he made up the story after reading about the pricing disparity between humans and canines. The example is still perfect. There is nothing surprising about the fact that the same medicine will be sold to dogs and people at different prices. It's airline seats all over again. People will pay more for their own medicine than they will for their pet's. So the profit-maximizing strategy is to charge one price for patients with two legs and another price for patients with four.

Price discrimination will become even more prevalent as technology enables firms to gather more information about their customers. It is now possible, for example, to charge different prices to customers ordering on-line rather than over the phone. Or, a firm can charge different prices to different on-line customers depending on the pattern of their past purchases. The logic behind firms like Priceline (a website where consumers bid for travel services) is that every customer could conceivably pay a different price for an airline ticket or hotel room. In an article entitled "How Technology Tailors Price Tags," the *Wall Street Journal* noted recently, "Grocery stores appear to be the model of one price for all. But even today, they post one price, charge another to shoppers willing to clip coupons and a third to those with frequent-shopper cards that allow stores to collect detailed data on buying habits."[7]

What can we infer from all of this? Consumers try to make themselves as well off as possible and firms try to maximize profits. Those are seemingly simple concepts, yet they can tell us a tremendous amount about how the world works.

The market economy is a powerful force for making our lives better. The only way firms can make profits is by delivering goods that we want to buy. They create new products—everything from thermal coffee mugs to lifesaving antibiotics. Or they take an existing product and make it cheaper or better. This kind of competition is fabulously good for consumers. In 1900, a three-minute phone call from New York to Chicago cost about $5.45. Now it costs less than a quarter. Profit inspires some of our greatest work, even in areas like higher education, the arts, and medicine. How many world leaders fly to North Korea when they need open-heart surgery?

At the same time, the market is amoral. Not immoral, simply amoral. The market rewards scarcity, which has no inherent relation to value. Diamonds are worth thousands of dollars a carat while water (if you are bold enough to drink it out of the tap) is nearly free. If there were no diamonds on the planet, we would be inconvenienced; if all the water disappeared, we would be dead. The market does not provide goods that we need; it provides goods that *we want to buy*. This is a crucial distinction. Our medical system does not provide health insurance for the poor. Why? Because they can't pay for it. Our most talented doctors do provide breast enhancements and face tucks for Hollywood stars. Why? Because they can pay for it. Meanwhile, firms can make a lot of money doing nasty things. Why do European crime syndicates kidnap young girls in Eastern Europe and sell them into prostitution in wealthier countries? Because it's profitable. The market is like evolution; it is an extraordinarily powerful force that derives its strength from rewarding the swift, the strong, and the smart. That said, it would be wise to remember that two of the most beautifully adapted species on the planet are the rat and the cockroach.

Our system uses prices to allocate scarce resources. Since there is a finite amount of everything worth having, the most basic function of any economic system is to decide who gets what. Who gets tickets to the Super Bowl? The people who are willing to pay the most. Who had the best seats for the Supreme Soviet Bowl in the old USSR (assuming some such event existed)? The individuals chosen by the Communist Party. Prices had nothing to do with it. If a Moscow butcher received a new shipment of pork, he slapped on the official state price for pork. And if that price was low enough that he had more customers than pork chops, he did not raise the price to earn some extra cash. He merely sold the chops to the first people in line. Those at the end of the line were out of luck. Capitalism and communism both ration goods. We do it with prices; the Soviets did it by waiting in line. (Of course, the communists had many black markets; it is quite likely that the butcher sold extra pork chops illegally out the back door of his shop.)

Because we use price to allocate goods, most markets are self-correcting. Periodically the oil ministers from the OPEC nations will meet in an exotic locale and agree to limit the global production of oil. Several things happen shortly thereafter: (1) Oil and gas prices start to go up; and (2) politicians begin falling all over themselves with ideas, mostly bad, for intervening in the oil market. But high prices are like a fever; they are both a symptom and a potential cure. While politicians are puffing away on the House floor, some other crucial things start to happen. We drive less. We get one heating bill and decide to insulate the attic. We go to the Ford showroom and walk past the Expeditions to the Escorts.

Things start happening on the supply side, too. Oil producers outside of OPEC start pumping more oil to take advantage of the high price; indeed, the OPEC countries usually begin cheating on their own production quotas. Domestic oil companies begin pumping oil from wells that were not economical when the price of petroleum was low. Meanwhile, a lot of very smart people begin working more seriously on finding and commercializing alternative sources of energy. The price of oil and gasoline begins to drift down as supply rises and demand falls.

If we fix prices in a market system, private firms will find some other way to compete. Consumers often look back nostalgically at the "early days" of airplane travel, when the food was good, the seats were bigger, and people dressed up when they traveled. This is not just nostalgia speaking; the quality of coach air travel has fallen sharply. But the price of air travel has fallen even faster. Prior to 1978, airline fares were fixed by the government. Every flight from Denver to Chicago cost the same, but American and United were still competing for customers. They used quality to distinguish themselves. When the industry was deregulated, price became the primary margin for competition, presumably because that is what consumers care more about. Since then, everything related to being in or near an airplane has become less pleasant, but the average fare, adjusted for inflation, has fallen by nearly half.

In 1995, I was traveling across South Africa, and I was struck by the remarkable service at the gas stations along the way. The attendants, dressed in sharp uniforms, often with bow ties, would scurry out to fill the tank, check the oil, wipe the windshields. The bathrooms were spotless—a far cry from some of the scary things I've seen driving across the USA. Was there some special service station mentality in South Africa? No. The price of gasoline was fixed by the government. So service stations, which were still private firms, resorted to bow ties and clean bathrooms.

Every market transaction makes all parties better off. Firms are acting in their own best interests, and so are consumers. This is a simple idea that has enormous power. Consider an inflammatory example: The problem with Asian sweatshops is that there are not enough of them. Adult workers take jobs in these unpleasant, low-wage manufacturing facilities voluntarily. (I am not writing about forced labor or child labor, both of which are different cases.) So one of two things must be true. Either (1) workers take unpleasant jobs in sweatshops because it is the best employment option they have; or (2) Asian sweatshop workers are persons of weak intellect who have many more attractive job offers but choose to work in sweatshops instead.

Most arguments against globalization implicitly assume number two. The protesters smashing windows in Seattle were trying to make the case that workers in the developing world would be better off if we curtailed international trade, thereby closing down the sweatshops that churn out shoes and handbags for those of us in the developed world. But how exactly does that make workers in poor countries better off? It does not create any new opportunities. The only way it could possibly improve social welfare is if fired sweatshop workers take new, better jobs—opportunities they presumably ignored when they went to work in a sweatshop. When was the last time a plant closing in the United States was hailed as good news for its workers?

Sweatshops are nasty places by Western standards. And yes, one might argue that Nike should pay its foreign workers better wages out of sheer altruism. But they are a symptom of poverty, not a cause. Nike pays a typical worker in one of its Vietnamese factories roughly $600 a year. That is a pathetic amount of money. It also happens to be twice an average Vietnamese worker's annual income.[8] Indeed, sweatshops played an important role in the development of countries like South Korea and Taiwan, as we will explore in Chapter 11.

As John F. Kennedy famously remarked, "Life is not fair." Neither is capitalism in some important respects. Is it a good system?

I will argue that a market economy is to economics what democracy is to government: a decent, if flawed, choice among many bad alternatives. Markets are consistent with our views of individual liberty. We may disagree over whether or not the government should compel us to wear motorcycle helmets, but most of us agree that the state should not tell us where to live, what to do for a living, or how to spend our money. True, there is no way to rationalize spending money on a birthday cake for my dog when the same money could have vaccinated several African children. But any system that forces me to spend money on vaccines instead of doggy birthday cakes can only be held together by oppression. The communist governments of the twentieth century controlled their economies by controlling their citizens' lives. They often wrecked both in the process. During the twentieth century, communist governments killed some 100 million of their own people in peacetime, either by repression or by famine.

Markets are consistent with human nature and therefore wildly successful at motivating us to reach our potential. I am writing this book because I love to write. I am writing this book because I believe that economics will be interesting to lay readers. And I am writing this book because I really want a summer home in Wisconsin. We work harder when we benefit directly from our work, and that hard work often yields significant social gains.

Last and most important, we can and should use government to modify markets in all kinds of ways. The economic battle of the twentieth century was between capitalism and communism. Capitalism won. Even my leftist brother-in-law does not believe in collective farming or government-owned steel mills (though he did once say that he would like to see a health care system modeled after the U.S. Post Office). On the other hand, reasonable people can disagree sharply over when and how the government should involve itself in a market economy or what kind of safety net we should offer to those whom capitalism treats badly. The economic battles of the twenty-first century will be over how unfettered our markets should be.

CHAPTER 2

Incentives Matter:

Why you might be able to save your face by cutting off your nose (if you are a black rhinoceros)

The black rhinoceros is one of the most endangered species on the planet. Fewer than 2,500 of them roam southern Africa, down from about 65,000 in 1970. This is an ecological disaster in the making. It is also a situation in which basic economics can tell us why the species is in such trouble—and perhaps even what we can do about it.

Why do people kill black rhinos? For the same reason they sell drugs or cheat on their taxes. Because they can make a lot of money relative to the risk of getting caught. In many Asian countries, the horn of the black rhino is believed to be a powerful aphrodisiac and fever reducer. It is also used to make the handles on traditional Yemenese daggers. As a result, a single rhino horn can fetch $30,000 on the black market—a princely sum in countries where per capita income is around $1,000 a year and falling. In other words, the black rhino is worth far more dead than alive to the people of impoverished southern Africa.

Sadly, this is a market that does not naturally correct itself. Unlike automobiles or personal computers, firms can't produce new black rhinos as they see the supply dwindling. Indeed, quite the opposite force is at work; as the black rhino becomes more and more imperiled, the black market price for rhino horn rises, providing even more incentive for poachers to hunt down the remaining animals. This vicious circle is compounded by another aspect of the situation that is common to many environmental challenges: Most black rhinos are communal property rather than private property. That may sound wonderful. In fact, it creates more conservation problems than it solves. Imagine that all of the black rhinos were in the hands of a single avaricious rancher who had no qualms about making rhino horns into Yemenese daggers. This rancher has not a single environmental bone in his body. Indeed, he is so mean and selfish that sometimes he kicks his dog just because it gives him utility. Would this ogre of a rhino rancher have let his herd fall from 65,000 to 2,500 in thirty years? Never. He would have bred and protected the animals so that he would always have a large supply of horns to ship off to market—much as cattle ranchers manage their herds. This has nothing to do with altruism; it has everything to do with maximizing the value of a scarce resource.

Communal resources, on the other hand, present some unique problems. First, the villagers who live in close proximity to these majestic animals usually derive no benefit from having them around. To the contrary, large animals like rhinos and elephants can cause massive damage to crops. To put yourself in the shoes of local villagers, imagine that the people of Africa suddenly took a keen interest in the future of the North American brown rat and that a crucial piece of the conservation strategy involved letting these creatures live and breed in your house. Further imagine that a poacher came along and offered you cash to show him where the rats were nesting in your basement. Hmm. True, millions of people around the world derive utility from conserving species like the black rhino or the mountain gorilla. But that can actually be part of the problem; it is easy to be a "free rider" and let someone else, or some other organization, do the work. Last year, how much time and money did you contribute to preserving endangered species?

Tour and safari operators, who do make a lot of money by bringing wealthy tourists to see rare wildlife, face a similar "free rider" problem. If one tour company invests heavily in conservation, other tour companies that have made no such investment still enjoy all the benefits of the rhinos that have been saved. So the firm that spends money on conservation actually suffers a cost disadvantage in the market. Their tours will have to be more expensive (or they will have to accept a lower profit margin) in order to recoup their conservation investment. Obviously there is a role for government here. But the governments in sub-Saharan Africa are low on resources at best and corrupt and dysfunctional at worst. The one party who has a clear and powerful incentive is the poacher, who makes a king's ransom by hunting down the remaining rhinos, killing them, and then sawing off their horns.

This is pretty depressing stuff. But economics also offers at least some insight into how the black rhino and other endangered species can be saved. An effective conservation strategy must properly align the incentives of the people who live in or near the black rhino's natural habitat. Translation: Give local people some reason to want the animals alive rather than dead. This is the premise of the budding eco-tourism industry. If tourists are willing to pay great amounts of money to spot and photograph black rhinos, and, more important, *if local citizens somehow share the profits from this tourism*, then the local population has a large incentive to keep such animals alive. This has worked in places like Costa Rica, a country that has protected its rain forests and other ecological features by setting aside more than 25 percent of the country as national parks. Tourism currently generates over $1 billion in annual revenue, accounting for 11 percent of the national income.[1]

Sadly, this process is working in reverse at the moment with the mountain gorilla, another seriously endangered species (made famous by Dian Fossey, author of *Gorillas in the Mist*). It is estimated that only 620 mountain gorillas are left in the dense jungles of East Africa. But the countries that make up this region—Uganda, Rwanda, Burundi, and Congo—are embroiled in a series of civil wars that have devastated the tourism trade. In the past, local inhabitants have preserved the gorillas' habitat not because they have any great respect for the mountain gorilla, but because they can make more money from tourists than they can by chopping down the forests that make up the gorillas' habitat. That has changed as the violence in the region grinds on. One local man told the *New York Times*, "[The gorillas] are important when they bring in tourists. If not, they are not. If the tourists don't come, we will try our luck in the forest. Before this, we were good timber cutters."[2]

Meanwhile, conservation officials are experimenting with another idea that is about as basic as economics can be. Black rhinos are killed because their horns fetch a princely sum. If there is no horn, then presumably there is no reason to poach the animals. Thus, some conservation officials have begun to capture black rhinos, saw off their horns, and then release the animals back into the wild. The rhinos are left mildly disadvantaged relative to some of their predators, but they are less likely to be hunted down by their most deadly enemy, man. Has it worked? The evidence is mixed. In some cases, poachers have continued to kill dehorned rhinos, for a number of possible reasons. Killing the animals without horns saves the poachers from wasting time tracking the same animal again. Also, there is some money to be made from removing and selling even the stump of the horn. And, sadly, dead rhinos, even without horns, make the species more endangered, which drives up the value of existing horn stocks.

All of this ignores the demand side of the equation. Should we allow trade in products made from endangered species? Most would say no. Making rhino-horn daggers illegal in countries like the United States lowers the overall demand, which diminishes the incentive for poachers to hunt down the animals. At the same time, there is a credible dissenting view. Some conservation officials argue that selling a limited amount of rhino horn (or ivory, in the case of elephants) that has been legally stockpiled would have two beneficial effects. First, it would raise money to help strapped governments pay for antipoaching efforts. Second, it would lower the market price for these illicit items and therefore diminish the incentive to poach the animals.

As with any complex policy issue, there is no right answer, but there are some ways of approaching the problem that are more fruitful than others. The point is that protecting the black rhino is at least as much about economics as it is about science. We know how the black rhino breeds, what it eats, where it lives. What we need to figure out is how to stop human beings from shooting them. That requires an understanding of how humans behave, not black rhinos.

Incentives matter. When we are paid on commission, we work harder; if the price of gasoline goes up, we drive less; if my three-year-old daughter learns that she will get an Oreo if she cries while I'm talking on the phone, then she will cry while I am talking on the phone. This was one of Adam Smith's insights in *The Wealth of Nations*: "It is not from the benevolence of the butcher, the brewer, or the baker that we expect our dinner, but from their regard to their own interest." Bill Gates did not drop out of Harvard to join the Peace Corps; he dropped out to found Microsoft, which made him one of the richest men on the planet and launched the personal computer revolution in the process—making all of us better off, too. Self-interest makes the world go around, a point that seems so obvious as to be silly. Yet it is routinely ignored. The old slogan "From each according to his abilities, to each according to his needs" made a wonderful folk song; as an economic system, it has led to everything from inefficiency to mass starvation. In any system that does not rely on markets, personal incentives are usually divorced from productivity. Firms and workers are not rewarded for innovation and hard work, nor are they punished for sloth and inefficiency.

How bad can it get? Economists reckon that by the time the Berlin Wall crumbled, some East German car factories were actually destroying value. Because the manufacturing process was so inefficient and the end product was so shoddy, the plants were producing cars worth less than the inputs used to make them. Basically, they took perfectly good steel and ruined it! These kinds of inefficiencies can also exist in nominally capitalist countries where large sectors of the economy are owned and operated by the state, such as India. By 1991, the Hindustan Fertilizer Corporation had been up and running for twelve years.[3] Every day, twelve hundred employees reported to work with the avowed goal of producing fertilizer. There was just one small complication: The plant had never actually produced any salable fertilizer. None. Government bureaucrats ran the plant using public funds; the machinery that was installed never worked properly. Nevertheless, twelve hundred workers came to work every day and the government continued to pay their salaries. The entire enterprise was an industrial charade. It limped along because there was no mechanism to force it to shut down. When government is bankrolling the business, there is no need to produce something and then sell it for more than it cost to make.

These examples seem funny in their own way, but they aren't. Right now, the North Korean economy is in such shambles that the country cannot feed itself, nor does it produce anything valuable enough to trade for sufficient food with the outside world. As a result, an ongoing famine has killed roughly two million people and left 60 percent of North Korean children malnourished. Journalists describe starving people eating grass and scouring railroad tracks for bits of coal or food that may have fallen from passing trains.

American policymakers routinely ignore the importance of incentives. The cause of California's chronic electricity shortage is simple enough: The demand for electricity is greater than the supply. Yet politicians initially refused to do the one thing that had to be part of any solution: allow the price of electricity to rise. Consumers were told to conserve electricity without having any financial incentive to do so. The sad reality is that the pocketbook is mightier than the conscience. It is one thing to feel a vague sense of guilt when you turn up the thermostat; it is another thing to know that doing so will cost you an extra $200 a month. (I have powerful childhood memories of my father, who has no great affection for the environment but could squeeze a nickel out of a stone, stalking around the house closing the closet doors and telling us that he was not paying to air-condition our closets.) Any long-term solution in California will have to allow the price of power to reflect its scarcity.

Meanwhile, American public education operates a lot more like North Korea than Silicon Valley. I will not wade into the school voucher debate, but I will discuss one striking phenomenon related to incentives in education that I have written about for *The Economist*.[4] The pay of American teachers is not linked in any way to performance; teachers' unions have consistently opposed any kind of merit pay. Instead, salaries in nearly every public school district in the country are determined by a rigid formula based on experience and years of schooling, factors that researchers have found to be generally unrelated to performance in the classroom. This uniform pay scale creates a set of incentives that economists refer to as adverse selection. Since the most talented teachers are also likely to be good at other professions, they have a strong incentive to leave education for jobs in which pay is more closely linked to productivity. For the least talented, the incentives are just the opposite.

The theory is interesting; the data are amazing. When test scores are used as a proxy for ability, the brightest individuals shun the teaching profession at every juncture. The brightest students are the least likely to choose education as a college major. Among students who do major in education, those with higher test scores are less likely to become teachers. And among individuals who enter teaching, those with the highest test scores are the most likely to leave the profession early. None of this proves that America's teachers are being paid enough. Many of them are not, especially those gifted individuals who stay in the profession because they love it. But the general problem remains: Any system that pays all teachers the same provides a strong incentive for the most talented among them to look for work elsewhere.

Human beings are complex creatures who are going to do whatever it takes to make themselves as well off as possible. Sometimes it is easy to predict how that will unfold; sometimes it is enormously complex. Economists often speak of "perverse incentives," which are the inadvertent incentives that can be created when we set out to do something completely different. In policy circles, this is sometimes called the "law of unintended consequences." Consider a well-intentioned proposal to require that all infants and small children be restrained in car seats while flying on commercial airlines. During the Clinton administration, FAA administrator Jane Garvey told a safety conference that her agency was committed to "ensuring that children are accorded the same level of safety in aircraft as are adults." James Hall, chairman of the National Transportation Safety Board at the time, lamented that luggage had to be stowed for takeoff while "the most precious cargo on that aircraft, infants and toddlers, were left unrestrained."[5] Garvey and Hall cited several cases in which infants might have survived crashes had they been restrained. Thus, requiring car seats for children on planes would prevent injuries and save lives.

Or would it? Using a car seat requires that a family buy an extra seat on the plane, which dramatically increases the cost of flying. Airlines no longer offer significant children's discounts; a seat is a seat, and it is likely to cost at least several hundred dollars. As a result, some families will choose to drive rather than fly. Yet driving—even with a car seat—is dramatically more dangerous than flying. As a result, requiring car seats on planes might result in more injuries and deaths to children (and adults), not fewer.

Consider another example in which good intentions led to a bad outcome because the incentives were not fully anticipated. Mexico City is one of the most polluted cities in the world; the foul air trapped over the city by the surrounding mountains and volcanoes has been described by the *New York Times* as "a grayish-yellow pudding of pollutants."[6] Beginning around 1990, the government launched a program to fight this pollution, much of which is caused by auto and truck emissions. A new law required that all cars stay off the streets one day a week on a rotating basis (e.g., cars with certain license plate numbers could not be driven on Tuesday). The logic of the plan was straightforward: Fewer cars on the road would lead to less air pollution.

So what really happened? As would be expected, many people did not like the inconvenience of having their driving days limited. They reacted in a way that analysts might have predicted but did not. Families who could afford a second car bought one, or simply kept their old car when buying a new one, so that they would always have one car that could be driven on any given day. This proved to be worse for emissions than no policy at all, since the proportion of old cars on the road went up, and old cars are dirtier than new cars. The net effect of the policy change was to put *more* polluting cars on the road, not fewer. A 1995 study found that overall gas consumption had increased. The policy was later dropped in favor of a mandatory emissions test.[7]

The wonder of the private sector, of course, is that incentives magically align themselves in a way that makes everyone better off. Right? Well, not exactly. From top to bottom, corporate America is a cesspool of competing and misaligned incentives. Have you ever seen some variation of the sign near the cash register at a fast-food restaurant that says, "Your meal is free if you don't get a receipt. Please see a manager"? Does Burger King have a passionate interest in providing a receipt so that your family bookkeeping will be complete? Of course not. Burger King does not want its employees stealing. And the only way employees can steal without getting caught is by performing transactions without recording them on the cash register—selling you a burger and fries without issuing a receipt and then pocketing the cash. This is what economists call a principal-agent problem. The principal (Burger King) employs an agent (the cashier) who has an incentive to do a lot of things that are not necessarily in the best interest of the firm. Burger King can either spend a lot of time and money monitoring its employees for theft, or it can provide an incentive for you to do it for them. That little sign by the cash register is an ingenious management tool.

Principal-agent problems are as much a problem at the top of corporate America as they are at the bottom, in large part because the agents who run America's large corporations (CEOs and other top executives) are not necessarily the principals who own those companies (the shareholders). I own shares in Starbucks, but I don't even know the CEO's name. How can I be sure that he (she?) is acting in my best interest? Indeed, there is ample evidence to suggest that corporate managers are no different from Burger King cashiers—they have some incentives that are not always in the best interest of the firm. They may steal from the cash register figuratively by showering themselves with private jets and country club memberships. Or they may make strategic decisions from which they benefit but shareholders do not. For example, a shocking two-thirds of all corporate mergers do not add value to the merged firms and a third of them leave shareholders worse off. Why would very smart CEOs engage so often in behavior that seems to make little financial sense?

One partial answer, economists have argued, is that CEOs benefit from mergers even when shareholders are left with losses. A CEO draws a lot of attention to himself by engineering a complex corporate transaction. He is left running a bigger company, which is almost always more prestigious, even if the new entity is less profitable than the merged companies were when they were on their own. Big companies have big offices, big salaries, and big airplanes. On the other hand, some mergers and takeovers make perfect strategic sense. As an uninformed shareholder with a large financial stake in the company, how do I tell the difference? If I don't even know the name of the CEO of Starbucks, how can I be sure that she (he?) is not spending the bulk of her day chasing attractive secretaries around her office? Hell, this is harder than being a manager at Burger King.

One answer that has emerged in recent years is the use of stock options as a management compensation tool. This is the CEO equivalent of the sign near the cash register asking if you received your receipt. Most American CEOs and other important executives now receive a large share of their compensation in the form of stock options. These stock options enable the recipient to purchase the company's stock in the future at some predetermined price, say $10. If the company is highly profitable and the stock does well, climbing to say $57, then those stock options are very valuable. (It is good to be able to buy something for $10 when it is selling on the open market for $57.) On the other hand, if the company's stock falls to $7, the options are worthless. There is no point in buying something for $10 when you can buy it on the open market for $3 less. The point of this compensation scheme is to align the incentives of the CEO with the interests of the shareholders. If the share price goes up, the CEO gets rich—but the shareholders do well, too. It's not a perfect strategy; wily CEOs can find ways to abuse the options game (just as cashiers can find new ways to steal from the register). But the overall strategy makes sense. Given that I don't know the name of the Starbucks CEO, I do hope that he or she has a large chunk of stock options.

The same strategy works for motivating boards of directors, the individuals elected by shareholders to govern publicly held companies. A study conducted by the consulting firm McKinsey & Company found that something as simple as having a company's directors hold large investments in the company's stock correlates with significantly better company performance.[8] McKinsey found that companies whose directors owned "meaningful equity stakes" in 1987 performed much better over the subsequent decade than companies whose directors did not. When McKinsey looked separately at companies that had significantly outperformed other firms in their business sector, they found that the median investment of outside directors at the star firms was five times as large as the stake owned by outside directors at the laggard firms.

One need not be a corporate titan to deal with principal-agent problems. There are plenty of situations in which we must hire someone whose incentives are similar but not identical to our own—and the distinction between "similar" and "identical" can make all the difference. Take real estate agents, a particular breed of scoundrel who purport to have your best interest at stake but may not, regardless of whether you are buying or selling a property. Let's look at the buy side first. The agent graciously shows you lots of houses and eventually you find one that is just right. So far, so good. Now it is time to bargain with the seller over the purchase price, often with your agent as your chief adviser. Yet your real estate agent will be paid a percentage of the eventual purchase price. The more you are willing to pay, the more your agent makes and the less time the whole process will take.

There are problems on the sell side, too, though they are more subtle. The better price you get for your house, the more money your agent will make. That is a good thing. But the incentives are still not perfectly aligned. Suppose you are selling a house in the $300,000 range. Your agent can list the house for $280,000 and sell it in about twenty minutes. Or she could list it for $320,000 and wait for a buyer who really loves the place. The benefit to you of pricing the house high is huge: $40,000. Your real estate agent may see things differently. Listing high would mean many weeks of showing the house, holding open houses, and baking cookies to make the place smell good. Lots of work, in other words. Assuming a 3 percent commission, your agent can make $8,400 for doing virtually nothing or $9,600 for doing many weeks of work. Which would you choose? On the buy side or the sell side, your agent's most powerful incentive is to get a deal done, whether it is at a price favorable to you or not.

Economics teaches us how to get the incentives right. As Gordon Gekko told us in *Wall Street*, greed is good, so make sure that you have it working on your side. Yet Mr. Gekko was not entirely correct. Greed can be very bad—even for people who are entirely selfish. Indeed, some of the most interesting problems in economics involve situations in which rational individuals acting in their own best interest do things that make themselves worse off. Yet their behavior is entirely logical.

The classic example is the prisoner's dilemma, a somewhat contrived but highly powerful model of human behavior. The basic idea is that two men have been arrested on suspicion of murder. They are immediately separated so that they can be interrogated without communicating with one another. The case against them is not terribly strong, and the police are looking for a confession. Indeed, the authorities are willing to offer a deal if one of the men rats out the other as the trigger man.

If neither man confesses, the police will charge them both with illegal possession of a weapon, which carries a five-year jail sentence. If both of them confess, then each will receive a twenty-five-year murder sentence. If one man rats out the other, then the snitch will receive a light three-year sentence as an accomplice and his partner will get life in prison. What happens?

The men are best off collectively if they keep their mouths shut. But that's not what they do. Each of them starts thinking. . . . Prisoner A figures that if his partner keeps his mouth shut, then he can get the light three-year sentence by ratting him out. Then it dawns on him: His partner is almost certainly thinking the same thing—in which case he had better confess to avoid having the whole crime pinned on himself. Indeed, his best strategy is to confess regardless of what his partner does: It either gets him the three-year sentence (if his partner stays quiet) or saves him from getting life in prison (if his partner talks).

Of course, Prisoner B has the same incentives. They both confess, and they both get twenty-five years in prison when they might have served only five. Yet neither prisoner has done anything irrational.

The amazing thing about this model is that it offers great insight into real-world situations in which unfettered self-interest leads to very poor outcomes. It is particularly applicable to the way in which renewable natural resources, such as fisheries, are exploited when many individuals are drawing from a common resource. For example, if Atlantic swordfish are harvested wisely, such as by limiting the number of fish caught each season, then the swordfish population will remain stable or even grow, providing a living for fishermen indefinitely. But no one "owns" the world's swordfish stocks, making it difficult to police who catches what. As a result, independent fishing boats start to act a lot like our prisoners under interrogation. They can either limit their catch in the name of conservation, or they can take as many fish as possible. What happens?

Exactly what the prisoner's dilemma predicts: The fishermen do not trust each other well enough to coordinate an outcome that would make them all better off. Rhode Island fisherman John Sorlien told the *New York Times* in a story on dwindling fish stocks, "Right now, my only incentive is to go out and kill as many fish as I can. I have no incentive to conserve the fishery, because any fish I leave is just going to be picked up by the next guy."[9] So the world's stocks of tuna, cod, swordfish, and lobster are fished away. Meanwhile, politicians often make the situation worse by bailing out struggling fishermen with assorted subsidies. This merely keeps boats in the water when some fishermen might otherwise quit.

Sometimes individuals need to be saved from themselves. One nice example of this is the lobstering community of Port Lincoln on Australia's southern coast. In the 1960s, the community set a limit on the number of traps that could be set and then sold licenses for those traps. Since then, any newcomer could enter the business only by buying a license from another lobsterman. This limit on the overall catch has allowed the lobster population to thrive. Ironically, Port Lincoln lobstermen catch more than their American colleagues while working less. Meanwhile, a license purchased in 1984 for $2,000 now fetches about $35,000. As Aussie lobsterman Daryl Spencer told the *Times*, "Why hurt the fishery? It's my retirement fund. No one's going to pay me $35,000 a pot if there are no lobsters left. If I rape and pillage the fishery now, in ten years my licenses won't be worth anything." Mr. Spencer is not smarter or more altruistic than his fishing colleagues around the world; he just has different incentives. Oddly, some environmental groups oppose these kinds of licensed quotas because they "privatize" a public resource. They also fear that the licenses will be bought up by large corporations, driving small fishermen out of business.

• • •

Two other points regarding incentives are worth noting. First, a market economy inspires hard work and progress not just because it rewards winners, but because it crushes losers. The 1990s were a great time to be involved in the Internet. They were bad years to be in the electric typewriter business. Implicit in Adam Smith's invisible hand is the idea of "creative destruction," a term coined by the Austrian economist Joseph Schumpeter. Markets do not suffer fools gladly. Take Wal-Mart, a remarkably efficient retailer that often leaves carnage in its wake. Americans flock to Wal-Mart because the store offers an amazing range of products cheaper than they can be purchased anywhere else. This is a very good thing. Being able to buy goods cheaper is essentially the same thing as having more income. At the same time, Wal-Mart is the ultimate nightmare for Al's Glass and Hardware in Pekin, Illinois—and for mom-and-pop shops everywhere else. The pattern is well established: Wal-Mart opens a giant store just outside of town; several years later, the small shops on Main Street are closed and boarded up.

Capitalism can be a brutal, cruel process. We look back and speak admiringly of technological breakthroughs like the steam engine, the spinning wheel, the telephone. But those advances made it a bad time to be, respectively, a blacksmith, a seamstress, or a telegraph operator. Creative destruction is not just something that might happen in a market economy. It is something that *must* happen. At the beginning of the twentieth century, half of all Americans worked in farming or ranching.[10] Now that figure is about one in a hundred and still falling. (Iowa is still losing roughly fifteen hundred farmers a year.) Note that two important things have *not* happened: (1) We have not starved to death; and (2) we do not have a 49 percent unemployment rate. Instead, American farmers have become so productive that we need far fewer of them to feed ourselves. The individuals who would have been farming ninety years ago are now fixing our cars, designing computer games, playing professional football, etc. Just imagine our collective loss of utility if Bill Gates, Steven Spielberg, and Oprah Winfrey were corn farmers.

Creative destruction is a tremendous positive force in the long run. The bad news is that people don't pay their bills in the long run. The folks at the mortgage company can be real sticklers about getting that check every month. When a plant closes or an industry is wiped out by competition, it can be years or even an entire generation before the affected workers and communities recover. Anyone who has ever driven through New England has seen the abandoned or underutilized mills that are monuments to the days when America still manufactured things like textiles and shoes. Or one can drive through Gary, Indiana, where miles of rusting steel plants are a reminder that the city was not always most famous for having more murders per capita than any other city in the United States.

Competition means losers, which goes a long way to explain why we embrace it heartily in theory and then often fight it bitterly in practice. A college classmate of mine worked for a congressman from Michigan shortly after our graduation. My friend was not allowed to drive his Japanese car to work, lest it be spotted in one of the Michigan congressman's reserved parking spaces. That congressman will almost certainly tell you that he is a capitalist. Of course he believes in markets—unless a Japanese company happens to make a better, cheaper car, in which case the staff member who bought that vehicle should be forced to take the train to work. This is nothing new; competition is always best when it involves other people. During the Industrial Revolution, weavers in rural England demonstrated, petitioned Parliament, and even burned down textile mills in an effort to fend off mechanization. Would we be better off now if they had succeeded and we still made all of our clothes by hand?

If you make a better mousetrap, the world will beat a path to your door; if you make the old mousetrap, it is time to start firing people. This helps to explain our ambivalence to international trade and globalization, to ruthless retailers like Wal-Mart, and even to some kinds of technology and automation. Competition also creates some interesting policy trade-offs. Government inevitably faces pressure to help firms and industries under siege from competition and to protect the affected workers. (For all our talk about free markets and survival of the fittest, when Chrysler Motors was on the brink of bankruptcy in 1980, the United States government bailed out the company by guaranteeing its loans.) Yet many of the things that minimize the pain inflicted by competition—bailing out firms or making it hard to lay off workers—slow down or stop the process of creative destruction. To quote my junior high school football coach: "No pain, no gain."

One other matter related to incentives vastly complicates public policy: It is not easy to transfer money from the rich to the poor. Congress can pass the laws, but wealthy taxpayers do not stand idly by. They change their behavior in ways that avoid as much taxation as possible—moving money around, making investments that shelter income, or, in extreme cases, moving to another jurisdiction. When Bjorn Borg dominated the tennis world, the Swedish government taxed his earnings at an extremely high rate. Borg did not lobby the Swedish government for lower taxes or write passionate op-eds about the role of taxes in the economy. He merely transferred his residence to Monaco, where the tax burden is much lower.

At least he was still playing tennis. Taxes provide a powerful incentive to avoid or reduce the activity that is taxed. In America, where much of our revenue comes from the income tax, high taxes discourage . . . income? Will people really stop or start working based on tax rates? Yes—especially when the worker involved is the family's second earner. Virginia Postrel, a columnist on economics for the *New York Times*, has declared that tax rates are a feminist issue. Because of the "marriage tax," second earners in families with high household incomes, who are more likely to be women, pay an average of 50 cents in taxes for every dollar they earn, which profoundly affects the decision to work or stay home. "By disproportionately punishing married women's work, the tax system distorts women's personal choices. And by discouraging valuable work, it lowers our overall standard of living," she writes. She offers some interesting evidence. As a result of the 1986 tax reform, marginal tax rates for women in the highest income brackets fell more sharply than tax rates for women with lower incomes, meaning that they saw a much sharper drop in the amount that the government takes from every paycheck. Did they respond differently from women who did not get the same large tax break? Yes, their participation in the work force jumped three times as much.[11]

On the corporate side, high taxes can have a similar effect. High taxes lower a firm's return on investment, thereby providing less incentive to invest in plants, research, and other activities that lead to economic growth. Once again we are faced with an unpleasant trade-off: Raising taxes to provide generous benefits to disadvantaged Americans can simultaneously discourage the kinds of productive investments that might make them better off.

If tax rates get high enough, individuals and firms may slip into the "underground economy" where they opt to break the law and avoid taxes entirely. Scandinavian countries, which offer generous government programs funded by high marginal tax rates, have seen large growth in the size of their black market economies. Experts estimate that the underground economy in Norway has grown from 1.5 percent of gross national product in 1960 to 18 percent in the mid-1990s. Cheating the tax man can be a vicious circle. As more individuals and firms slip into the underground economy, tax rates must go up for everyone else to provide the same level of government revenue. Higher taxes in turn cause more flight to the underground economy—and so on.[12]

The challenge of transferring money from rich to poor is not just on the taxation side. Government benefits create perverse incentives, too. Generous unemployment benefits diminish the incentive to find work. Welfare policy, prior to reform in 1996, offered cash payments only to unemployed single women with children, which implicitly punished poor women who were married or employed—two things that the government generally does not try to discourage.

This is not to suggest that all government benefits go to poor people. They don't. The largest federal entitlement programs are Social Security and Medicare, which go to all Americans, even the very rich. By providing guaranteed benefits in old age, both programs may discourage personal savings. Indeed, this is the subject of a long-simmering debate. Some economists argue that government old-age benefits cause us to save less (thereby lowering the national savings rate) because we need to set aside less money for retirement. Others argue that Social Security and Medicare do not reduce our personal savings; they merely allow us to pass along more money to our children and grandchildren. Empirical studies have not found a clear answer one way or the other. This is not merely an esoteric squabble among academics. As we shall explore later in the book, a low savings rate can limit the pool of capital available to make the kinds of investments that allow us to improve our standard of living.

None of this should be interpreted as a blanket argument against taxes or government programs. Rather, economists spend much more time than politicians thinking about what kind of taxes we should collect and how we should structure government benefits. For example, both a gasoline tax and an income tax generate revenue. Yet they create profoundly different incentives. The income tax will discourage some people from working, which is a bad thing. The gasoline tax will discourage some people from driving, which can be a very good thing. Indeed, "green taxes" collect revenue by taxing activities that are detrimental to the environment and "sin taxes" do the same thing for the likes of cigarettes, alcohol, and gambling.

In general, economists tend to favor taxes that are broad, simple, and fair. A simple tax is easily understood and collected; a fair tax implies only that two similar individuals, such as two people with the same income, will pay similar taxes; a broad tax means that revenue is raised by imposing a small tax on a very large group rather than imposing a large tax on a very small group. A broad tax is harder to evade because fewer activities are exempted, and, since the tax rate is lower, there is less incentive to evade it anyway. We should not, for example, impose a large tax on the sale of red sports cars. The tax could be evaded, easily and legally, by buying another color—*in which case everybody is made worse off.* The government collects no revenue and sports car enthusiasts do not get to drive their favorite color car. This phenomenon, whereby taxes make individuals worse off without making anyone else better off, is referred to as "dead weight loss."

It would be preferable to tax all sports cars, or even all cars, because more revenue could be raised with a much smaller tax. Then again, a gasoline tax collects revenue from drivers, just as a tax on new cars does, but it also provides an incentive to conserve fuel. Those who drive more pay more. So now we're raising a great deal of revenue with a tiny tax and doing a little something for the environment, too. Many economists would go yet one step further: We should tax the use of all kinds of carbon-based fuels, such as coal, oil, and gasoline. Such a tax would raise revenue from a broad base while creating an incentive to conserve non-renewable resources and curtailing the CO_2 emissions that cause global warming.

Sadly, this thought process does not lead us to the optimal tax. We have merely swapped one problem for another. A tax on red sports cars would be paid only by the rich. A carbon tax would be paid by rich and poor alike, but it would probably cost the poor a larger fraction of their income. Taxes that fall more heavily on the poor than the rich, so-called regressive taxes, often offend our sense of justice. (Progressive taxes, such as the income tax, fall more heavily on the rich than the poor.) Here, as elsewhere, economics does not give us a "right answer"—only an analytical framework for thinking about important questions. Indeed the most efficient tax of all—one that is perfectly broad, simple, and fair (in the narrow, tax-related sense of the word)—is a lump-sum tax, which is imposed uniformly on every individual in a jurisdiction just for being. Margaret Thatcher actually tried it with the "poll tax." What happened? Britons rioted in the streets at the prospect of the rich paying the same as the poor, the employed paying the same as the unemployed. Obviously good economics is not always good politics.

Meanwhile, not all benefits are created equal either. One of the biggest poverty-fighting tools in recent years has been the earned income tax credit (EITC), an idea that economists have pushed for decades because it creates a far better set of incentives than traditional social welfare programs. Most social programs offer benefits to individuals who are not working. The EITC does just the opposite; it uses the income tax system to subsidize low-wage workers so that their total income is raised above the poverty line. A worker who earns $11,000 and is supporting a family of four might get an additional $8,000 through the EITC and matching state programs. The idea was to "make work pay." Indeed, the system provides a powerful incentive for individuals to get into the labor force, where it is hoped they can learn skills and advance to higher-paying jobs. Of course, the program has an obvious problem too. Unlike welfare, the EITC does not help individuals who cannot find work at all; in reality, those are the folks who are likely to be most desperate.

When I applied to graduate school many years ago, I wrote an essay expressing my puzzlement at how a country that could put a man on the moon could still have people sleeping on the streets. Part of that problem is political will; we could take a lot of people off the streets tomorrow if we made it a national priority. But I have also come to realize that NASA had it easy. Rockets conform to the unchanging laws of physics. We know where the moon will be at a given time; we know precisely how fast a spacecraft will enter or exit the earth's orbit. If we get the equations right, the rocket will land where it is supposed to—always. Human beings are more complex than that. A recovering drug addict does not behave as predictably as a rocket in orbit. We don't have a formula for persuading a sixteen-year-old not to drop out of school. But we do have a powerful tool: We know that people seek to make themselves better off, however they may define that. Our best hope for improving the human condition is to understand why we act the way we do and then plan accordingly. Programs, organizations, and systems work better when they get the incentives right. It is like rowing downstream.

CHAPTER 3

Government and the Economy:
Government is your friend (and a round
of applause for all those lawyers)

W hy did I sell my Honda Civic in 1998? Two reasons: (1)
It didn't have a cup holder; and (2) my wife was pregnant, and I had become fearful that our whole family
would get flattened by a Chevy Suburban. I could have
gotten beyond the cup holder problem. But putting a car seat in a vehicle that weighed a quarter as much as the average SUV was not an option.
So we bought a Ford Explorer and became part of the problem for all of
those people still driving Honda Civics.*

The point is this: My decision to buy and drive an SUV affects
everyone else on the road, yet none of those people has a say in my decision. I do not have to compensate all the owners of Honda Civics for the
fact that I am putting their lives slightly more at risk. Nor do I have to
compensate asthmatic children who will be made worse off by the
exhaust I generate as I cruise around the city getting nine miles to the
gallon. And I have never mailed off a check to people in New Orleans
who may someday find their houses underwater because my CO_2 emissions are melting the polar ice caps. Yet these are real costs associated
with driving a less fuel-efficient car.

*When our Ford Explorer rolled over at sixty-five mph on an interstate three years
later, we bought a Volvo.

My decision to buy a Ford Explorer causes what economists refer to as an externality, which means that the private costs of my behavior are different from the social costs. When my wife and I went to the Bert Weinman Ford Dealership and the salesman, Angel, asked, "What is it going to take for me to put you in this car?", we tallied up the costs of driving an Explorer rather than a Civic: more gas, more expensive insurance, higher car payments. There was nothing on our tally sheet about asthmatic children, melting polar ice caps, or pregnant women driving Hyundais. Are these costs associated with driving an Explorer? Yes. Do we have to pay them? No. Therefore, they did not figure into our decision (other than as a vague sense of guilt as we contemplated telling our environmentally conscious relatives who live in Boulder, Colorado, and flush the toilet only once a day in order to conserve water).

When an externality—the gap between the private cost and the social cost of some behavior—is large, individuals have an incentive to do things that make them better off at the expense of others. The market, left alone, will do nothing to fix this problem. In fact, the market "fails" in the sense that it encourages individuals and firms to cut corners in ways that make society worse off as a result. If this concept were really as dry as most economics textbooks make it seem, then movies like *A Civil Action* and *Erin Brockovich* would not have made millions at the box office. After all, both of these stories are about simple externalities: A large, multinational company does something to endanger the local water supply, possibly poisoning families. *There is no market solution in this case; the market is the problem.* The polluting company can produce its product more cheaply by dumping the by-products on nearby vacant land than by paying to dispose of them properly. Customers, most of whom live far away and are unaware of (or indifferent to) the pollution, will actually reward the company by buying more of its product, which will be cheaper than what can be produced by competitors that pay to dispose of their waste in a more responsible way. The only redress in these recent film examples (both based on true stories) was through a nonmarket, government-supported mechanism: the courts. And, of course, John Travolta and Julia Roberts look good doing it.

Consider a more banal example, but one that raises the ire of most city dwellers: people who don't pick up after their dogs. In a perfect world, we would all carry pooper scoopers because we derive utility from behaving responsibly. But we don't live in a perfect world. From the narrow perspective of some individual dog walkers, it's easier ("less costly" in economist speak) to ignore Fido's unsightly pile and walk blithely on. (For those who think this is a trivial example, an average of 650 people a year break bones or are hospitalized in Paris after slipping in dog waste, according to the *New York Times*.)[1] The pooper-scooper decision can be modeled like any other economic decision; a dog owner weighs the costs and benefits of behaving responsibly and then scoops or does not scoop. But who speaks for the woman running to catch the bus the next morning who makes one misstep and is suddenly having a very bad day? No one, which is why most cities have laws requiring pet owners to pick up after their animals.

Thankfully there is a broader point: One crucial role for government in a market economy is dealing with externalities—those cases in which individuals or firms engage in private behavior that has broader social consequences. I noted in Chapter 1 that all market transactions are voluntary exchanges that make the involved parties better off. That's still true, but note the word "involved" that has left me some wiggle room. The problem is that all of the individuals *affected* by a market transaction may not be sitting at the table when the deal is struck. Our neighbor Stuart, with whom we share an adjoining wall, is an avid bongo drum player. I'm sure that both he and the music shop owner were both pleased the last time he purchased a new set of bongos. (Based on the noise involved, he may have even purchased some kind of high-tech amplifier.) *But I am not happy about this transaction.*

Externalities are at the root of all kinds of policy issues, from the mundane to those that literally threaten the planet:

- *The Economist* has suggested somewhat peevishly that families traveling with small children on airplanes should be required to fly at the back of the plane so that other passengers might enjoy a "child-free zone." An editorial in the magazine noted, "Children, just like cigarettes or mobile phones, clearly impose a negative externality on people who are near them. Anybody who has suffered a 12-hour flight with a bawling baby in the row immediately ahead or a bored youngster viciously kicking their seat from behind, will grasp this as quickly as they would love to grasp the youngster's neck. Here is a clear case of market failure: parents do not bear the full costs (indeed young babies travel free), so they are too ready to take their noisy brats with them. Where is the invisible hand when it is needed to administer a good smack?"[2]

- Mobile phone use is under stricter scrutiny, both in public places, such as restaurants and commuter trains, where the behavior is fabulously annoying, but also in vehicles, where it has been linked to a higher rate of accidents.

- In Chicago, Mayor Richard Daley attempted to impose a 1-cent tax on every $2 of take-out food purchases, arguing that the "litter tax" would reimburse the city for the costs of picking up litter, much of which consists of discarded fast-food containers. The mayor's economics were sound—litter is a classic externality—but a judge ruled the ordinance unconstitutional because it was "vague and lacking in uniformity" in the way it dealt with different kinds of fast-food containers.

- Global warming will be one of the most difficult international challenges in coming years in large part because firms that emit large amounts of greenhouse gases pay only a small share of the cost of those emissions. Indeed, even the countries in which they reside do not bear the full cost of the pollution. A steel plant in Pennsylvania emits CO_2 that may one day flood Bangladesh. (Meanwhile, acid rain caused by U.S. emissions is already killing Canadian forests.) The same thing is true in all kinds of factories all around the world. Thus, any solution to global warming will have to raise the cost of emitting greenhouse gases in a way that is binding upon all of the earth's polluters—not the easiest of tasks.

It is worth noting that there can be positive externalities as well; an individual's behavior can have a positive impact on society for which he or she is not fully compensated. My office window looks out across the Chicago River at the Wrigley Building and the Tribune Tower, two of the most beautiful buildings in a city renowned for its architecture. On a clear day, the view of the skyline, and of these two buildings in particular, is positively inspiring. But I have never paid for the utility that I get from this wonderful architecture. I don't mail a check to the Tribune Company every time I glance out the window. Or, in the realm of economic development, a business may invest in a downtrodden neighborhood in a way that attracts other kinds of investment. Yet this business is not compensated for anchoring what may become an economic revitalization, which is why local governments often offer subsidies for such investment.

Some activities have both positive and negative externalities. Cigarettes kill people who smoke them; that is old news. Responsible adults are free to smoke or not smoke as they choose. But cigarette smoke can also harm those who happen to be lingering nearby, which is why most office buildings consider smoking to be slightly less acceptable than running through the halls naked. Meanwhile, all fifty states filed suit against the tobacco industry (and subsequently accepted large settlements) on the grounds that smokers generate extra health care costs that must be borne by state governments. In other words, my taxes go to remove part of some smoker's lung. (Private insurance companies do not have this problem; they simply recoup the extra cost of insuring smokers by charging them higher premiums.)

At the same time, smokers do provide a benefit to the rest of us. They die young. According to the American Lung Association, the average smoker dies seven years earlier than the average nonsmoker, which means that smokers pay into Social Security and private pension funds for all of their working lives but then don't stick around very long to collect the accumulated benefits. Nonsmokers, on average, get to share the extra money left in the pot. The good folks at Philip Morris have even quantified this benefit for us. In 2001, they released a report on the Czech Republic (just as parliament was considering raising cigarette taxes) showing that premature deaths from smoking save the Czech government roughly $28 million a year in pension and old-age housing benefits. The net benefit of smoking to the government, including taxes and subtracting public health costs, was reckoned to be $148 million.[3]

How does a market economy deal with externalities? Sometimes the government regulates the affected activity. The federal government issues thousands of pages of regulations every year on everything from groundwater contamination to poultry inspection. The states have their own regulatory structures; California, for example, has a strict set of emissions standards for automobiles. Local governments have zoning laws that forbid private property owners from impinging on their neighbors by constructing buildings that may be unsafe, inappropriate for the neighborhood, or simply ugly. The island of Nantucket allows only a few select colors of exterior paint lest irresponsible property owners use neon colors that would destroy the quaint character of the island. I live in a historic neighborhood in which every external change to our homes—from the color of new windows to the size of a flower box—must be approved by an architecture committee.

There is another approach to dealing with externalities that tends to be favored in some cases by economists: tax the offending behavior rather than banning it. I've conceded that my Ford Explorer was a menace to society. As Cornell economist Robert Frank noted in an op-ed for the *New York Times*, we are locked in an SUV arms race. "Any family can only choose the size of its own vehicle. It cannot dictate what others buy. Any family that unilaterally bought a smaller vehicle might thus put itself at risk by unilaterally disarming," he wrote.[4] He penned those sentiments before Daimler-Chrysler announced plans to produce the Unimog, *an SUV that will weigh more than six tons, or roughly the same as a Tyrannosaurus rex or two Chevy Suburbans.* Should SUVs be banned? Should Detroit be ordered to manufacture safer, more fuel-efficient cars?

Economists, including Mr. Frank, would argue not. The primary problem with SUVs—and all vehicles, for that matter—is that they are too cheap to drive. A Daimler-Chrysler marketing executive said of the Unimog, "Even in Scottsdale, Arizona, moms will want to take it to the grocery store. It's a head-turning vehicle."[5] The private cost of driving a Unimog to the grocery store is obviously far lower than the social cost. *So raise the private cost.* As Mr. Frank writes, "The only practical remedy, given the undeniable fact that driving bulky, polluting vehicles causes damage to others, is to give ourselves an incentive to take this damage into account when deciding what vehicles to buy." If the real cost to society of having an Explorer on the road is 75 cents a mile instead of the 50 cents a mile that it costs the vehicle's owner to operate the vehicle, then tack on a tax that equates the two. This might be accomplished with a gas tax, or an emissions tax, or a weight tax, or some combination thereof. The result will make driving a Unimog to the grocery store a lot less attractive.

But now we have entered strange terrain. Is it appropriate to allow some drivers to pay for the privilege of driving a vehicle so bulky that it might run over a Hyundai without even spilling the sixty-four-ounce drink in the monster cup holder? Yes, for the same reason that most of us eat ice cream even though it causes heart disease. We weigh the health costs of Starbucks Almond Fudge against that divine, creamy taste and decide to have a pint every once in a while. We don't quit ice cream entirely, nor do we have it with every meal. Economics tells us that the environment requires the same kinds of trade-offs as everything else in life. We should raise the cost of driving an SUV (or any vehicle) to reflect its true social cost and then let individual drivers decide if it still makes sense to commute forty-five miles to work in a Chevy Tahoe.

Taxing behavior that generates a negative externality creates a lot of good incentives. First, it limits the behavior. If the cost of driving a Ford Explorer goes to 75 cents a mile, then there will be fewer Explorers on the road. As important, those people who are still driving them—and paying the full social freight—will be those who value driving an SUV the most, perhaps because they actually haul things or drive off-road. Second, a gas-guzzler tax raises revenue, which a ban on certain kinds of vehicles does not. That revenue might be used to pay for some of the costs of global warming (such as research into alternative energy sources, or at least building a dike around New Orleans). Or it might be used to reduce some other tax, such as the income or payroll tax, that discourages behavior we would rather encourage.

Third, a tax that falls most heavily on hulking, fuel-hungry vehicles will encourage Detroit to build more fuel-efficient cars, albeit with a carrot rather than a stick. If Washington arbitrarily bans vehicles that get less than eighteen miles per gallon without raising the cost of driving those vehicles, then Detroit will produce a lot of vehicles that get—no big surprise here—about eighteen miles a gallon. Not twenty, not twenty-eight, not sixty using new solar technology. On the other hand, if consumers are going to be stuck with a tax based on fuel consumption and/or the mass of the vehicle, then they will have very different preferences when they step into the showroom. The automakers will respond quickly, and the Unimog will be sent where it belongs, to some kind of museum for mutant industrial products.

Is taxing externalities a perfect solution? No, far from it. The auto example alone has a number of problems, the most obvious of which is getting the size of the tax right. Scientists are not yet in complete agreement on how quickly global warming is happening, let alone what the costs might be, or, many steps beyond that, what the real cost of driving a Unimog for a mile might be. Is the right tax $.75, $2.21, $3.07? You will never get a group of scientists to agree on that, let alone the Congress of the United States. There is an equity problem, too. I have stipulated correctly that if we raise the cost of driving SUVs, then those who value them most will continue to drive them. But our measure of how much we value something is how much we are willing to pay for it—and the rich can always pay more for something than everyone else. If the cost of driving an Explorer goes to $9 a gallon, then the people driving them might be hauling wine and cheese to beach parties on Nantucket while a contractor in Chicago who needs a truck to haul lumber and bricks can no longer afford it. Who really "values" that truck more? (Clever politicians might get around the equity issue by using a tax on gas guzzlers to offset a tax that falls heavily on the middle class, such as the payroll tax, in which case our Chicago contractor would pay more for his truck but less to the IRS.) And last, the process of finding and taxing externalities can get out of control. Every activity generates an externality at some level. Any thoughtful policy analyst knows that some individuals who wear spandex in public should be taxed, if not jailed. I live in Chicago, where hordes of pasty people, having spent the winter indoors on the couch, flock outside in skimpy clothing on the first day in which the temperature rises above fifty degrees. This can be a scary experience for those forced to witness it and is certainly something that young children should never have to experience. Still, a tax on spandex is probably not practical.

I've wandered from my original, more important point. Anyone who tells you that markets left to their own devices will always lead to socially beneficial outcomes is talking utter nonsense. Markets alone fail to make us better off when there is a large gap between the private cost of some activity and the social cost. Reasonable people can and should debate what the appropriate remedy might be. Often it will involve government.

But let's back up for a moment. Government does not just fix the rough edges of capitalism; it makes markets possible in the first place. You will get a lot of approving nods at a cocktail party by asserting that if government would simply get out of the way, then markets would deliver prosperity around the globe. Indeed, entire political campaigns are built around this issue. Anyone who has ever waited in line at the Department of Motor Vehicles, applied for a building permit, or tried to pay the nanny tax would agree. There is just one problem with that cocktail party sentiment: It's wrong. Good government makes a market economy possible. Period. And bad government, or no government, dashes capitalism against the rocks, which is one reason that billions of people live in dire poverty around the globe.

To begin with, government sets the rules. Countries without functioning governments are not oases of free market prosperity. They are places in which it is expensive and difficult to conduct even the most simple business. Nigeria has one of the world's largest reserves of oil and natural gas, yet firms trying to do business there face a problem known locally as BYOI—Bring Your Own Infrastructure.[6] Angola is rich with oil and diamonds, but the wealth has financed over a decade of civil war, not economic prosperity. In 1999, Angola's rulers spent $900 million in oil revenues to purchase weapons. Never mind that one child in three dies before the age of five and life expectancy is a shocking forty-two years.[7] These are not countries in which the market economy has failed; they are countries in which the government has failed to develop and sustain the institutions necessary to support a market economy. A recent report issued by the United Nations Development Program placed much of the blame for world poverty on bad government. Without good governance, reliance on trickle-down economic development and a host of other strategies will not work, the report concluded.[8]

The reality is that nobody ever likes the umpire, but you can't play the World Series without one. So what are the rules for a functional market economy? First, the government defines and protects property rights. You own things: your home, your car, your dog, your golf clubs. Within reasonable limits, you can do with that property as you wish. You can sell it, or rent it, or pledge it as collateral. Most important, you can make investments in your property having full confidence that the returns from that investment will also belong to you. Imagine a world in which you spend all summer tending to your corn crop and then your neighbor drives by in his combine, waves cheerily, and proceeds to harvest the whole crop for himself. Does that sound contrived? Not if you're a musician—because that is pretty much what Napster did by allowing individuals to download music without paying any compensation to the musicians who created it or the record companies that owned the copyrights. The music industry successfully sued Napster for facilitating piracy.

Property rights are not just about houses, cars, and things you can stack in a closet. Some of the most important property rights involve ownership of ideas, artwork, formulas, inventions, and even surgical procedures. This book is as good an example as any. I write the text. My agent sells it to a publisher, who contracts to have the book printed and distributed. The book is sold in private stores, where private security guards are hired to handle the massive, potentially unruly crowds trying to get a signed copy. At every juncture, only private parties are involved. These would appear to be straightforward market transactions; government could only get in the way. Indeed, I might curse the government for taxing my income, taxing the sale of the book, even taxing the salary that I pay the nanny to look after my daughters while I write.

In fact, the whole transaction is made possible by one thing: copyright law, which is a crucial form of property right for those of us who write for a living. The United States government guarantees that after I invest my time in producing a manuscript, no company can steal the text and publish it without compensating me. Any professor who photocopies it to use it in a class must pay the publisher a royalty first. Indeed, the government enforces similar rights for Microsoft software, and a related property right, a patent, for the pharmaceutical company that invented Viagra. The case of patents is an interesting one that is often mischaracterized. The ingredients in Viagra cost pennies a pill, but because Pfizer has a patent on Viagra giving it a monopoly on the right to sell the product for twenty years, the company sells each pill for as much as $7. This huge markup, which is common with new HIV/AIDS drugs and other lifesaving products, is often described as some kind of social injustice perpetrated by rapacious companies—the "big drug companies" that Al Gore demonized in his presidential campaign. What would happen if other companies were allowed to sell Viagra, or if Pfizer were forced to sell the drug more cheaply? The price would fall to the point where it was much closer to the cost of production. Indeed, when a drug comes off patent—the point at which generic substitutes become legal—the price usually falls by 80 or 90 percent.

So why do we allow Pfizer to fleece Viagra users? Because if Viagra did not get patent protection, then Pfizer never would have made the large investments that were necessary to invent the drug in the first place. The real cost of breakthrough drugs is the research and development—scouring the world's rain forests for exotic tree barks with medicinal properties—not making the pills once the formula is discovered. The same is true with drugs for any other illness, no matter how serious or even life-threatening.* The average cost of bringing a new drug to market is somewhere in the area of $600 million. And for every successful drug, there are many expensive research forays that end in failure. Is there a way to pro-

---

* I cannot fully explain why the pharmaceutical companies were so resistant to providing low-cost HIV/AIDS drugs to Africa. These countries will never be able to pay the high prices charged in the developed world, so the companies would not be forgoing profits by selling the drugs cheaply. In places like South Africa, it's either cheap drugs or no drugs. This would appear to be a perfect opportunity for price discrimination: Make the drugs cheap in Cape Town and expensive in New York. True, price discrimination could create an opportunity for a black market; drugs sold cheaply in Africa could be resold illegally at high prices in New York. But that seems a manageable problem relative to the huge public relations cost of denying important drugs to large swathes of the world's population.

vide affordable drugs to low-income Americans—or poor individuals elsewhere in the world—without destroying the incentive to invent those drugs? Yes; the government could buy out the patent when a new drug is invented. The government would pay a firm up front a sum equal to what the firm would have earned over the course of its twenty-year patent. After that, the government would own the property right and could charge whatever price for the drugs it deemed appropriate. It's an expensive solution that comes with some problems of its own. For example, which drug patents would the government buy? Is arthritis serious enough to justify using public funds to make a new drug more affordable? How about asthma? Still, this kind of plan is at least consistent with the economic reality: Individuals and firms will make investments only when they are guaranteed to reap what they sow, literally or figuratively.

I recently stumbled on a curious example of how ambiguous property rights can stifle economic development. I was working on a long story on American Indians for *The Economist*. Having spent time on a handful of reservations, I noticed that there was very little private housing stock. Tribal members lived either in houses that had been financed by the federal government or in trailers. Why? One principal reason is that it is difficult, if not impossible, to get a conventional home mortgage on an Indian reservation because the land is owned communally. A tribal member may be given a piece of land to use, but he or she does not own it; the tribe does. What that means to a commercial bank is that a mortgage that has fallen delinquent cannot be foreclosed. If a bank is denied that unpleasant but necessary option, then the lender is left without any effective collateral on its loan. A trailer, on the other hand, is different. If you fall delinquent on your payments, the company can show up one day and haul it off the reservation. But trailers, unlike conventional housing, do not support local building trades. They are assembled thousands of miles away in a factory and then transported to the reservation. That process does not provide jobs for roofers, and masons, and drywallers, and electricians—which is what America's Indian reservations need more than anything else.

Government lowers the cost of doing business in the private sector in all kinds of ways: by providing uniform rules and regulations, such as contract law; by rooting out fraud; by circulating a sound currency. Government builds and maintains infrastructure—roads, bridges, locks and dams—that makes private commerce less costly. E-commerce may be a modern wonder, but let's not lose sight of the fact that after you order a book on Amazon, it will be dispatched from a distribution center in a truck barreling along Interstate 80. In the 1950s and 1960s, new roads, including the interstate highway system, accounted for a significant fraction of new capital created in the United States. And that investment in infrastructure is associated with large increases in productivity in industries that are vehicle-intensive.[9]

Effective regulation and oversight make markets more credible. Because of the diligence of the Securities and Exchange Commission (SEC), one can buy shares in a new company listed on the NASDAQ with a reasonable degree of certainty that neither the company nor the traders on the stock exchange are engaging in fraud. In short, government is responsible for the rule of law. (Failure of the rule of law is one reason why nepotism, clans, and other family-centered behavior are so common in developing countries; in the absence of binding contractual agreements, business deals can be guaranteed only by some kind of personal relationship.) Jerry Jordan, president of the Federal Reserve Bank of Cleveland, recently mused on something that is obvious but too often taken for granted: Our sophisticated institutions, both public and private, make it possible to undertake complex transactions with total strangers. He noted:

> It seems remarkable, when you think about it, that we often take substantial amounts of money to our bank and hand it over to people we have never met before. Or that securities traders can send millions of dollars to people they don't know in countries they have never been in. Yet this occurs all the time. We trust that the infrastructure is set in place that allows us not to worry that the person at the bank who takes our money doesn't just pocket it. Or that when we use credit cards to buy a new CD or tennis racquet over the Internet, from a business that is located in some other state

> or country, we are confident we will get our merchandise,
> and they are confident they will get paid.[10]

Shakespeare may have advised us to get rid of all the lawyers, but he was a playwright, not an economist. The reality is that we all complain about lawyers until we have been wronged, at which point we run out and hire the best one we can find. Government enforces the rules in a reasonably fair and efficient manner. Is it perfect? No. But rather than singing the praises of the American justice system, let me simply provide a counterexample from India. Abdul Waheed filed a lawsuit against his neighbor, a milk merchant named Mohammad Nanhe, who had built several drains at the edge of his property that emptied into Mr. Waheed's front yard. Mr. Waheed did not like the water draining onto his property, in part because he had hoped to add a third room to his cement house and he was worried that the drains would create a seepage problem. So he sued. The case came to trial in June 2000 in Moradabad, a city near New Delhi.[11]

There is one major complication with this civil dispute: The case was filed thirty-nine years ago; Mr. Waheed is dead and so is Mr. Nanhe. (Their relatives have inherited the case.) By one calculation, if no new cases were filed in India, it would still take 324 years to clear all the existing cases from the docket. These are not just civil cases. In late 1999, a seventy-five-year-old man was released from a Calcutta jail after waiting thirty-seven years to be tried on murder charges. He was released because the witnesses and investigating officer were all dead. (A judge had declared him mentally incompetent to stand trial in 1963 but the action was somehow lost.) *Bear in mind that by developing world standards, India has relatively good government institutions.* In Somalia, these kinds of disputes are not resolved in the courts.

All the while, government enforces antitrust laws that forbid companies from conspiring together in ways that erase the benefits of competition. Having three airlines that secretly collude when setting fares is no better than having one slovenly monopoly. The bottom line is that all these institutions form the tracks on which capitalism runs. Thomas Friedman, foreign affairs columnist for the *New York Times*, made this point in a recent column. "Do you know how much your average Russian would give for a week of Joel Klein and Janet Reno busting Russia's oligarchs and monopolists?" he queried.[12] He pointed out that with many of the world's economies plagued by endemic corruption, particularly in the developing world, he has found that foreigners often envy us for . . . hold on to your latte here . . . our Washington bureaucrats; "that is, our institutions, our courts, our bureaucracy, our military, and our regulatory agencies—the SEC, the Federal Reserve, the FAA, the FDA, the FBI, the EPA, the IRS, the INS, the U.S. Patent Office and the Federal Emergency Management Agency," he wrote.

The government has another crucial role: It provides a wide array of goods, so-called "public goods," that make us better off but would not otherwise be provided by the private sector. Suppose I decide to buy an antimissile system to protect myself from missiles lobbed by rogue nations. (It would be similar to the DirectTV satellite dish, only a lot more expensive.) I ask my neighbor Etienne if he would like to share the cost of this system; he says no, knowing full well that my missile defense will shield his house from any missiles that North Korea may send our way. Etienne, and most of my other neighbors, have a powerful incentive to be "free riders" on my system. At the same time, I do not want to pay the full cost of the system myself. In the end, we get no missile defense system even though it might have made us all better off.

Public goods have two salient characteristics. First, the cost of offering the good to additional users—even thousands or millions of people— is very low or even zero. Think of that missile defense system; if I pay to knock Saddam Hussein's missiles out of the sky, the millions of people who live relatively close to me in the Chicago metropolitan area get that benefit free. The same is true of a radio signal or a lighthouse or a large park; once it is operational for one person, it can serve thousands more at no extra cost. Second, it is very hard, if not impossible, to exclude persons who have not paid for the good from using it. How exactly do you tell a ship's captain that he can't use a lighthouse? Do you make him close his eyes as he sails by? ("Attention USS *Britannica*: You are peeking!") I once had a professor at Princeton who began his lecture on public goods by saying, "Okay, who are the suckers who actually contribute to public radio?"

(Note: He now has a prominent position in the Bush administration.)

Free riders can cripple enterprises. Author Stephen King recently attempted an experiment in which he offered his new novel directly to readers via the Internet. The plan was that he would offer monthly installments for readers to download in exchange for a $1 payment based on the honor system. He warned that the story would fold if fewer than 75 percent of readers made the voluntary payment. "If you pay, the story rolls. If you don't, it folds," he wrote on the website. The outcome was sadly predictable to economists who have studied these kinds of problems. The story folded. At the time "The Plant" went into hibernation, only 46 percent of readers had paid to download the last chapter offered.

That is the basic problem if public goods are left to private enterprise. Firms cannot force consumers to pay for these kinds of goods, no matter how much utility they may derive from them or how often they use them. (Remember the lighthouse.) And any system of voluntary payments falls prey to the free riders. Think about the following:

- Basic research. We have already discussed the powerful incentives that profits create for pharmaceutical companies and the like. But not all important scientific discoveries have immediate commercial applications. Exploring the universe or understanding how human cells divide or seeking subatomic particles may be many steps removed from launching a communications satellite or developing a drug that shrinks tumors or finding a cleaner source of energy. As important, this kind of research must be shared freely with other scientists in order to maximize its value. In other words, you won't get rich—or even cover your costs in most cases—by generating knowledge that may someday significantly advance the human condition. Most of America's basic research is done either directly by the government at places like NASA and the National Institutes for Health or at research universities, which are nonprofit institutions that receive federal funding.
- Law enforcement. There is no shortage of private security firms— "rent-a-cops" as we used to call them in college as they aggressively sought out twenty-year-old beer drinkers. But there is a limit to

what they can or will do. They will only defend your property against some kind of trespass. They will not proactively seek out criminals who might someday break into your house; they will not track Mexican drug kingpins or stop felons from entering the country or solve other crimes so that the perpetrator does not eventually attack you. All of these things would make you and your property safer in the long run, but they have inherent free rider problems. If I pay for this kind of security, everyone else in the country benefits at no cost. Everywhere in the world, most kinds of law enforcement are undertaken by government.

- Parks and open space. Chicago's lakefront is the city's greatest asset. For some thirty miles along Lake Michigan, there are parks and beaches owned by the city and protected from private development. If this is the best use of the land, which I firmly believe it is, then why wouldn't a private landowner use it for the same purposes? After all, we've just stipulated that private ownership of an asset ensures that it will be put to its most productive use. If I owned thirty miles of lakefront, why couldn't I charge bicyclists and roller bladers and picnickers in order to make a healthy profit on my investment? Two reasons: First, it would be a logistical nightmare to patrol such a large area and charge admission. More important, many of the people who value an open lakefront don't actually use it. They may enjoy the view from the window of a high-rise apartment or as they drive along Lake Shore Drive. A private developer would never collect anything from these people and would therefore undervalue the open space. This is true for many of America's natural resources. You have probably never been to Prince William Sound in Alaska and may never go there. Yet you almost certainly cared when the *Exxon Valdez* ran aground and despoiled the area. Government can make us collectively better off by protecting these kinds of resources.

Last, government redistributes wealth. We collect taxes from some citizens and provide benefits to others. Contrary to popular opinion, most government benefits do not go to the poor; they go to the middle class in the form of Medicare and Social Security. Still, government has the legal authority to play Robin Hood; other governments around the world, such as the European countries, do so quite actively. What does economics have to say about this? Not much, unfortunately. The most important questions related to income distribution require philosophical or ideological answers, not economic ones. Consider the following question: Which would be a better state of the world, one in which every person in America earned $25,000—enough to cover the basic necessities—or the status quo, in which some Americans are wildly rich, some are desperately poor, and the *average* income is somewhere around $30,000? The latter describes a bigger economic pie; the former would be a smaller pie more evenly divided.

Economics does not provide the tools for answering philosophical questions related to income distribution. For example, economists cannot prove that taking a dollar forcibly from Bill Gates and giving it to a starving child would improve overall social welfare. Most people intuitively believe that to be so, but it is theoretically possible that Bill Gates would lose more utility from having the dollar taken from him than the starving child would gain. This is an extreme example of a more general problem: We measure our well-being in terms of utility, which is a theoretical concept, not a measurement tool that can be quantified, compared among individuals, or aggregated for the nation. We cannot say, for example, that Candidate A's tax plan would generate 120 units of utility for the nation while Candidate B's tax plan would generate only 111.

Consider the following question posed by Amartya Sen, winner of the 1998 Nobel Prize in Economics.[13] Three men have come to you looking for work. You have only one job to offer; the work cannot be divided among the three of them and they are all equally qualified. One of your goals is to make the world a better place by hiring the man who needs the job the most.

The first man is the poorest of the three. If improving human welfare is your primary aim, then presumably he should get the job. Or maybe not. The second man is not the poorest, but he is the unhappiest because he has only recently become poor and he is not accustomed to the deprivation. Offering him the job will cause the greatest gain in happiness.

The third man is neither the poorest nor the unhappiest. But he has a chronic health problem, borne stoically for his whole life, that can be cured with the wages from the job. Thus, giving him the job would have the most profound effect on an individual's quality of life.

Who should get the job? As would be expected of a Nobel Prize winner, Mr. Sen has many interesting things to say about this dilemma. But the bottom line is that there is no right answer. The same thing is true—contrary to what politicians on both sides of the political spectrum will tell you—with issues related to the redistribution of wealth in a modern economy. Will a tax increase that funds a better safety net for the poor but lowers overall economic growth make the country better off? That is a matter of opinion, not economic expertise. (Note that every presidential administration is able to find very qualified economists to support its ideological positions.) Liberals (in the American sense of the word) often ignore the fact that a growing pie, even if unequally divided, will almost always make even the small pieces larger. The developing world needs economic growth (to which international trade contributes heavily) to make the poor better off. Period. One historical reality is that government policies that ostensibly serve the poor can have inadvertent consequences that make them less effective or even counterproductive.

Meanwhile, conservatives often blithely assume that we should all rush out into the street and cheer for any policy that makes the economy grow faster, neglecting the fact that there are perfectly legitimate intellectual grounds for supporting other policies, such as protecting the environment or redistributing income, that may diminish the overall size of the pie. Indeed, some recent evidence suggests that our sense of well-being is determined at least as much by our relative wealth as it is by our absolute level of wealth. In other words, we derive utility not just from having a big television but from having a television that is as big as or bigger than the neighbors'.

Good government matters. The more sophisticated our economy becomes, the more sophisticated our government institutions need to be. The Internet is a perfect example. The private sector will be the engine of growth for the web economy, but it will be the government that roots out fraud, makes on-line transactions legally binding, sorts out property rights (such as domain names), settles disputes, and deals with issues that we have not even thought about yet.

One sad irony of September 11 and the subsequent anthrax attacks was that one simple-minded view of government, that "taxpayers know better what to do with their money than the government does," was exposed for its hollowness. Individual taxpayers cannot gather intelligence, track down a fugitive in the mountains of Afghanistan, do research on bioterrorism, or protect planes and airports. It is true that if the government takes money out of my paycheck, then there are things that would have given me utility that I can no longer buy. But it is also true that there are things that would make me better off that I cannot buy for myself. I cannot build a missile defense system, or protect endangered species, or stop global warming, or install traffic lights, or regulate the New York Stock Exchange, or negotiate lower trade barriers with China. Government enables us to work collectively to do those things.

CHAPTER 4

Government and the Economy II:

The army was lucky to get that screwdriver for $500

By now you are probably ready to extol the virtues of bureaucracy at your next dinner party. Not so fast. If government were so wonderful, then the most government-intensive countries in the world—places like North Korea and Cuba—would be economic powerhouses. They're not. Government is good at doing some things and tragically bad at doing others. Government can deal with significant externalities—or it can regulate an economy to the point of ruin. Government can provide essential public goods—or it can squander enormous tax revenues on ineffective programs and pet projects. Government can transfer money from the wealthy to the disadvantaged—or it can transfer money from common folk to the politically well-connected. In short, government can be used to create the foundations for a vibrant market economy or to stifle highly productive behavior. The wisdom, of course, lies in telling the difference.

There is an old joke, one of Ronald Reagan's favorites, that goes something like this. A Soviet woman is trying to buy a Lada, one of the cheap automobiles made in the former Soviet Union. The dealer tells her that there is a shortage of these cars, despite their reputation for shoddy quality. Still, the woman insists on placing an order. The dealer gets out a large, dusty ledger and adds the woman's name to the long waiting list. "Come back two years from now on March 17th," he says.

The woman consults her calendar. "Morning or afternoon?" she asks.

"What difference does it make?" the surly dealer replies. "That's two years from now!"

"The plumber is coming that day," she says.

If the USSR taught us anything, it is that monopoly stifles any need to be innovative or responsive to customers. And government is one very large monopoly. Why is the clerk at the Department of Motor Vehicles plodding and surly? Because she can be. *What would your business look like if your customers, by law, could not go anywhere else?* It would certainly make me think twice about working late, or, for that matter, working at all on warm summer days when the Cubs were playing at home.

Government operations are often described as inefficient. In fact, they operate exactly as we would expect given their incentives. Think about the Department of Motor Vehicles, which has a monopoly on the right to grant driver's licenses. What is the point of being friendly, staying open longer, making customers comfortable, adding clerks to shorten lines, keeping the office clean, or interrupting a personal call when a customer comes to the window? *None of these things will produce even one more customer!* Every single person who needs a driver's license already comes to the DMV and will continue to come no matter how unpleasant the experience. There are limits, of course. If service becomes bad enough, then voters may take action against the politician in charge. But that is an indirect, cumbersome process. Compare that to your options in the private sector. If a rat scampered across the counter at your favorite Chinese take-out restaurant, you would (presumably) just stop ordering there. End of problem. The restaurant will get rid of the rats or go out of business. Meanwhile, if you stop going to the Department of Motor Vehicles, you may end up in jail.

This contrast was illustrated to me quite sharply several weeks ago when a check I was expecting from Fidelity, the mutual fund company, failed to show up in the mail. (I needed the money to pay back my mother, who can be a fierce creditor.) Day after day went by—no check. Meanwhile, my mother was "checking in" with increasing frequency. One of two parties was guilty, Fidelity or the U.S. Postal Service, and I was getting progressively more angry. Finally I called Fidelity to demand proof that the check had been mailed. I was prepared to move all of my (relatively meager) assets to Vanguard, Putnam, or some other mutual fund company (or at least make the threat). Instead, I spoke with a very friendly customer assistant who explained that the check had been mailed two weeks earlier but apologized profusely for my inconvenience anyway. She canceled the check and issued another one in a matter of seconds. Then she apologized some more for a problem that, it was now apparent, her company did not cause.

The culprit was the post office. So I got even angrier and then . . . I did nothing. What exactly was I supposed to do? The local postmaster does not accept complaints by phone. I did not want to waste time writing a letter (which might never arrive anyway). Nor would it help to complain to our letter carrier, who has never been consumed by the quality of his service. Roughly once a month he gets "off" by a house and delivers every family's mail to the house one door to the west. This is a problem, since my neighbor to the west spends months at a time at his summer home in Canada (during which time I am mercifully spared the noise of those bongo drums). The point, carefully disguised in this diatribe, is that the U.S. Postal Service has a monopoly on the delivery of first-class mail. And it shows.

There are two broader lessons to be learned from this. First, government should not be the sole provider of a good or service unless there is a compelling reason to believe that the private sector will fail in that role. That leaves plenty for government to do in areas ranging from public health to national defense. Having just lambasted the Department of Motor Vehicles, I must admit that issuing driver's licenses is probably a function that should remain in the hands of government. Private firms issuing driver's licenses might not compete only on price and quality of service; they would have a powerful incentive to attract customers by issuing licenses to drivers who don't deserve them.

Still, that leaves a lot of things that government should *not* be doing. Delivering mail is one of them. A century ago the government may have had legitimate reasons for being in the mail business. The U.S. Postal Service indirectly assisted underdeveloped regions of the country by guaranteeing mail delivery at a subsidized rate (since delivering mail to remote areas is more expensive than delivering to a metropolitan area but the stamp costs the same). The technology was different, too. In 1820, it was unlikely that more than one private firm would have made the massive investment necessary to build a system that could deliver mail anywhere in the country. (A private monopoly is no better—and perhaps worse—than a government monopoly.) Times have changed. FedEx and UPS have proved that private firms are perfectly capable of building worldwide delivery infrastructures.

Is there a huge economic cost associated with mediocre mail service? Probably not. But imagine the U.S. Postal Service controlling other important sectors of the economy. Elsewhere in the world, the government runs steel mills, coal mines, banks, hotels, airlines. All the benefits that competition can bring to these businesses are lost, and citizens are made worse off as a result. (Food for thought: One of the largest government monopolies remaining in the United States is public education.)

There is a second more subtle point. Even if government has an important role to play in the economy, such as building roads and bridges, it does not follow that government must actually do the work. Government employees do not have to be the ones pouring cement. Rather, government can plan and finance a new highway and then solicit bids from private contractors to do the work. If the bidding process is competitive (a big "if" in many cases), then the project will go to the firm that can do the best work at the lowest cost. In short, a public good is delivered in a way that harnesses all the benefits of the market.

Even the Central Intelligence Agency has taken this lesson to heart. The CIA needs to be on the cutting edge of technology, yet it cannot provide the same incentives to innovate as the private sector can. Someone who makes a breakthrough discovery at the CIA will not find himself or herself worth hundreds of millions of dollars six months later, as might happen at a Silicon Valley startup. So the CIA decided to use the private sector for its own ends.[1] In 1999, the CIA used money appropriated by Congress to open its own venture capital firm, named In-Q-It (in a sly reference to Q, the technology guru who develops gadgets for James Bond). An In-Q-It executive explained that the purpose of the venture was to "move information technology to the agency more quickly than traditional Government procurement processes allow." Like any other venture capital firm, In-Q-It will make investments in small firms with promising new technologies. In-Q-It and the firms it bankrolls will make money—perhaps a lot of money—if these technologies turn out to have valuable commercial applications. At the same time, the CIA will retain the right to use any new technology with potential intelligence-gathering applications. A Silicon Valley entrepreneur funded by In-Q-It may develop a better way to encrypt data on the Internet—something that e-commerce firms would snap up. Meanwhile, the CIA would end up with a better way to safeguard information sent to Washington by covert operatives around the world.

In the private sector, markets tell us where to devote our resources. Not long ago I was in the center field seats at a Chicago White Sox game when I spotted a vendor walking through the stands wearing what was prominently advertised as the Margarita Space Pak. This piece of technology enabled the vendor to make frozen margaritas on the spot; somehow he mixes the drinks in his backpack-like device and then pours them through a hose into the awaiting plastic cup. The ostensible social benefit of this breakthrough technology is that baseball fans can now enjoy margaritas, rather than just beer, without leaving their seats. I suspect that some of our country's top engineering minds—a scarce resource—devoted their time and effort to creating the Margarita Space Pak, which means that they were *not* spending their time searching for a cheaper, cleaner source of energy or a better way to deliver nutrients to malnourished children in Africa. Does the world need the Margarita Space Pak? No. Could the engineering minds that created it have been put to some more socially useful purpose? Yes. But—this is an important point—*that's my opinion and I don't run the world.*

When government controls some element of the economy, scarce resources are allocated by autocrats or bureaucrats or politicians rather than by the market. In the former Soviet Union, massive steel plants churned out tons of steel, but the average citizen couldn't buy soap or decent cigarettes. In hindsight, it should not have been a surprise that the USSR was the first to send a rocket into orbit (and equally obvious that it would not invent the Margarita Space Pak). The government could simply mandate that resources be spent on the space program, even if people would rather have had fresh vegetables or tube socks. Some of these resource allocation decisions were tragic. For example, Soviet central planners did not consider birth control to be an economic priority. The Soviet government could have made contraceptives available to all; any country that can build intercontinental ballistic missiles has the know-how to make a birth control pill, or at least a condom. But contraception simply was not where central planners chose to channel the country's resources, leaving abortion as the only form of family planning. In the years of communism, there were roughly two abortions for every single live birth. Since the collapse of the Soviet Union, Western contraceptives have become widely available and the abortion rate has fallen by half.

Even in democratic countries, the political process can devote resources to some pretty strange places. I recently interviewed a technology expert about the government's plans to build a high-speed particle accelerator in the early 1990s (a good example of basic research). The accelerator would bring jobs and federal money to the location that landed the project. The two leading sites were northern Illinois and somewhere in Texas. According to the fellow I was speaking with, Illinois was the more attractive site because it already had a particle accelerator and a major federal laboratory. Much of the scientific infrastructure was in place and would not have to be duplicated. Despite that, the project was sited in Texas. "Why?" I asked. This guy looked at me as if I were some kind of idiot. "Because George Bush was president," he answered, as if there could be no more obvious reason to put a giant particle accelerator in Texas. In the end, the government spent roughly $1 billion on the project and then abandoned it.

The private sector allocates resources where they will earn the highest return. In contrast, the government allocates resources wherever the political process sends them. (Consider a recent front-page headline in the *Wall Street Journal*: "Industries that Backed Bush Are Now Seeking Return on Investment.") [2] Sometimes this is a necessary but imperfect process; military bases get built or closed in a way that reflects the makeup of the Senate Armed Services Committee as much as or more than the military needs of the country. A private army is not an option, so this is the best we can reasonably expect. But the less the economy is left to politics, the better. Powerful politicians should not be deciding, for example, who gets bank credit and who does not. Yet that is exactly what happens in autocratic nations like China and in democratic countries like Indonesia where politicians play "crony capitalism." Projects that have the potential to be highly profitable do not get financing while dubious undertakings sponsored by the president's brother-in-law are lavished with government funds. Consumers lose in two ways. First, their tax money is squandered when projects that never should have been funded in the first place go bust (or when the whole banking system needs to be bailed out because it is full of rotten, politically motivated loans). Second, the economy does not develop as quickly or efficiently as it might because credit (a finite resource) is channeled away from worthwhile projects: car plants don't get built; students don't get loans; entrepreneurs don't get funding. As a result, resources are squandered and the economy does not perform anywhere near its potential.

Government need not run steel mills or parcel out bank loans to meddle in the economy. The more subtle and pervasive kind of government involvement is regulation. Markets work because resources flow to where they are valued most. Government regulation inherently interferes with that process. In the world painted by economics textbooks, entrepreneurs cross the road to earn higher profits. In the real world, government officials will be standing by the road demanding a toll, if not blocking the crossing entirely. The entrepreneurial firm may have to obtain a license to cross the road, or have its vehicle emissions tested by the Department of Transportation as it crosses the road, or prove to the INS that the workers crossing the road are U.S. citizens. Some of these regulations may make us better off. It's good to have government officials blocking the road when the "entrepreneur" is carrying seven kilos of cocaine. But every single regulation carries a cost, too.

Milton Friedman, who is a delightful writer and the most articulate spokesman for a less intrusive government (and a far more subtle thinker than many of the writers who haunt the op-ed pages these days purporting to have inherited his mantle), makes this point in *Capitalism and Freedom* by recounting an exchange between an economist and a representative of the American Bar Association at a large meeting of lawyers.[3] The economist was arguing before the group that admission to the bar should be less restrictive. Allowing more lawyers to practice, including those who might not be the sharpest knives in the drawer, would lower the cost of legal services, he argued. After all, some legal procedures, such as basic wills and real estate closings, do not require the services of a brilliant Constitutional scholar. He argued by analogy that it would be absurd for the government to require that all automobiles be Cadillacs. At that point, a lawyer in the audience rose and said, "The country cannot afford anything but Cadillac lawyers!"

In fact, demanding only "Cadillac lawyers" completely misses all that economics seeks to teach us about trade-offs. In a world with only Cadillacs, most people would not be able to afford any transportation at all. Sometimes there is nothing wrong with allowing people to drive Dodge Neons.

For a striking international example of the effects of regulation on the economy, consider the recent civil unrest in Delhi, India.[4] Delhi is one of the most polluted cities in the world. After the Supreme Court of India made a major decision regarding industrial pollution, thousands of Delhi residents took to the streets in violent protest. "Mobs torched buses, threw stones, and blocked major roads," the *New York Times* reported. Here is the twist: *The protesters were supporting the polluters.* The Supreme Court held the city of Delhi in contempt for failing to close some ninety thousand small factories that pollute the area. Those factories employ roughly a million people who will be thrown out of work. The headline on the story nicely encapsulated the tradeoff: "A Cruel Choice in New Delhi: Jobs vs. a Safer Environment."

How about DDT, one of the nastier chemicals mankind has unleashed on the environment? DDT is a "persistent organic pollutant" that works its way into and up the food chain, wreaking havoc along the way. Should this noxious pesticide be banned from the planet? *The Economist* has made a convincing argument that it should not.[5] Much of the developing world is ravaged by malaria; some 300 million people suffer from the disease every year and more than a million die. (Of course, malaria is not a disease that we are particularly sensitive to in the developed world, since it was eradicated in North America and Europe fifty years ago.) Harvard economist Jeffrey Sachs has estimated that sub-Saharan Africa would be almost a third richer today if malaria had been eradicated in 1965. Now, back to DDT, which is the most cost-effective way of controlling the mosquitoes that spread the disease. The next best alternative is not only less effective but also four times as expensive. Do the health benefits of DDT justify its environmental costs? Maybe. At a minimum, we ought to reject the grossly oversimplified argument that any chemical that harms the environment should be banned.

Meanwhile, not all regulations are created equal. The relevant question is not always whether or not government should involve itself in the economy; the more important issue may be how the subsequent regulation is structured. University of Chicago economist and Nobel laureate Gary Becker spends his summers on Cape Cod, where he is a fond consumer of striped bass.[6] Because the stocks of this fish are dwindling, the government has imposed a limit on the total commercial catch of striped bass allowed every season. Mr. Becker has no problem with that; he would like to be able to eat striped bass ten years from now, too.

Instead, he raised the issue in his regular column for *Business Week* of how the government chose to limit the total catch. At the time he was writing, the government had imposed an aggregate quota on the quantity of striped bass that could be harvested every season. Mr. Becker wrote, "Unfortunately, this is a very poor way to control fishing because it encourages each fishing boat to catch as much as it can early in the season, before other boats bring in enough fish to reach the aggregate quota that applies to all of them." Everybody loses: The fishermen get low prices for their fish when they sell into a glut early in the season; then, after the aggregate quota is reached early in the season, consumers are unable to get any striped bass at all. Several years later, Massachusetts did change its system so that the striped bass quota is divided among individual fishermen; the total catch is still limited but individual fishermen can fulfill their quota anytime during the season.

The key to thinking like an economist is recognizing the trade-offs inherent to fiddling with markets. Regulation can disrupt the movement of capital and labor, raise the cost of goods and services, inhibit innovation, and otherwise shackle the economy (such as by letting mosquitoes escape alive). *And that is just the regulation inspired by good intentions.* At worst, regulation can become a powerful tool for self-interest as firms work the political system to their own benefit. After all, if you can't beat your competitors, then why not have the government hobble them for you? University of Chicago economist George Stigler won the Nobel Prize in Economics in 1982 for his trenchant observation and supporting evidence that firms and professional associations often seek regulation as a way of advancing their own interests.

Consider a recent regulatory campaign in my home state of Illinois. The state legislature is being pressured to enact more stringent licensing requirements for manicurists. Is this a grassroots lobbying campaign being waged by the victims of pedicures gone terribly awry? (One can just imagine them limping in pain up the capital steps.) Not exactly. The lobbying is being done by the Illinois Cosmetology Association on behalf of established spas and salons that would rather not compete with a slew of immigrant upstarts. The number of nail salons grew 23 percent in just one year in the late 1990s with discount salons offering manicures for as little as $6, compared to $25 in a full-service salon. Stricter licensing requirements—which almost always exempt existing service providers—would limit this fierce competition by making it more expensive to open a new salon.

Milton Friedman has pointed out that the same thing happened on a wider scale in the 1930s. After Hitler came to power in 1933, large numbers of professionals fled Germany and Austria for the United States. Many professions erected barriers such as "good citizenship" requirements and language exams that had a tenuous connection to the quality of service provided. Friedman pointed out that the number of foreign-trained physicians licensed to practice in the United States in the five years after 1933 was the same as in the five years before—which would have been highly unlikely if licensing requirements existed only to screen out incompetent doctors but quite likely if the licensing requirements were used to ration the number of foreign doctors allowed into the profession.

By global standards, the United States has a relatively lightly regulated economy (though try making that argument at a Chamber of Commerce meeting). Indeed, one sad irony of the developing world is that governments fail in their most basic tasks, such as defining property rights and enforcing the law, while piling on other kinds of heavy-handed regulation. In theory, this kind of regulation could protect consumers from fraud, improve public health, or safeguard the environment. On the other hand, economists have asked whether this kind of regulation is less of a "helping hand" for society and more of a "grabbing hand" for corrupt bureaucrats whose opportunities to extort bribes rise along with the number of government permits and licenses required for any endeavor.

A group of economists studied the "helping hand" versus "grabbing hand" question by examining the procedures, costs, and expected delays associated with starting up a new business in seventy-five different countries.[7] The range was extraordinary. Registering and licensing a business in Canada requires a mere two procedures compared to twenty in Bolivia. The time required to open a new business legally ranges from two days, again in Canada, to six months in Mozambique. The cost of jumping through these assorted government hoops ranges from 0.4 percent of per capita GDP in New Zealand to 260 percent of per capita GDP in Bolivia. The study found that in poor countries like Vietnam, Mozambique, Egypt, and Bolivia an entrepreneur has to give up an amount equal to one to two times his annual salary (not counting bribes and the opportunity cost of his time) just to get a new business licensed.

So are consumers safer and healthier in countries like Mozambique than they are in Canada or New Zealand? No. The authors find that compliance with international quality standards is lower in countries with more regulation. Nor does this government red tape appear to reduce pollution or raise health levels. Meanwhile, excessive regulation pushes entrepreneurs into the underground economy, where there is no regulation at all. It is hardest to open a new business in countries where corruption is highest, suggesting that excessive regulation is a potential source of income for the bureaucrats who enforce it.

•　　•　　•

Let's step out of our cynical mode for a moment and return to the idea that government has the capacity to do many good things. Even then, when government is doing the things that it is theoretically supposed to do, government spending must be financed by levying taxes, and taxes exert a cost on the economy. This "fiscal drag," as Burton Malkiel has called it, stems from two things. First, taxes take money out of our pockets, which necessarily diminishes our purchasing power and therefore our utility. True, the government can create jobs by spending billions of dollars on jet fighters, but we are paying for those jets with money from our paychecks, which means that we buy fewer televisions, we give less to charity, we take fewer vacations. Thus, government is not necessarily creating jobs; it may be simply moving them around, or, on net, destroying them. This effect of taxation is less obvious than the new defense plant at which happy workers churn out shiny airplanes. (When we turn to macroeconomics later in the book, we will examine the Keynesian premise that government can increase economic growth by stoking the economy during economic downturns.)

Second, and more subtly, taxation causes individuals to change their behavior in ways that make the economy worse off without necessarily providing any revenue for the government. Think about the income tax, which can be as high as 50 cents for every dollar earned by the time all the relevant state and federal taxes are tallied up. Some individuals who would prefer to work if they were taking home every dollar they earn may decide to leave the labor force when the marginal tax rate is 50 percent. *Everybody loses in this situation.* Someone whose preference is to work quits his or her job (or does not start working in the first place), yet the government raises no revenue.

As we noted in Chapter 2, economists refer to this kind of inefficiency associated with taxation as "dead weight loss." It makes you worse off without making anyone else better off. Imagine that a burglar breaks into your home and steals assorted personal possessions; in his haste, he makes off with wads of cash but also a treasured family photo album. There is no deadweight loss associated with the cash he has stolen; every dollar purloined from you makes him better off by a dollar. (Perversely, it is simply a transfer of wealth in the eyes of our amoral economists.) On the other hand, the stolen photo album is pure deadweight loss. It means nothing to the thief, who tosses it in a dumpster when he realizes what he has taken. Yet it is a tremendous loss to you. Any kind of taxation that discourages productive behavior will cause some deadweight loss.

Taxes can discourage investment, too. An entrepreneur who is considering making a risky investment may do so when the expected return is $100 million but not when the expected return, diminished by taxation, is only $60 million. An individual may pursue a graduate degree that will raise her income by 10 percent. But that same investment, which is costly in terms of tuition and time, may not be worthwhile if her after-tax income—what she actually sees after all those deductions on the paycheck—only goes up 5 percent. (On the day my younger brother got his first paycheck, he came home, opened the envelope, and then yelled, "Who the hell is FICA?") Or consider a family that has a spare $1,000 and is deciding between buying a big-screen television and squirreling the money away in an investment fund. These two options have profoundly differently impacts on the economy in the long run. Choosing the investment makes capital available to firms that build plants, conduct research, train workers. These investments are the macro equivalents of a college education; they make us more productive in the long run and therefore richer. Buying the television, on the other hand, is current consumption. It makes us happy today but does nothing to make us richer tomorrow.

Yes, money spent on a television keeps workers employed at the television factory. But if the same money were invested, it would create jobs somewhere else, say for scientists in a laboratory or workers on a construction site, while also making us richer in the long run. Think about the college example. Sending students to college creates jobs for professors. Using the same money to buy fancy sports cars for high school graduates would create jobs for auto workers. The crucial difference between these scenarios is that a college education makes a young person more productive for the rest of his or her life; a sports car does not. Thus, college tuition is an investment; buying a sports car is consumption (though buying a car for work or business might be considered an investment).

So back to our family with a spare $1,000. What will they choose to do with it? Their decision will depend on the *after-tax* return the family can expect to earn by investing the money rather than spending it. The higher the tax, such as a capital gains tax, the lower the return on the investment—and therefore the more attractive the television becomes.

Taxation discourages both work and investment. Many economists will argue that cutting taxes and rolling back regulation will unleash productive forces in the economy. This is true. The most ardent "supply-siders" will argue further that tax cuts can actually raise the amount of revenue collected by the government because we all will work harder, earn higher incomes, and end up paying more in taxes even though tax rates have fallen. This is the idea behind the Laffer curve, which provided the intellectual underpinnings for the large Reagan-era tax cuts. Economist Arthur Laffer theorized in 1974 that high tax rates discourage so much work and investment that cutting taxes will earn the government more revenue, not less. (He first sketched a graph of this idea on a restaurant napkin while having dinner with a group of journalists and politicians. In one of life's delicious ironies, it was Dick Cheney's napkin.)[8] At some level of taxation, this relationship must be true. If the personal income tax is 95 percent, for example, then no one is going to do a whole lot of work beyond what is necessary to subsist. Cutting the tax rate to 50 percent would almost certainly boost government revenues.

But would the same relationship hold true in the United States, where tax rates were much lower to begin with? The Reagan tax cuts provided an answer: no. The large tax cuts did not boost government revenues; they led to a decade and a half of large budget deficits. Mr. Laffer's conjecture did appear to hold true for the wealthiest Americans, who ended up sending more money to the Treasury after their tax rates were cut. Of course, this may be mere coincidence. As we shall explore in Chapter 6, highly skilled workers saw their wages rise sharply over the last several decades as the economy increasingly demanded more brains than brawn. Thus, the wealthiest Americans may have paid more in taxes because their incomes went up sharply, not because they were working harder in response to lower tax rates.

In the United States, where tax rates are low relative to the rest of the world, supply-side economics is a chimera: We cannot cut taxes *and* have more money to spend on government programs. Still, the proponents of smaller government have a point. Lower taxes can lead to more investment, which causes a faster long-term rate of economic growth. It is facile to dismiss this as a policy that strictly favors the rich. A growing pie is important—perhaps even most important—for those with the smallest slices. When the economy grows slowly or sinks into recession, it is steelworkers and busboys who are laid off, not brain surgeons and university professors. Rebecca Blank, a University of Michigan economist and member of the Council of Economic Advisers in the Clinton administration, looked back on the remarkable economic expansion of the 1990s and noted:

> I believe that the first and most important lesson for anti-poverty warriors from the 1990s is that sustained economic growth is a wonderful thing. To the extent that policies can help maintain strong employment growth, low unemployment, and expanding wages among workers, these policies may matter as much or more than the dollars spent on targeted programs for the poor. If there are no job opportunities, or if wages are falling, it is much more expensive—both in terms of dollars spent and political capital—for government programs alone to lift people out of poverty.[9]

So, for two chapters now I have danced around the obvious "Goldilocks" question: Is the role that government plays in the United States economy too big, too small, or just about right? I can finally offer a simple, straightforward, and unequivocal answer: It depends whom you ask. There are smart and thoughtful economists who would like to see a larger, more activist government; there are smart and thoughtful economists who would prefer a smaller government; and there is a continuum of thinkers in between.

In some cases, the experts disagree over factual questions, just as eminent surgeons may disagree over the appropriate remedy for opening a clogged artery. For example, there is an ongoing dispute over the effects of raising the minimum wage. Theory suggests that there must be a trade-off: A higher minimum wage obviously helps those workers whose wages are raised; at the same time, it hurts some low-wage workers who lose their jobs (or never get hired in the first place) because firms cut back on the number of workers they employ at the new higher wage. Economists disagree (and present competing research) over how many jobs are lost when the minimum wage goes up. This is a crucial piece of information if one is to make an informed decision on whether or not raising the minimum wage is a good policy for helping low-wage workers. Over time, it is a question that can be answered with good data and solid research. (As one policy analyst once pointed out to me, it may be easy to lie with statistics, but it's a lot easier to lie without them.)

More often, economics can merely frame issues that require judgments based on morals, philosophy, and politics—somewhat as a doctor lays out the options to a patient. The physician can outline the medical issues related to treating an advanced cancer with chemotherapy. The treatment decision ultimately resides with the patient, who will interject his or her own views on quality of life versus longevity, willingness to experience discomfort, family situation, etc.—all perfectly legitimate considerations that have nothing to do with medicine or science. Yet making that decision still requires excellent medical advice.

In that vein of thought, we can present a framework for thinking about the role of the government in the economy.

Government has the potential to enhance the productive capacity of the economy and make us much better off as a result. Government creates and sustains the legal framework that makes markets possible; it raises our utility by providing public goods that we are unable to purchase for ourselves; it fixes the rough edges of capitalism by correcting externalities, particularly in the environmental realm. Thus, the notion that smaller government is always better government is simply wrong.

That said, reasonable people can agree with everything above and still disagree over whether the U.S. government should be bigger or smaller. It is one thing to believe, in theory, that government has the capacity to spend resources in ways that will make us better off; it is another to believe that the fallible politicians who make up Congress are going to choose to spend money that way. Is a German-Russian museum in Lawrence Welk's birthplace of Strasburg, North Dakota, really a public good? Congress allocated $500,000 for the museum in 1990 (and then withdrew it in 1991 when there was a public outcry). How about a $100 million appropriation to search for extraterrestrial life? Searching for ET meets the definition of a public good, since it would be impractical for each of us to mount his or her own individual search for life in outer space. Still, I suspect that many Americans would prefer to see their money spent elsewhere.

If I were to poll one hundred economists, nearly every one of them would tell me that significantly improving primary and secondary education in this country would lead to large economic gains. But the same group would be divided over whether or not we should spend more money on public education. Why? Because they would disagree sharply over whether pouring more money into the existing system would improve student outcomes.

Some government activity shrinks the size of the pie but still may be socially desirable. Transferring money from the rich to the poor is technically "inefficient" in the sense that sending a check for $1 to a poor family may cost the economy $1.25 when the deadweight costs of taxation are taken into account. The relatively high taxation necessary to support a strong social safety net falls most heavily on those with productive assets, including human capital, making countries like France a good place to be a child born into a poor family and a bad place to be an Internet entrepreneur (which in turn makes it a bad place to be a high-tech worker). Overall, policies that guarantee some pie for everybody will slow the growth of the pie itself. Per capita income in the United States is higher than the per capita income in France; the United States also has far more children living in poverty.

Having said all that, reasonable people can disagree over the appropriate level of social spending. First, they may have different preferences about how much wealth they are willing to trade off for more equality. The United States is a richer but more unequal place than most of Europe. Second, the notion of a simple trade-off between wealth and equality oversimplifies the dilemma of helping the most disadvantaged.

Economists who care deeply about the poorest Americans may disagree over whether the poor would be helped more by expensive government programs, such as universal health care, or by lower taxes that would encourage economic growth and put more low-income Americans to work at higher wages.

Last, some government involvement in the economy is purely destructive. Heavy-handed government can be like a millstone around the neck of a market economy. Good intentions can lead to government programs and regulations whose benefits are grossly outweighed by their costs. Bad intentions can lead to all kinds of laws that serve special interests or corrupt politicians. This is especially true in the developing world, where much good could be done just by getting government out of areas of the economy where it does not belong. As Jerry Jordan, president and CEO of the Federal Reserve Bank of Cleveland, has noted, "What separates the economic 'haves' from the 'have-nots' is whether the role of an economy's institutions—particularly its public institutions—is to facilitate production or to confiscate it."[10]

In short, government is like a surgeon's scalpel: It is an intrusive tool that can be used for good or for ill. Wielded carefully and judiciously, it will facilitate the body's remarkable ability to heal itself. In the wrong hands, or wielded overzealously with even the best of intentions, it can cause great harm.

CHAPTER 5

Economics of Information:

McDonald's didn't create a better hamburger

W hen Bill Clinton ran for president in 1992, he floated the idea of Hope Scholarships. The Clinton plan (based on an earlier experiment at Yale) was seemingly elegant: Students could borrow money for college and then repay the loans after graduation with a percentage of their annual income rather than the usual fixed payments of principal plus interest. Graduates who went on to become investment bankers would owe more in student loans than graduates who counseled disadvantaged teens in poor neighborhoods, which was exactly the point. The plan was designed to address the concern that students graduating with large debts are forced to do well rather than do good. After all, it is hard to become a teacher or a social worker after graduating with $50,000 in student loans.

In theory, the program would finance itself. Administrators could determine the average postgraduation salary for eligible students and then calculate the percentage of income they would have to pay in order for the program to recoup its costs—say 1.5 percent of annual income for fifteen years. Students who became brain surgeons would pay back more than average; students who fought tropical diseases in Togo would pay less. On average, the high and low earners would cancel each other out and the program would break even.

There was just one problem: The Hope Scholarships had no hope of working, at least not without a large, ongoing government subsidy. The problem was a crucial asymmetry of information: Students know more about their future career plans than loan administrators do. College students never know their future plans with certainty, but most have a good idea whether their postgraduation income will be more or less than average—which is enough to determine if a Hope Scholarship would be more or less expensive than a conventional loan. Aspiring Wall Street barons would avoid the program because it's a bad deal for them. Who wants to pay back 1.5 percent of $5 million every year for fifteen years when a conventional loan would be much cheaper? Meanwhile, the world's future kindergarten teachers and Peace Corps volunteers would opt in.

The result is called adverse selection; future graduates sort themselves in or out of the program based on private information about their career plans. In the end, the program attracts predominantly low earners. The repayment calculations, based on the average postgraduation salary, no longer apply and the program cannot recover its costs. One may assume that Mr. Clinton ignored what his advisers almost certainly told him about the Yale experiment: It was quietly canceled after five years, both because repayments fell short of projections and because the administrative costs were prohibitive.

What we don't know *can* hurt us. Economists study how we acquire information, what we do with it, and how we make decisions when all we get to see is a book's cover. Indeed, the Swedish Academy of Sciences recognized this point in 2001 by awarding the Nobel Prize in Economics to George Akerlof, Michael Spence, and Joseph Stiglitz for their seminal work on the economics of information. Their work explores the problems that arise when rational people are forced to make decisions based on incomplete information, or when one party to a transaction knows more than another. Their insights are relevant to some of our most pressing social issues, from genetic screening to discrimination in the workplace.

Consider a small law firm interviewing two job candidates, one male and one female. Both candidates are recent Harvard Law School graduates and are eminently qualified for the position. If the "best" candidate for the job is the one who will earn the most money for the firm, which seems a reasonable assumption, then I will argue that the rational choice is to hire the man. The interviewer has no specific information on the family plans of the candidates at hand (and is forbidden by law from asking about them), but can make a reasonable inference based on what everyone knows about America at the beginning of the twenty-first century: Women still bear the bulk of child-rearing responsibilities. Demographics suggest that both candidates are likely to start families in the near future. Yet only the female candidate will take paid maternity leave. More important, she may not return to work after having the child, which leaves the firm with the cost of finding, hiring, and training another lawyer.

Is any of this certain? No. The male candidate may have dreams of staying home with his five children; the female candidate may have decided years ago that she has no interest in having children. But these are not the most likely scenarios. The female candidate is punished because the firm has no information on her specific circumstances but good data on broad social trends. Is this fair? No. (And it's not legal either.) *Yet the firm's logic makes sense.* In other words, it is rational to discriminate in this case, which turns the whole idea of discrimination on its head. Discrimination is usually irrational. As Nobel laureate Gary Becker pointed out in *The Economics of Discrimination*, employers with a "taste for discrimination" sacrifice profits because they pass over minorities in favor of less qualified whites.[1] A patient who refuses to see an eminent black doctor because of his skin color is a fool. A law firm that minimizes employee turnover by playing the statistical averages may offend our sensibilities and violate federal law—but it is not foolish.

When we approach this situation as an information problem, there are several crucial insights. First, firms are not the only villains. When professional women choose to have a child, take paid maternity leave, and then quit their companies, they impose a cost, arguably unfair, on their firms. *More important, they impose a cost on other women.* Firms that feel they have been "burned" by employees who take maternity leave and then quit are more likely to discriminate against young women in the hiring process (particularly those who are already pregnant) and less likely to offer generous maternity benefits. The good news is that there is a quick and easy solution: a generous but refundable maternity package. Keep it if you come back to work, return it if you don't. That simple policy change gives us nearly everything we want. Firms no longer have to be concerned about paying benefits to women who will not return to work. Indeed, it becomes possible to offer more generous benefits without providing an incentive for workers to take the money and run. Women, in turn, do not face the same level of discrimination in the hiring process.

Of course, the best long-term solution is to change behavior at the household level. If and when men assume a larger share of child-care responsibilities, it will change the "profile" of job applicants. An interviewer will no longer be able to rationally infer that female applicants are more likely to leave the firm than male applicants. Thus, the incentive for firms to discriminate against young women in the hiring process will go away completely. At the same time, firms with a higher fraction of men leaving early for soccer practice and doctor's appointments will be more sympathetic to the challenges of balancing work and family, making the workplace more hospitable for all workers with children, male or female.

This chapter is not about discrimination. It is about information, which lies at the heart of many discrimination-related problems. Information matters, particularly when we don't have all that we need. Markets tend to favor the party that knows more. (Have you ever bought a used car?) But if the imbalance, or asymmetry of information, becomes too large, then markets can break down entirely. This was the fundamental insight of 2001 Nobel laureate George Akerlof, an economist at the University of California, Berkeley. His paper entitled "The Market for Lemons" used the used-car market to make its central point. Any individual selling a used car knows more about its quality than someone looking to buy it. This creates an adverse selection problem, just as it did with the Hope Scholarships. Car owners who are happy with their vehicles are less likely to sell them. Thus, used-car buyers anticipate hidden problems and demand a discount. But once there is a discount built into the market, owners of high-quality cars become even less likely to sell them—which guarantees the market will be full of lemons. In theory, the market for high-quality used cars will not work, much to the detriment of anyone who may want to buy or sell such a car. (In practice, such markets often do work for reasons explained by the gentlemen with whom Mr. Akerlof shared his Nobel prize; more on that in a moment.)

"The Market for Lemons" is characteristic of the kinds of ideas recognized by the Nobel committee. It is, in the words of the Royal Swedish Academy of Sciences, "a simple but profound and universal idea, with numerous implications and widespread applications." Health care, for example, is plagued with information problems. Consumers of health care—the patients—almost always have less information about their care than their doctors do. Indeed, even after we see a doctor, we may not know whether we were treated properly. This asymmetry of information is at the heart of our health care woes.

Under the old "fee for service" system (before the appearance of health maintenance organizations, or HMOs), doctors charged a fee for each procedure they performed. Patients did not pay for these extra tests and procedures; their insurance companies did. At the same time, medical technology was presenting all kinds of new medical options. It was an expensive combination: Doctors had an incentive to perform expensive medical procedures and patients had no reason to disagree. If you walked into your doctor's office with a headache and the doctor suggested a CAT scan, you would almost certainly agree "just to be sure." Neither you nor your doctor was acting unethically. When cost is not a factor, it makes perfect sense to rule out brain cancer even when the only symptom is a headache the morning after the holiday office party.

Health maintenance organizations were designed to control costs by changing the incentives. Under many HMO plans, general practitioners are paid a fixed fee per patient per year, regardless of what services they provide. They may be restricted in the kinds of tests and services they can prescribe and may even be paid a bonus if they refrain from sending their patients to see specialists. That changes things. Now when you walk into the doctor's office (still at a disadvantage in terms of information about your own health) and say, "I'm dizzy, my head hurts, and I'm bleeding out my ear," the doctor consults the HMO treatment guidelines and tells you to take two aspirin. As exaggerated as that example may be, the basic point is valid: The person who knows most about your medical condition may have an economic incentive to deny you care. Complaints about too much spending have been replaced by complaints about too little spending. Every HMO customer has a horror story about wrangling with bureaucrats over acceptable expenses. In the most extreme (and anecdotal) stories, patients are denied lifesaving treatments by HMO bean counters.

Some doctors are willing to do battle with the insurance companies on behalf of their patients. Others simply break the rules by disguising treatments that are not covered by insurance as treatments that are. (Patients aren't the only ones suffering from an asymmetry of information.) Politicians have jumped into the fray, too, demanding things like disclosure of the incentives paid to doctors by insurance companies and even a patient's bill of rights. To be fair, HMOs and their assorted spinoffs have slowed the explosive growth in health care spending. But the information problem at the heart of health care has not gone away: (1) The patient, who does not pay the bill, demands as much care as possible; (2) the insurance company maximizes profits by paying for as little care as possible; and (3) it is very costly for either the patient or the insurance company to prove the "right" course of treatment. In short, information makes health care different from the rest of the economy. When you walk into an electronics store to buy a big-screen TV, you can observe which picture looks clearest. You then compare price tags, knowing that the bill will arrive at your house eventually. In the end, you weigh the benefits of assorted televisions (whose quality you can observe) against the costs (that you will have to pay) and you pick one. *Brain surgery really is different.*

But we're not done with health care yet. The doctor may know more about your health than you do, but you know more about your long-term health than your insurance company does. You may not be able to diagnose rare diseases, but you know whether or not you lead a healthy lifestyle, if certain diseases run in your family, if you are engaging in risky sexual behavior, if you are likely to become pregnant, etc. This information advantage has the potential to wreak havoc on the insurance market.

Insurance is about getting the numbers right. Some individuals require virtually no health care. Others may have chronic diseases that require hundreds of thousands of dollars of treatment. The insurance company makes a profit by determining the average cost of treatment for all of its policyholders and then charging slightly more. When Aetna writes a group policy for twenty thousand fifty-year-old men, and the average cost of health care for a fifty-year-old man is $1,250 a year, then presumably the company can set the annual premium at $1,300 and make $50—*on average*—for each policy underwritten. Aetna will make money on some policies and lose money on others, but overall the company will come out ahead—if the numbers are right.

Is this example starting to look like the Hope Scholarships or the used-car market? It should. The $1,300 policy is a bad deal for the healthiest fifty-year-old men and a very good deal for the overweight smokers with a family history of heart disease. So, the healthiest men are most likely to opt out of the program; the sickest guys are most likely to opt in. As that happens, the population of men on which the original premium was based begins to change; on average, the remaining men are less healthy. The insurance company studies its new pool of middle-aged men and reckons that the annual premium must be raised to $1,800 in order to make a profit. Do you see where this is going? At the new price, more men—the most healthy of the unhealthy—decide that the policy is a bad deal, so they opt out. The sickest guys cling to their policies as tightly as their disease-addled bodies will allow. Once again the pool changes and now even $1,800 does not cover the cost of insuring the men who sign up for the program. In theory, this adverse selection could go on until the market for health insurance fails entirely.

That does not actually happen. Insurance companies usually insure large groups whose individuals are not allowed to select in or out. If Aetna writes policies for all General Motors employees, for example, then there will be no adverse selection. The policy comes with the job, and all workers, healthy and unhealthy, are covered. They have no choice. Aetna can calculate the average cost of care for this large pool of men and women and then charge a premium sufficient to make a profit.

Writing policies for individuals, however, is a much scarier undertaking. Companies rightfully fear that the people who have the most demand for health coverage (or life insurance) are those who need it most. *This will be true no matter how much an insurance company charges for its policies.* At any given price—even $5,000 a month—the individuals who expect their medical costs to be higher than the cost of the policy will be the most likely to sign up. Of course, the insurance companies have some tricks of their own, such as refusing coverage to individuals who are sick or likely to become sick in the future. This is often viewed as some kind of cruel and unfair practice perpetrated on the public by the insurance industry. On a superficial level, it does seem perverse that sick people have the most trouble getting health insurance. But imagine if insurance companies did not have that legal privilege. A (highly contrived) conversation with your doctor might go something like this:

> DOCTOR: I'm afraid I have bad news. Four of your coronary arteries are fully or partially blocked. I would recommend open-heart surgery as soon as possible.
> PATIENT: Is it likely to be successful?
> DOCTOR: Yes, we have excellent outcomes.
> PATIENT: Is the operation expensive?
> DOCTOR: Of course it's expensive. We're talking about open-heart surgery.
> PATIENT: Then I should probably buy some health insurance first.
> DOCTOR: Yes, that would be a very good idea.

Insurance companies ask applicants questions about family history, health habits, smoking, dangerous hobbies, and all kinds of other personal things. When I applied for term life insurance, a representative from the company came to my house and drew blood to make sure that I was not HIV-positive. He asked whether my parents were alive, if I scuba-dive, if I race cars. (Yes, yes, no.) I peed in a cup; I got on a scale; I answered questions about tobacco and illicit drug use—all of which seemed reasonable given that the company was making a commitment to pay my wife a large sum of money should I die in the near future.

Insurance companies have another subtle tool. They can design policies, or "screening" mechanisms, that elicit information from their potential customers. This insight, which is applicable to all kinds of other markets, earned Joseph Stiglitz, an economist at Columbia University and a former chief economist of the World Bank, a share of the 2001 Nobel Prize. How do firms screen customers in the insurance business? They use a deductible. Customers who consider themselves likely to stay healthy will sign up for policies that have a high deductible. In exchange, they are offered cheaper premiums. Customers who privately know that they are likely to have costly bills will avoid the deductible and pay a higher premium as a result. (The same thing is true when you are shopping for car insurance and you have a sneaking suspicion that your sixteen-year-old son is an even worse driver than most sixteen-year-olds.) In short, the deductible is a tool for teasing out private information; it forces customers to sort themselves.

Any insurance question ultimately begs one explosive question: How much information is too much? I guarantee that this will become one of the most nettlesome policy problems in coming years. Here is a simple exercise. Pluck one hair from your head. (If you are totally bald, take a swab of saliva from your cheek.) That sample contains your entire genetic code. In the right hands (or the wrong hands), it can be used to determine if you are predisposed to heart disease, certain kinds of cancer, depression, and—if the science continues at its current blistering pace—all kinds of other diseases. With one strand of your hair, a researcher (or insurance company) may soon be able to determine if you are at risk for Alzheimer's disease—twenty-five years before the onset of the disease. This creates a dilemma. If genetic information is shared widely with insurance companies, then it will become difficult, if not impossible, for those most prone to illness to get any kind of coverage. In other words, the people who need health insurance most will be the least likely to get it—not just the night before surgery, but ever. Individuals with a family history of Huntington's disease, a hereditary degenerative brain disorder that causes premature death, are already finding it hard or impossible to get life insurance. On the other hand, if insurance companies are forbidden from gathering such information, they will be crushed by adverse selection. Individuals who know that they are at high risk of getting sick in the future will be the ones who load up on generous insurance policies.

A recent editorial in *The Economist* noted this looming quandary: "Governments thus face a choice between banning the use of test results and destroying the industry, or allowing their use and creating an underclass of people who are either uninsurable or cannot afford to insure themselves." *The Economist*, which is hardly a bastion of left-wing thought, suggested that the private health insurance market may eventually find this problem intractable, leaving government with a much larger role to play. The editorial concluded: "Indeed, genetic testing may become the most potent argument for state-financed universal health care."[2]

This chapter started with the most egregious information-related problems—cases in which missing information cripples markets and causes individuals to behave in ways that have serious social implications. Economists are also intrigued by more mundane examples of how markets react to missing information. We spend our lives shopping for products and services whose quality we cannot easily determine. (You had to pay for this book before you were able to read it.) In the vast majority of cases, consumers and firms create their own mechanisms to solve information problems. Indeed, therein lies the genius of McDonald's that inspired the title of this chapter. The "golden arches" have as much to do with information as they do with hamburgers. Every McDonald's hamburger tastes the same, whether it is sold in Moscow, Mexico City, or Cincinnati. That is not a mere curiosity; it is at the heart of the company's success. Suppose you are driving along Interstate 80 outside of Omaha, having never been in the state of Nebraska, when you see a McDonald's. Immediately you know all kinds of things about the restaurant. You know that it will be clean, safe, and inexpensive. You know that it will have a working bathroom. You know that it will be open seven days a week. You may even know how many pickles are on the double cheeseburger. *You know all of these things before you get out of your car in a state you've never been in.*

Compare that to the billboard advertising Chuck's Big Burger. Chuck's may offer one of the best burgers west of the Mississippi. Or it might be a likely spot for the nation's next large *E. coli* outbreak. How would you know? If you lived in Omaha, then you might be familiar with Chuck's reputation. But you don't; you are driving through Nebraska at nine o'clock at night. (What time does Chuck's close, anyway?) If you are like millions of other people, even those who find fast food relatively unappealing, you will seek out the golden arches because you know what lies beneath them. McDonald's sells hamburgers, fries, and, most important, predictability.

This idea underlies the concept of "branding" whereby companies spend enormous sums of money to build an identity for their products. Branding solves a problem for consumers: How do you select products whose quality or safety you can determine only after you use them (and sometimes not even then)? Hamburgers are just one example. The same rule applies in everything from vacations to fashion. Will you have fun on your cruise? Yes, because it is Royal Caribbean—or Celebrity or Viking or Cunard. I have a poor sense of fashion, so I am reassured that when I buy a Tommy Hilfiger shirt I will look reasonably presentable when I leave the house. Michelin tire advertisements feature babies playing inside of Michelin tires with the tag line "Because so much is riding on your tires." The implicit message is clear enough. Meanwhile, Firestone has most likely destroyed much of the value of its brand as the result of the link between faulty tires and deadly rollovers in Ford Explorers.

Branding has come under assault as a tool by which avaricious multinational corporations persuade us to pay extortionate premiums for goods that we don't need. Economics tells a different story: Branding helps to provide an element of trust that is necessary for a complex economy to function. Modern business requires that we conduct major transactions with people whom we've never met before. I regularly mail off checks to Fidelity even though I do not know a single person at the company. Harried government regulators can only protect me from the most egregious kinds of fraud. They do not protect me from shoddy business practices, many of which are perfectly legal. Businesses routinely advertise their longevity. That sign outside the butcher proclaiming "Since 1927" is a politic way of saying, "We wouldn't still be here if we ripped off our customers."

Brands do the same thing. Like reputations, they are built over time. Indeed, sometimes the brand becomes more valuable than the product itself. In 1997, Sara Lee, a company that sells everything from underwear to breakfast sausages, declared that it would begin selling off its manufacturing facilities. No more turkey farms or textile mills. Instead, the company would focus on attaching its prestigious brand names—Champion, Hanes, Coach, Jimmy Dean—to products manufactured by outside firms. One business magazine noted, "Sara Lee believes that its soul is in its brands, and that the best use of its energies is to breathe commercial life into the inert matter supplied by others."[3] The irony is lovely: Sara Lee's strategy for growth and profits was to produce nothing.

Branding can be a very profitable strategy. In competitive markets, prices are driven relentlessly toward the cost of production. If it costs 10 cents to make a can of soda and I sell it for $1, someone is going to come along and sell it for 50 cents. Soon enough, someone else will be peddling it for a quarter, then 15 cents. Eventually, some ruthlessly efficient corporation will be peddling soda for 11 cents a can. From the consumer's standpoint, this is the beauty of capitalism. From the producer's standpoint, it is "commodity hell." Consider the sorry lot of the American farmer. A soybean is a soybean; as a result, an Iowa farmer cannot charge even one penny above the market price for his crop. Once transportation costs are taken into account, every soybean in the world sells for the same price, which, in most years, is not a whole lot more than it cost to produce.

How does a firm save its profits from the death spiral of competition? By convincing the world (rightfully or not) that its mixture of corn syrup and water is different from everyone else's mixture of corn syrup and water. Coca-Cola is not soda; it's Coke. Producers of branded goods create a monopoly for themselves—and price their products accordingly—by persuading consumers that their products are like no other. Nike shoes are not pieces of leather sewn together by poorly paid workers in Vietnam; they are Michael Jordan's shoes. Even farmers have taken this message to heart. At the supermarket, one finds (and pays a premium for) Sunkist oranges, Angus beef, Tyson chickens.

Sometimes we gather information by paying outsiders to certify quality. Roger Ebert's job is to see lots of bad movies so that I don't have to. When he sees the occasional gem, he gives it a "thumbs up." In the meantime, I am spared from seeing the likes of *Tom Cats*, a film that Mr. Ebert awarded zero stars. I pay for this information in the form of my subscription to the *Chicago Sun-Times*. *Consumer Reports* provides the same kind of information on consumer goods; Underwriters Laboratories certifies the safety of electrical appliances; Morningstar evaluates the performance of mutual funds. And then there is Oprah's book club, which has the capacity to send obscure books rocketing up the best-seller lists.

Meanwhile, firms will do whatever they can to "signal" their own quality to the market. This was the insight of 2001 Nobel laureate Michael Spence, an economist at Stanford University. Suppose that you are choosing an investment adviser after a good stroke of fortune in the Powerball Lottery. The first firm you visit has striking wood paneling, a marble lobby, original Impressionist paintings, and executives wearing handmade Italian suits. Do you think: (1) My fees will pay for all this very nice stuff—what a ripoff!; or (2) wow, this firm must be extremely successful and I hope they will take me on as a client. Most people would choose 2. (If you're not convinced, think about it the other way: how would you feel if your investment adviser worked in a dank office with fifteen-year-old government-surplus WANG word processors?)

The trappings of success—the paneling, the marble, the art collection—have no inherent relation to the professional conduct of the firm. Rather, we interpret them as "signals" that reassure us that the firm is top-notch. They are to markets what a peacock's bright feathers are to a prospective mate: a good sign in a world of imperfect information.

Here is a related question that economists like to ponder: Harvard graduates do very well in life, but is that because they learned things at

Harvard that made them successful, or is it because Harvard finds and admits talented students who would have done extraordinarily well in life anyway? In other words, does Harvard add great value to its students, or does it simply provide an elaborate "signaling" mechanism that allows bright students to advertise their talents to the world by being admitted to Harvard? Alan Krueger, a Princeton economist, and Stacy Dale, an economist at the Mellon Foundation, have done an interesting study to get at this question.[4] They note that graduates of highly selective colleges earn higher salaries later in life than graduates of less selective colleges. For example, the average student who entered Yale, Swarthmore, or the University of Pennsylvania in 1976 earned $92,000 in 1995; the average student who entered a moderately selective college, such as Penn State, Denison, or Tulane, earned $22,000 less. That is not a particularly surprising finding, nor does it get at the question of whether the students at schools like Yale and Princeton would earn more than their peers at less competitive schools even if they played beer pong and watched television for four years.

So Mr. Krueger and Ms. Dale took their analysis one step further. They examined the outcomes of students who were admitted to both a highly selective school and a moderately selective school. Some of those students headed to places like the Ivy League; others chose their less selective option. Mr. Krueger and Ms. Dale's chief finding is best summarized by the title of the paper: "Children Smart Enough to Get into Elite Schools May Not Need to Bother." The average earnings of students admitted to both a highly selective school and a moderately selective school were roughly the same regardless of which type of college they attended. (The one exception was students from lower-income families for whom attending a more selective school increased earnings significantly.) Overall, the quality of student appears to matter more later in life than the quality of the university he or she attended.

Is it irrational to spend $100,000 or more to attend an Ivy League University? Not necessarily. At a minimum, a Princeton or Yale diploma is the résumé equivalent of Roger Ebert's "thumbs up." It pronounces you highly qualified so that others in life—employers, spouses, in-laws— will have fewer doubts. And there is always the possibility that you may learn something while huddling for four years with the world's great minds. Still, Mr. Krueger offers this advice to students applying to college: "Don't believe that the only school worth attending is one that would not admit you. . . . Recognize that your own motivation, ambition and talents will determine your success more than the college name on your diploma."

The notion that bright, motivated individuals (with similarly motivated parents) will do well, however or wherever they are schooled, is often lost on America's school reformers. In Illinois, each fall is greeted with the release of the state's school report cards. Every school in the state is evaluated based on how well its students have performed on a battery of standardized exams. The media quickly seize on these school report cards to identify the state's "best" schools, most of which are usually in affluent suburbs. But does this process really tell us anything about which schools are the most effective? Not necessarily. "In many suburban communities, students would do well on standardized tests even if they went to school and sat in a closet every day for four years," says University of Rochester economist Eric Hanushek, an expert on the somewhat tenuous relationship between school inputs and student outcomes. There is a fundamental piece of missing information: How much value is really being added at these "high-performing schools"? Do they have exceptional teachers and administrators, or are they repositories for privileged students who would do well on standardized tests regardless of where they went to school? It's the Harvard question all over again.

This chapter started with a serious social issue, and so it will end. Racial profiling is an information problem. There are two simple questions at the heart of the issue. First, does race or ethnicity—alone or in conjunction with some other circumstance—convey meaningful information? If so, what do we do about it? The answer to the first question gets most of the attention. After the attacks of September 11, one could certainly make the case that thirty-five-year-old Arab men posed a greater risk to the country than sixty-five-year-old Polish women. Police officers have long argued that race can be a tip-off; well-dressed white kids in poor black neighborhoods are often looking to buy drugs. Criminal organizations have racial or ethnic affiliations. At the same time President Clinton was declaring racial profiling "morally indefensible," the website of his drug czar, Barry McCaffrey, was doing just that. In Denver, the site noted, the heroin dealers are predominantly Mexican nationals. In Trenton, crack dealers are predominantly African-American males and the powdered cocaine dealers are predominantly Latino.[5]

Indeed, we all profile in our own way. We are taught from a young age that one should never judge a book by its cover. *But we must; it is often all we get to see.* Imagine you are walking in a parking garage at night when you hear footsteps behind you. Ideally, you would ask this person for a résumé; you and he would sit down for coffee and discuss his goals, his job, his family, his political philosophy, and, most important, the reason he is walking behind you in a dark parking garage. Then, after this fruitful discussion, you would decide whether or not to hit the panic button on your key ring. The reality, of course, is different. You get one quick glance over your shoulder. What information matters? Sex? Race? Age? Briefcase? Clothing?

From a social policy standpoint, however, all of that is a red herring. The question that matters is: Are we willing to systematically harass individuals who fit a broad racial or ethnic profile that may, on average, have some statistical support but will still be wrong far more often than it is right? Most people would answer no. We've built a society that values civil liberties even at the expense of social order. Opponents of racial profiling always seem to get dragged into the quagmire of whether or not it is good police work. *It doesn't matter.* If economics teaches us anything, it's that we ought to weigh costs and benefits. The costs of harassing ten or twenty or one hundred law-abiding people to catch one more drug dealer are not worth it. Might that change in the case of a sustained terrorist attack on the United States? Sadly, yes.

In the world of Econ 101, all parties have "perfect information." The graphs are neat and tidy; consumers and producers know everything they could possibly want to know. The world outside of Econ 101 is more interesting, albeit messier. A state patrolman who has pulled over a 1990 Grand Am with a broken taillight on a deserted stretch of Florida highway does not have perfect information. Nor does a young family looking for a safe and dependable nanny or an insurance company seeking to protect itself from the extraordinary costs of HIV/AIDS. Information matters. Economists study what we do with it, and, sometimes more important, what we do without it.

CHAPTER 6

Productivity and Human Capital:

Why is Bill Gates so much richer than you are?

Bill Gates is adding onto his house. The software mogul moved into his $100 million dollar mansion in 1997; now it needs some tweaking. The 37,000-square-foot home has a twenty-seat theater, a reception hall, parking for twenty-eight cars, an indoor trampoline pit, and all kinds of computer gadgetry, such as phones that ring only when the person being called is nearby. But the house is not quite big enough.[1] According to documents filed with the zoning board in suburban Medina, Washington, Mr. Gates and his wife would like to add another bedroom and some additional play and study areas for their children.

There are a lot of things one might infer from Mr. Gates's building plans, but one of them is fairly obvious: It is good to be Bill Gates. The world is a fascinating playground when you have $50 billion or so. One might also ponder some larger questions: Why do some people have indoor trampolines and private jets while others sleep in bus station bathrooms? How is it that at the end of the longest economic boom in American history, many Americans lack the basic necessities? Nine years of continuous economic growth only dented the poverty rate. Roughly 11 percent of Americans are poor, which is an improvement from a recent peak of 15 percent in 1993 but not significantly better than it was during any year in the 1970s. Meanwhile, one in five American children—

and a staggering 40 percent of black children—live in poverty. Of course, America is the rich guy on the block. At the dawn of the third millennium, vast swathes of the world's population—some three billion people—are desperately poor.

Economists study poverty and income inequality. They seek to understand who is poor, why they are poor, and what can be done about it. Any discussion of why Bill Gates is so much richer than the men and women sleeping in steam tunnels must begin with a concept economists refer to as human capital. Human capital is the sum total of skills embodied within an individual: education, intelligence, charisma, creativity, work experience, entrepreneurial vigor, even the ability to throw a baseball fast. It is what you would be left with if someone stripped away all of your assets—your job, your money, your home, your possessions—and left you on a street corner with only the clothes on your back. How would Bill Gates fare in such a situation? Very well. Even if Microsoft perished and his wealth were confiscated, other companies would snap him up as a consultant, a board member, a CEO, a motivational speaker. (When Steve Jobs was fired from Apple, the company that he founded, he turned around and founded Pixar; only later did Apple invite him back.) How would Tiger Woods do? Just fine. If someone lent him golf clubs, he could be winning tournaments by the weekend.

How would Bubba, who dropped out of school in tenth grade and has a methamphetamine addiction, fare? Not so well. The difference is human capital; Bubba doesn't have much. (Ironically, some very rich individuals, such as the sultan of Brunei, might not do particularly well in this exercise either; the sultan is rich because his kingdom sits atop an enormous oil reserve.) The labor market is no different from the market for anything else; some kinds of talent are in greater demand than others. The more nearly unique a set of skills, the better compensated their owner will be. Alex Rodriguez will earn $250 million over ten years playing baseball for the Texas Rangers because he can hit a round ball traveling ninety-plus miles an hour harder and more often than other people can. "A Rod" will help the Rangers win games, which will fill stadiums, sell merchandise, and earn television revenues. Virtually no one else on the planet can do that as well as he can.

As with other aspects of the market economy, the price of a certain skill bears no inherent relation to its social value, only its scarcity. I once interviewed Robert Solow, winner of the 1987 Nobel Prize in Economics and a noted baseball enthusiast. I asked if it bothered him that he received less money for winning the Nobel Prize than Roger Clemens, who was pitching for the Red Sox at the time, earned in a single season. "No," Solow said. "There are a lot of good economists, but there is only one Roger Clemens." That is how economists think.

Who is wealthy in America, or at least comfortable? Software programmers, hand surgeons, nuclear engineers, writers, accountants, bankers, teachers. Sometimes these individuals have natural talent; more often they have acquired their skills through specialized training and education. In other words, they have made significant investments in human capital. Like any other kind of investment—from building a manufacturing plant to buying a bond—money invested today in human capital will yield a return in the future. A very good return. A college education is reckoned to yield about 10 percent, meaning that if you put down money today for college tuition, you can expect to earn that money back plus about 10 percent a year in higher earnings. Few people on Wall Street make better investments than that on a regular basis.

Human capital is an economic passport—literally, in some cases. When I was an undergraduate in the late 1980s, I met a young Palestinian man named Gamal Abouali. Gamal's family, who lived in Kuwait, were insistent that their son finish his degree in three years instead of four. This required taking extra classes each quarter and attending school every summer, all of which seemed rather extreme to me at the time. What about internships and foreign study, or even a winter in Colorado as a ski bum? I had lunch with Gamal's father once, and he explained that the Palestinian existence was itinerant and precarious. Mr. Abouali was an accountant, a profession that he could practice nearly anywhere in the world—because, he explained, that is where he might end up. The family had lived in Canada before moving to Kuwait; they could easily be somewhere else in five years, he said.

Gamal was studying engineering, a similarly universal skill. The sooner he had his degree, his father insisted, the more secure he would be. Not only would the degree allow him to earn a living, but it might also enable him to find a home. In some developed countries, the right to immigrate is based on skills and education—human capital.

Mr. Abouali's thoughts were strikingly prescient. After Saddam Hussein's retreat from Kuwait in 1990, most of the Palestinian population, including Gamal's family, was expelled because the Kuwaiti government felt that the Palestinians had been sympathetic to the Iraqi aggressors. I have since lost track of Gamal and his family, as has my undergraduate college. Wherever they are, Gamal has an engineering degree and his father is an accountant.

The opposite is true at the other end of the labor pool. The skills necessary to ask, "Would you like fries with that?" are not scarce. There are probably 150 million people in this country capable of selling value meals at McDonald's. Fast-food restaurants need only pay a wage high enough to put warm bodies behind all of their cash registers. That may be $5.50 an hour when the economy is slow or $9 an hour when the labor market is especially tight; it will never be $400 an hour, which is the kind of fee that a top trial lawyer can command. Excellent trial lawyers are scarce; burger flippers are not. The most insightful way to think about poverty, in this country or anywhere else in the world, is as a dearth of human capital. True, people are poor in America because they cannot find good jobs. But that is the symptom, not the illness. The underlying problem is a lack of skills, or human capital. The poverty rate for high school dropouts in America is twelve times the poverty rate for college graduates. Why is India one of the poorest countries in the world? Primarily because 35 percent of the population is illiterate (down from almost 50 percent a decade ago).[2] Or individuals may suffer from conditions that render their human capital less useful. A high proportion of America's homeless population suffer from substance abuse, disability, or mental illness.

A healthy economy matters, too. It was easier to find a job in 2001 than it was in 1975 or 1932. A rising tide does indeed lift all boats; economic growth is a very good thing for poor people. Period. Conversely, a bad economy is usually most devastating for workers at the shallow end of the labor pool. But even at high tide, low-skilled workers are clinging to driftwood while their better-skilled peers are having cocktails on their yachts. A robust economy does not transform valet parking attendants into college professors. Investments in human capital do that. Macro factors control the tides; human capital determines the quality of the boat.

Consider this thought experiment. Imagine that on some Monday morning we dropped off 100,000 high school dropouts on the corner of State Street and Madison Street in Chicago. It would be a social calamity. Government services would be stretched to capacity or beyond; crime would go up. Businesses would be deterred from locating in downtown Chicago. Politicians would plead for help from the state or the federal government: *Either give us enough money to support these people or help us get rid of them.* When business leaders in Sacramento, California, decided to crack down on the homeless, one strategy was offering them one-way bus tickets out of town.[3] (Atlanta reportedly did the same before the 1996 Olympics.)

Now imagine the same corner and let's drop off 100,000 graduates from America's top universities. The buses arrive at the corner of State and Madison and begin unloading lawyers, doctors, artists, geneticists, software engineers, and a lot of smart, motivated people with general skills. Many of these individuals would find jobs immediately. (Remember, human capital embodies not only classroom training but also perseverance, honesty, creativity—virtues that lend themselves to finding work.) Some of these highly skilled graduates would start their own businesses; entrepreneurial flair is certainly an important component of human capital. Some of them would leave for other places; highly skilled workers are more mobile than their low-skilled peers. In some cases, firms would relocate to Chicago or open up offices and plants in Chicago to take advantage of this temporary glut of talent. Economic pundits would later describe this freak unloading of buses as a boon for Chicago's economic development, much as waves of immigration helped America to develop.

If this example sounds contrived, consider the case of the Naval Air Warfare Center (NAWC) in Indianapolis, a facility that produced advanced electronics for the navy until the late 1990s. NAWC, which employed roughly 2,600 workers, was slated to be closed as part of the military downsizing. We're all familiar with these plant-closing stories. Hundreds or thousands of workers lose their jobs; businesses in the surrounding community begin to wither because so much purchasing power has been lost. Someone comes on camera and says, "When the plant closed back in [some year], this town just began to die." But NAWC was a very different story.[4] One of its most valuable assets was its workforce, some 40 percent of whom were scientists or engineers. Astute local leaders, led by Mayor Stephen Goldsmith, believed that the plant could be sold to a private buyer. Seven companies filed bids; Hughes Electronics was the winner.

On a Friday in January 1997, the NAWC employees went home as government employees; the following Monday, 98 percent of them came to work as Hughes employees. (And NAWC became HAWC.) The Hughes executives I interviewed said that the value of the acquisition lay in the people, not just the bricks and mortar. Hughes was buying a massive amount of human capital that it could not easily find anywhere else. That contrasts sharply with the plant closings that Bruce Springsteen sings about, where workers with limited education find that their narrow sets of skills have no value once the mill/mine/factory/plant is gone. The difference is human capital. Indeed, economists can even provide empirical support for those Springsteen songs. Labor economist Robert Topel has estimated that experienced workers lose 25 percent of their earnings capacity in the long run when they are forced to change jobs by a plant closing.

Now is an appropriate time to dispatch one of the most pernicious notions in public policy: the lump of labor fallacy. This is the mistaken belief that there is a fixed amount of work to be done in the economy, and therefore every new job must come at the expense of a job lost somewhere else. If I am unemployed, the mistaken argument goes, then I will find work only if someone else works less, or not at all. This is how the French government believes the world works, and it is wrong. Jobs are created anytime an individual provides a new good or service, or finds a better (or cheaper) way of providing an old one.

The numbers prove the point. The United States economy produced tens of millions of new jobs in the 1990s, including virtually the entire Internet sector. (Some of those jobs are still around.) Millions of women entered the labor force in the second half of the twentieth century, yet our unemployment rate is still low by historical standards. Similarly, huge waves of immigrants have come to work in America throughout our history without any long-run increase in unemployment. Are there short-term displacements? Absolutely; some workers lose jobs or see their wages depressed when they are forced to compete with new entrants to the labor force. But more jobs are created than lost. Remember, new workers must spend their earnings elsewhere in the economy, creating new demand for other products. The economic pie gets bigger, not merely resliced.

Here is the intuition: Imagine a farming community in which numerous families own and farm their own land. Each family produces just enough to feed itself; there is no surplus harvest or unfarmed land. Everyone in this town has enough to eat; on the other hand, no one lives particularly well. Every family spends large amounts of time doing domestic chores. They make their own clothes, teach their own children, make and repair their own farm implements, etc. Suppose a guy wanders into town looking for work. In scenario one, this guy has no skills. There is no extra land to farm, so the community tells him to get back on the train. Maybe they even buy him a one-way ticket out of town. This town has "no jobs."

Now consider scenario two: The guy who ambles into town has a Ph.D. in agronomy. He has designed a new kind of plow that improves corn yields. He trades his plow to farmers in exchange for a small share of their harvests. Everybody is better off. The agronomist can support himself; the farmers have more to eat, even after paying for their new plows (or else they wouldn't buy the plows). And this community has just created one new job: plow salesman. Soon thereafter, a carpenter arrives at the train station. He offers to do all the odd jobs that limit the amount of time farmers can spend tending to their crops. Yields go up again because farmers are able to spend more time doing what they do best: farming. And another new job is created.

At this point, farmers are growing more than they can possibly eat themselves, so they "spend" their surplus to recruit a teacher to town.

That's another new job. She teaches the children in the town, making the next generation of farmers better educated and more productive than their parents. Over time, our contrived farming town, which had "no jobs" at the beginning of this exercise, has romance novelists, firefighters, professional baseball players, and even engineers who design Margarita Space Paks. This is the one-page economic history of the United States. Rising levels of human capital enabled an agrarian nation to evolve into places as rich and complex as Manhattan and Silicon Valley.

Not all is rosy along the way, of course. Suppose one of our newly educated farmers designs a plow that produces even better yields, putting the first plow salesman out of business—creative destruction. True, this technological breakthrough eliminates one job in the short run. In the long run, though, the town is still better off. Remember, all the farmers are now richer (as measured by higher corn yields), enabling them to hire the unemployed agronomist to do something else, such as develop new hybrid seeds (which will make the town richer yet). Technology displaces workers in the short run but does not lead to mass unemployment in the long run. Rather, we become richer, which creates demand for new jobs elsewhere in the economy. Of course, educated workers fare much better than uneducated workers in this process. They are more versatile in a fast-changing economy, making them more likely to be left standing after a bout of creative destruction.

Human capital is about much more than earning more money. It makes us better parents, more informed voters, more appreciative of art and culture, more able to enjoy the fruits of life. It can make us healthier because we eat better and exercise more. (Meanwhile, good health is an important component of human capital.) Educated parents are more likely to put their children in car seats and teach them about colors and letters before they begin school. In the developing world, the impact of human capital can be even more profound. Economists have found that a year of additional schooling for a woman in a low-income country is associated with a 5 to 10 percent reduction in her child's likelihood of dying in the first five years of life.[5]

Similarly, our total stock of human capital—everything we know as a people—defines how well off we are as a society. We benefit from the fact that we know how to prevent polio or make stainless steel—even if virtually no one reading this book would be able to do either of those things if left stranded on a deserted island. Economist Gary Becker, who was awarded the Nobel Prize for his work in the field of human capital, reckons that the stock of education, training, skills, and even the health of people constitutes about 75 percent of the wealth of a modern economy. Not diamonds, buildings, oil, or fancy purses—but things that we carry around in our heads. "We should really call our economy a 'human capitalist economy,' for that is what it mainly is," Mr. Becker said in a recent speech. "While all forms of capital—physical capital, such as machinery and plants, financial capital, and human capital—are important, human capital is the most important. Indeed, in a modern economy, human capital is by far the most important form of capital in creating wealth and growth."[6]

There is a striking correlation between a country's level of human capital and its economic well-being. At the same time, there is a striking *lack* of correlation between natural resources and standard of living. Countries like Japan and Switzerland are among the richest in the world despite having relatively poor endowments of natural resources. Countries like Nigeria are just the opposite; enormous oil wealth has done relatively little for the nation's standard of living. In some cases, the mineral wealth of Africa has financed bloody civil wars that would have otherwise died out. In the Middle East, Saudi Arabia has most of the oil while Israel, with no natural resources to speak of, has the highest per capita income.

High levels of human capital create a virtuous cycle; well-educated parents invest heavily in the human capital of their children. Low levels of human capital have just the opposite effect. Disadvantaged parents beget disadvantaged children, as any public school teacher will tell you. Mr. Becker points out, "Even small differences among children in the preparation provided by their families are frequently multiplied over time into large differences when they are teenagers. This is why the labor market cannot do much for school dropouts who can hardly read and never developed good work habits, and why it is so difficult to devise policies to help these groups."[7]

• • •

Why does human capital matter so much? To begin with, human capital is inextricably linked to one of the most important ideas in economics: productivity. Productivity is the efficiency with which we convert inputs into outputs. In other words, how good are we at making things? Does it take 2,000 hours for a Detroit autoworker to make a car or 210 hours? Can an Iowa corn farmer grow thirty bushels of corn on an acre of land or 210 bushels? The more productive we are, the richer we are. The reason is simple: The day will always be twenty-four hours long; the more we produce in those twenty-four hours, the more we consume. Productivity is determined in part by natural resources—it is easier to grow wheat in Kansas than it is in Vermont—but in a modern economy, productivity is more affected by technology, specialization, and skills, all of which are a function of human capital.

America is rich because Americans are productive. We are better off today than at any other point in the history of civilization because we are better at producing goods and services than we have ever been, including things like health care and entertainment. The bottom line is that we work less and produce more. In 1870, the typical household required 1,800 hours of labor just to acquire its annual food supply; today, it takes about 260 hours of work. Over the course of the twentieth century, the average work year has fallen from 3,100 hours to about 1,730 hours. All the while, real gross domestic product (GDP) per capita—an inflation-adjusted measure of how much each of us produces, on average—has increased from $4,800 to $31,500. Even the poor are living extremely well by historical standards. *The poverty line is now at a level of real income that was attained only by those in the top 10 percent of the income distribution a century ago.* As John Maynard Keynes once noted, "In the long run, productivity is everything."

Productivity is the concept that takes the suck out of Ross Perot's "giant sucking sound." He reasoned that if we opened our borders to free trade with Mexico, then millions of jobs would flee south of the border. Why wouldn't a firm relocate to Mexico when the average Mexican factory worker earns a fraction of the wages paid to American workers? The answer is productivity. Can American workers compete against foreign workers who earn half as much or less? *Yes, most of us can.* We produce more than Mexican workers—much more in many cases—because we are better-educated, because we are healthier, because we have better access to capital and technology, and because we have more efficient government institutions and better public infrastructure. Can a Vietnamese peasant with two years of education do your job? Probably not.

Of course, there are industries in which American workers are not productive enough to justify their relatively high wages, such as manufacturing textiles and shoes. These are industries that require relatively unskilled labor, which is more expensive in this country than in the developing world. Can a Vietnamese peasant sew basketball shoes together? Yes—and for a lot less than the American minimum wage.

While Ross Perot was warning that most of the U.S. economy would migrate to Guadalajara, mainstream economists predicted that NAFTA would have a modest but positive effect on American employment. Some jobs would be lost to Mexican competition; more jobs would be created as exports to Mexico increased. We are now nearly a decade into NAFTA, and that is exactly what happened. Economists reckon that the effect on overall employment was positive, albeit very small relative to the size of the U.S. economy.

Will our children be better off than we are? Yes, if they are more productive than we are, which has been the pattern throughout American history. Productivity *growth* is what improves our standard of living. If productivity grows at 2 percent a year, then we will become 2 percent richer every year. Why? Because we can take the same inputs and make 2 percent more stuff. (Or we could make the same amount of stuff with 2 percent fewer inputs.) One of the most interesting debates in economics at the moment is whether or not the American economy has undergone a sharp increase in the rate of productivity growth. Some economists, including Alan Greenspan, have argued that investments in information technology have led to permanently higher rates of productivity growth. Others, such as Robert Gordon at Northwestern University, believe that productivity growth has not changed significantly when one interprets the data properly.

This is not merely an esoteric subject that economists like to debate while quaffing sherry in overstuffed chairs. From 1947 to 1975, productivity grew at an annual rate of 2.7 percent a year. From 1975 until the mid-1990s, for reasons that are still not fully understood, productivity growth slowed to 1.4 percent a year. That may seem like a trivial difference; in fact, it has a profound effect on our standard of living. One handy trick in finance and economics is the rule of 72; divide 72 by a rate of growth (or a rate of interest) and the answer will tell you roughly how long it will take for a growing quantity to double (e.g., the principal in a bank account paying 10 percent interest will double in seven years). When productivity grows at 2.7 percent a year, our standard of living doubles every twenty-seven years. At 1.4 percent, it doubles every fifty-one years.

Productivity growth makes us richer, regardless of what is going on in the rest of the world. If productivity grows at 4 percent in Japan and 2 percent in the United States, *then both countries are getting richer.* To understand why, go back to our simple farm economy. If one farmer is raising 2 percent more corn and hogs every year and his neighbor is raising 4 percent more, then they are eating more every year (or trading more away). If this disparity goes on for a long time, one of them will become significantly richer than the other, which may become a source of envy or political friction, but they are both growing steadily better off. The important point is that productivity growth, like so much else in economics, is not a zero-sum game.

What would be the effect on America if 500 million people in India became more productive and gradually moved from poverty to the middle class? We would become richer, too. Poor villagers currently subsisting on $1 a day cannot afford to buy our software, our cars, our music, our books, our agricultural exports. If they were wealthier, they could. Meanwhile, some of those 500 million people, whose potential is currently wasted for lack of education, would produce goods and services that are superior to what we have now, making us better off. One of those newly educated peasants might be the person who discovers an AIDS vaccine or a process for reversing global warming. To paraphrase the United Negro College Fund, 500 million minds are a terrible thing to waste.

Productivity growth depends on investment—in physical capital, in human capital, in research and development, and even in things like more effective government institutions. These investments require that we give up consumption in the present in order to be able to consume more in the future. If you skip buying a BMW and invest in a college education instead, your future income will be higher. Similarly, a software company may forgo paying its shareholders a dividend and plow its profits back into the development of a new, better product. The government may collect taxes (depriving us of some current consumption) to fund research in genetics that improves our health in the future. In each case, we spend resources now so that we will become more productive later. When we turn to the macroeconomy—our study of the economy as a whole—one important concern will be whether or not we are investing enough as a nation to continue growing our standard of living.

Our legal, regulatory, and tax structures also affect productivity growth. High taxes, bad government, poorly defined property rights, or excessive regulation can diminish or eliminate the incentive to make productive investments. Collective farms, for example, were a very bad way to organize agriculture. Social factors, such as discrimination, can profoundly affect productivity. A society that does not educate its women or that denies opportunities to members of a particular race or caste or tribe is leaving a vast resource fallow. Productivity growth also depends a great deal on innovation and technological progress, neither of which is understood perfectly. Why did the Internet explode onto the scene in the mid-1990s rather than the late 1970s? How is it that we have cracked the human genome yet we still do not have a clean source of energy? In short, fostering productivity growth is like raising children: We know what kinds of things are important even if there is no blueprint for raising an Olympic athlete or a Harvard scholar.

The study of human capital has profound implications for public policy. Most important, it can tell us why we haven't all starved to death. The earth's population has grown to six billion; how have we been able to feed so many mouths? In the eighteenth century, Thomas Malthus famously predicted a dim future for mankind because he believed that as society grew richer, it would continuously squander those gains through population growth—having more children. These additional mouths would gobble up the surplus. In his view, mankind was destined to live on the brink of subsistence, recklessly procreating during the good times and then starving during the bad. As Paul Krugman has pointed out, for fifty-five of the last fifty-seven centuries, Malthus was right. The world population grew, but the human condition did not change significantly.

Only with the advent of the Industrial Revolution did humans begin to grow steadily richer. Even then, Malthus was not far off the mark. As Gary Becker points out, "Parents did spend more on children when their incomes rose—as Malthus predicted—but they spent a lot more on each child and had fewer children, as human capital theory predicts."[8] The economic transformations of the Industrial Revolution, namely the large productivity gains, made parents' time more expensive. As the advantages of having more children declined, modern humans began investing their rising incomes in the *quality* of their children, not merely the *quantity*.

One of the fallacies of poverty is that developing countries are poor because they have rapid population growth. In fact, the causal relationship is best understood going the other direction: Poor people have many children because the cost of bearing and raising children is low. Birth control, no matter how dependable, works only to the extent that families prefer fewer children. As a result, one of the most potent weapons for fighting population growth is creating better economic opportunities for women, which starts by educating girls. Taiwan doubled the number of girls graduating from high school between 1966 and 1975. Meanwhile, the fertility rate dropped by half. In the developed world, where women have enjoyed an extraordinary range of new economic opportunities over the last half century, fertility rates have fallen near or below replacement level, which is 2.1 births per woman.

We began this chapter with a discussion of Bill Gates's home, which is, I am fairly certain, bigger than yours. At the dawn of the third millennium, America is a profoundly unequal place. Is the nation growing more unequal? That answer, by almost any measure, is yes. Between 1979 and 1997, the average income of the richest fifth of the population jumped from nine times the income of the poorest fifth to around fifteen times.[9]

As America's longest economic boom in history unfolded, the rich got richer while the poor ran in place, or even got poorer. Average income (adjusted for inflation) for the poorest fifth of Americans actually fell 3 percent between 1979 and 1997 before turning up sharply at the end of the 1990s.[10] Looking at accumulated wealth, rather than just annual income, presents an even more skewed picture. Most economists would agree that the gap between America's rich and poor is growing larger.

Why? Human capital offers the most insight into this social phenomenon. The last several decades have been a real-life version of *Revenge of the Nerds*. Skilled workers in America have always earned higher wages than unskilled workers; that difference has started to grow at a remarkable rate. In short, human capital has become more important, and therefore better rewarded, than ever before. One simple measure of the importance of human capital is the gap between the wages paid to high school graduates and the wages paid to college graduates. College graduates earned an average of 40 percent more than high school graduates at the beginning of the 1980s; now they earn 80 percent more. Individuals with graduate degrees do even better than that. The twenty-first century is an especially good time to be a rocket scientist.

Our economy is evolving in ways that favor skilled workers. For example, the shift toward computers in nearly every industry favors workers who either have computer skills or are smart enough to learn them on the job. Technology makes smart workers more productive while making low-skilled workers redundant. ATMs replaced bank tellers; self-serve pumps replaced gas station attendants; automated assembly lines replaced workers doing mindless, repetitive tasks. Indeed, the assembly line at General Motors encapsulates the major trend in the American economy. Computers and sophisticated robots now assemble the major components of a car—which creates high-paying jobs for people who write software and design robots while reducing the demand for workers with no specialized skills other than a willingness to do an honest day's work.

Meanwhile, international trade puts low-skilled workers in greater competition with other low-skilled workers around the globe. In the long run, international trade is a powerful force for good; in the short run, it has victims. Trade, like technology, makes high-skilled workers better off because it provides new markets for our high-tech exports. Boeing sells aircraft to Singapore, Microsoft sells software to Europe, McKinsey & Company sells consulting services to Latin America. Again, this is more good news for people who know how to design a fuel-efficient jet engine or explain total quality management in Spanish. On the other hand, it puts our low-tech workers in competition with low-priced laborers in Vietnam. Nike can pay workers $1 a day to make shoes in a Vietnamese sweat shop. You can't make Boeing airplanes that way.

There is still disagreement about the degree to which different causes are responsible for this shifting gap in wages. Unions have grown less powerful, giving blue-collar workers less clout at the bargaining table. Meanwhile, high-wage workers are logging more hours on the job than their low-wage counterparts, which exacerbates the total earnings gap.[11] In any case, the rise in income inequality is real. Should we care? Economists have traditionally argued that we should not for two basic reasons. First, income inequality sends important signals in the economy. The growing wage gap between high school and college graduates, for example, will motivate many students to get college degrees. Similarly, the spectacular wealth earned by entrepreneurs provides an incentive to take the risks necessary for leaps in innovation, many of which have huge payoffs for society. Economics is about incentives, and the prospect of getting rich is a big incentive.

Second, many economists argue that we should not care about the gap between rich and poor as long as everybody is living better. In other words, we should care about how much pie the poor are getting, not how much pie they are getting relative to Bill Gates. In his 1999 presidential address to the American Economics Association, Robert Fogel, a Nobel Prize–winning economic historian, pointed out that our poorest citizens have amenities unknown even to royalty a hundred years ago. (Over 90 percent of public housing residents have a color television, for example.) Envy may be one of the seven deadly sins, but it is not something to which economists have traditionally paid much attention. My utility should depend on how much I like my car, not on whether or not my neighbor is driving a Jaguar.

Of course, common sense suggests otherwise. H. L. Mencken once noted that a wealthy man is a man who earns $100 a year more than his wife's sister's husband. Some economists have belatedly begun to believe that he was on to something.[12] David Neumark and Andrew Postlewaite looked at a large sample of American sisters in an effort to understand why some women choose to work outside of the home and others do not. When the researchers controlled for all the usual explanations—unemployment in local labor market, a woman's education and work experience, etc.—they found powerful evidence to support H. L. Mencken's wry observation: A woman in their sample was significantly more likely to seek paid employment if her sister's husband earned more than her own.

Cornell economist Robert Frank, author of *Luxury Fever*, has made a persuasive case that relative wealth—the size of my pie compared to my neighbor's—is an important determinant of our utility. He offered survey respondents a choice between two worlds: (A): You earn $110,000 and everyone else earns $200,000. Or (B): You earn $100,000 and everyone else earns $85,000. As he explains, "The income figures represent real purchasing power. Your income in World A would command a house 10 percent larger than the one you could afford in World B, 10 percent more restaurant dinners and so on. By choosing World B, you'd give up a small amount of absolute income in return for a large increase in relative income." You would be richer in World A; you would be less wealthy in World B but richer than everyone else. Which scenario would make you happier? Mr. Frank found that a majority of Americans would choose B. In other words, relative income does matter. Envy may be part of the explanation. It is also true, Mr. Frank points out, that in complex social environments we seek ways to evaluate our performance. Relative wealth is one of them.

There is a second, more pragmatic concern about rising income inequality. Might the gap between rich and poor—ethics aside—become large enough that it begins to inhibit economic growth? Is there a point at which income inequality stops motivating us to work harder and becomes counterproductive? This might happen for all kinds of reasons. The poor might become disenfranchised to the point that they reject important political and economic institutions, such as property rights or the rule of law. A lopsided distribution of income may cause the rich to squander resources on increasingly frivolous luxuries (e.g., doggy birthday cakes) when other kinds of investments, such as human capital for the poor, would yield a higher return. Or class warfare may lead to measures that punish the rich without making the poor any better off.[13] Some studies have indeed found a negative relationship between income inequality and economic growth; others have found just the opposite. Over time, data will inform this relationship. But the larger philosophical debate will rage on: If the pie is growing, how much should we care about the size of the pieces?

The subject of human capital begs some final questions. Will the poor always be with us, as Jesus once admonished? Does our free market system make poverty inevitable? Must there be losers if there are huge economic winners? No, no, and no. Economic development is not a zero-sum game; the world does not need poor countries in order to have rich countries, nor must some people be poor in order for others to be rich. Families who live in public housing on the South Side of Chicago are not poor because Bill Gates lives in a big house. *They are poor despite the fact that Bill Gates lives in a big house.* For a complex array of reasons, America's poor have not shared in the productivity gains spawned by DOS and Windows. Bill Gates did not take their pie away; he did not stand in the way of their success or benefit from their misfortunes. Rather, his vision and talent created an enormous amount of wealth that not everybody got to share. There is a crucial distinction between a world in which Bill Gates gets rich by stealing other people's crops and a world in which he gets rich by growing his own enormous food supply that he shares with some people and not others. The latter is a better representation of how a modern economy works.

In theory, a world in which every individual was educated, healthy, and productive would be a world in which every person lived comfortably. Perhaps we will never cure the world of the assorted physical and mental illnesses that prevent some individuals from reaching their full potential. But that is biology, not economics. Economics tells us that there is no theoretical limit to how well we can live or how widely our wealth can be spread.

Can that really be true? If we all had Ph.D.s, who would pass out the towels at the Four Seasons? Probably no one. As a population becomes more productive, we begin to substitute technology for labor. We use voice mail instead of secretaries, washing machines instead of maids, ATMs instead of bank tellers, databases instead of file clerks, vending machines instead of shopkeepers, backhoes instead of ditch diggers. (I recently visited a grocery store in Boulder, Colorado, that was experimenting with a self-serve checkout line.) The motivation for this development harks back to a concept from Chapter 1: opportunity cost. Highly skilled individuals can do all kinds productive things with their time. Thus, it is fabulously expensive to hire an engineer to bag groceries. (How much would you have to be paid to pass out towels at the Four Seasons?) There are far fewer domestic servants in the United States than in India, even though the United States is a richer country. India is awash with low-skilled workers who have few other employment options; America is not, making domestic labor relatively expensive (as anyone with a nanny can attest). Who can afford a butler who would otherwise earn $50 an hour writing computer code?

When we cannot automate menial tasks, we may relegate them to students and young people as a means for them to acquire human capital. I caddied for more than a decade (most famously for George W. Bush, long before he was the mature world leader that he is today); my wife waited tables. These jobs provide work experience, which is an important component of human capital. But suppose there was some unpleasant task that could not be automated away, nor could it be done safely by young people at the beginning of their careers. Imagine, for example, a highly educated community that produces all kinds of valuable goods and services but generates a disgusting sludge as a by-product. Further imagine that collecting the sludge is disgusting, mind-numbing work. Yet if the sludge is not collected, then the whole economy will grind to a halt. If everyone has a Harvard degree, who hauls away the sludge?

The sludge hauler does. And he or she, incidentally, would be one of the best-paid workers in town. If the economy depends on hauling this stuff away, and no machine can do the task, then the community would have to induce someone to do the work. The way to induce people to do anything is to pay them a lot. The wage for hauling sludge would get bid up to the point that some individual—a doctor, or an engineer, or a writer—would be willing to leave a more pleasant job to haul sludge. Thus, a world rich in human capital may still have unpleasant tasks— proctologist springs to mind—but no one has to be poor.

Human capital creates opportunities. It makes us richer and healthier; it makes us more complete human beings; it enables us to live better while working less. Most important from a public policy perspective, human capital separates the haves from the have-nots. Marvin Zonis, a professor at the University of Chicago Graduate School of Business and a consultant to businesses and governments around the world, made this point wonderfully in a recent speech to the Chicago business community. "Complexity will be the hallmark of our age," he noted. "The demand everywhere will be for ever higher levels of human capital. The countries that get that right, the companies that understand how to mobilize and apply that human capital, and the schools that produce it . . . will be the big winners of our age. For the rest, more backwardness and more misery for their own citizens and more problems for the rest of us."[14]

CHAPTER 7

Financial Markets:

What economics can tell us about getting rich quick (and losing weight, too!)

When I was an undergraduate many years ago, a new diet swept through one of the sororities on campus. This was no ordinary diet; it was the grapefruit and ice cream diet. The premise, as the name would suggest, was that one could lose weight by eating large amounts of grapefruit and ice cream. The diet did not work, of course, but the incident has always stuck with me. I was fascinated that a very smart group of women had tossed aside common sense to embrace a diet that could not possibly work. No medical or dietary information suggested that eating grapefruit and ice cream would cause weight loss. Still, it was an appealing thought. Who wouldn't want to lose weight by eating ice cream?

I was reminded of the grapefruit and ice cream diet recently when one of my neighbors began to share his investment strategy. He had taken a big hit over the past year because his portfolio was laden with Internet and tech stocks, he explained, but he was plunging back into the market with a new and improved strategy. He was studying the charts of past market movements for shapes that would signal where the market was going next. I cannot remember the specific shapes he was looking for. I was distracted at the time, both because I was watering flowers and because my mind was screaming, "Grapefruit and ice cream!" My smart neighbor, who is both a doctor and a university faculty member, was venturing far from the halls of science with his investment strategy, and that is the broader lesson. When it comes to personal finance (and losing weight), intelligent people will toss good sense aside faster than you can say "miracle diet." The rules for investing successfully are strikingly simple, but they require discipline and short-term sacrifice. The payoff is a slow, steady accumulation of wealth (with plenty of setbacks along the way) rather than a quick windfall. So, faced with the prospect of giving up consumption in the present for plodding success in the future, we eagerly embrace faster, easier methods—and are then shocked when they don't work.

This chapter is not a primer on personal finance. There are some excellent books on investment strategies. Burton Malkiel, who was kind enough to write the foreword for this book, has written one of the best: *A Random Walk down Wall Street*. Rather, this chapter is about what a basic understanding of markets—the ideas covered in the first two chapters—can tell us about personal investing. Any investment strategy must obey the basic laws of economics, just as any diet is constrained by the realities of chemistry, biology, and physics. To borrow the title of Wally Lamb's best-selling novel: I know this much is true.

At first glance, the financial markets are remarkably complex. Stocks and bonds are complicated enough, but then there are options, futures, options on futures, interest rate swaps, government "strips," and an array of other products so arcane that new Ph.D.s in mathematics routinely head for Wall Street rather than the Ivory Tower. At the Chicago Mercantile Exchange, it is now possible to buy or sell a futures contract based on the average temperature in Los Angeles. Across town at the Chicago Board of Trade, one can buy and sell the right to emit SO_2. Yes, it's actually possible to make (or lose) money by trading smog. The details of these contracts can be mind-numbing, yet at bottom, most of what is going on is fairly straightforward. Financial instruments, like every other good or service in a market economy, must create some value. Both the buyer and seller must perceive themselves as better off by entering into the deal. All the while, entrepreneurs seek to introduce financial products that are cheaper, faster, easier, or otherwise better than what already exists. Mutual funds were a financial innovation; so were the index funds that Burt Malkiel helped to make popular. That said, all financial instruments—no matter how complex the bells and whistles—are based on four simple needs:

Raising capital. One of the fascinating things in life, particularly in America, is that we can spend large sums of money that don't belong to us. Financial markets enable us to borrow money. Sometimes this means that Visa and Mastercard indulge our eagerness to consume today what we cannot afford until next year (if then); more often—and more significant to the economy—borrowing makes possible all kinds of investment. We borrow to pay college tuition. We borrow to buy homes. We borrow to build plants and equipment or to launch new businesses. We borrow to do things that make us better off even after we've paid the cost of borrowing.

Sometimes we raise capital without borrowing; we may sell shares of our business to the public. Thus, we trade an ownership stake (and therefore a claim on future profits) in exchange for cash. Or companies and governments may borrow directly from the public by issuing bonds. These transactions may be as simple as a new car loan or as complex as a multibillion-dollar bailout by the International Monetary Fund. *The bottom line never changes: Individuals, firms, and governments need capital to do things today that they could not otherwise afford; the financial markets provide it to them—at a price.*

Modern economies cannot survive without credit. Indeed, the international development community has begun to realize that making credit available to entrepreneurs in the developing world, even loans as small as $50 or $100, can be a powerful tool for fighting poverty. Opportunity International is one such "microcredit" lender. In 2000, the organization made nearly 325,000 low-collateral or noncollateral loans in twenty-four developing countries. The average loan size was a seemingly paltry $195. Esther Gelabuzi, a widow in Uganda with six children, represents a typical story. She is a professional midwife, and she used a tiny loan by Western standards to set up a clinic (still without electricity). She has since delivered some fourteen hundred babies, charging patients from $6 to $14 each. Opportunity International claims to have created some 430,000 jobs. As impressive, the repayment rate on the micro-loans is 96 percent.

Storing, protecting, and making profitable use of excess capital. The sultan of Brunei earned billions of dollars in oil revenues in the 1970s. Suppose he had stuffed that cash under his mattress and left it there. He would have had several problems. First, it is very difficult to sleep with billions of dollars stuffed under the mattress. Second, with billions of dollars stuffed under the mattress, the dirty linens would not be the only thing that disappeared every morning. Nimble fingers, not to mention sophisticated criminals, would find their way to the stash. Third, and most important, the most ruthless and efficient thief would be inflation. If the sultan of Brunei stuffed $1 billion under his mattress in 1970, it would be worth only $226 million today.

Thus, the sultan's first concern would be protecting his wealth, both from theft and from inflation, each of which diminishes his purchasing power in its own way. His second concern would be putting his excess capital to some productive use. The world is full of prospective borrowers, all of whom are willing to pay for the privilege. When economists slap fancy equations on the chalkboard, the symbol for the interest rate is r, not i. Why? Because the interest rate is considered to be the rental rate—r—on capital. And that is the most intuitive way to think about what is going on. Individuals, companies, and institutions with surplus capital are renting it to others who can make more productive use of it. The Harvard University endowment is roughly $19 billion. This is the Ivy League equivalent of rainy-day money; stuffing it under the mattresses of students and faculty would be both impractical and a waste of a tremendous resource. Instead, Harvard employs nearly two hundred professionals to manage this hoard in a way that generates a healthy return for the university (6 percent over inflation for the past nine years) while providing capital to the rest of the world.[1] Harvard buys stocks and bonds, invests in venture capital funds, and otherwise puts $19 billion in the hands of people and institutions around the globe who can do productive things with it.

Financial markets do more than take capital from the rich and lend it to everyone else. They enable each of us to smooth consumption over our lifetimes, which is a fancy way of saying that we don't have to spend income at the same time we earn it. Shakespeare may have admonished us to be neither borrowers nor lenders; the fact is that most of us will be both at some point. If we lived in an agrarian society, we would have to eat our crops reasonably near the harvest or find some way to store them. Financial markets are a more sophisticated way of managing the harvest. We can spend income now that we have not yet earned—as by borrowing for college or a home—or we can earn income now and spend it later, as by saving for retirement. The important point is that earning income has been divorced from spending it, allowing us much more flexibility in life.

Insuring against risk. Life is a risky proposition. We risk death just getting into the bathtub, not to mention commuting to work or bungee jumping with friends. Let us consider the ways you might face financial ruin: natural disaster, illness or disability, fraud or theft. One of our primary impulses as human beings is to minimize these risks. Financial markets help us to do that. The most obvious examples are health, life, and auto insurance. As we noted in Chapter 4, insurance companies charge more for your policy than they expect to pay out to you, on average. But "average" is a really important term here. You are not worried about average outcomes; you are worried about the worst things that could possibly happen to you. A bad draw—the tree that falls in an electrical storm and crushes your home—could be devastating. Thus, most of us are willing to pay a predictable amount—even one that is more than we expect to get back—in order to protect against the unpredictable.

Almost anything can be insured. Aon, a Chicago-based insurance company, wrote a policy for the St. Louis Cardinals baseball team during the 2000 season protecting it against an injury to Mark McGwire, its star player. McGwire, who is one of baseball's best home-run hitters, sells tickets. If he gets hurt, then some St. Louis fans will stay home. So Aon agreed to insure the Cardinals against those potential lost ticket sales. If McGwire was put on the team's disabled list, then Aon paid the Cardinals $20 for every empty seat below the team's average attendance with McGwire in the lineup. "To quantify on an underwriting basis what

McGwire is worth was very simple," an Aon executive told *Crain's Chicago Business.*[2]

The financial markets provide an array of other products that look complicated but basically function like an insurance policy. A futures contract, for example, locks in a sale price for a commodity—anything from electrical power to soybean meal—at some defined date in the future. On the floor of the Board of Trade, one trader can agree to sell another trader a thousand bushels of corn for $3.27 a bushel in March of 2003. What's the point? The point is that producers and consumers of these commodities have much to fear from future price swings. Corn farmers can benefit from locking in a sale price while their corn is still in the ground—or even before they plant it. Might the farmers get a better price by waiting to sell the crop until harvest? Absolutely. Or they might get a much lower price, leaving them without enough money to pay the bills. They, like the rest of us, are willing to pay a price for certainty.

Meanwhile, big purchasers of commodities can benefit from being on the other side of the trade. Airlines use futures contracts to lock in a predictable price for jet fuel; fast-food restaurants can enter into futures contracts for ground beef, pork bellies (most of which are made into bacon), and even cheddar cheese. I don't know any Starbucks executives personally, but I have a pretty good idea what keeps them awake at night: the world price of coffee beans. Americans will pay $3.50 for a grande skim decaf latte, but probably not $6.50, which is why I would be willing to bet the royalties from this book that Starbucks uses the financial markets to protect itself from sudden swings in the price of coffee.

Other products deal with other risks. Consider one of my personal favorites: catastrophe bonds.[3] Wall Street dreamed up these gems to help insurance companies hedge their natural disaster risk. Remember, the insurance company writes a check when a tree falls on your house; if a lot of trees fall on a lot of houses, then the company, or even the entire industry, has a problem. Insurance companies can minimize that risk by issuing catastrophe bonds. These bonds pay a significantly higher rate of interest than other corporate bonds because there is a twist: If hurricanes or earthquakes do serious damage to a certain area during a specified period of time, then the investors forfeit some or all of their principal.

The United Services Automobile Association did one of the first deals in the late 1990s tied to the hurricane season on the East Coast. If a single hurricane caused $1.5 billion in claims or more, then the catastrophe bond investors lost all their principal. The insurance company, on the other hand, was able to offset its claims losses by avoiding repayment on its debt. If a hurricane did between $1 billion and $1.5 billion in damage, then investors lost a fraction of their principal.

If hurricanes did relatively little damage that year, then the bondholders got their principal back plus nearly 12 percent in interest—a very nice return for a bond. The beauty of this product lies in the way it spreads risk. The insurance company avoids ruin by sharing the costs of a natural disaster with a broad group of investors, each of whom will take a relatively small hit if the East Coast is battered by hurricane after hurricane.

Indeed, one role of the financial markets is to allow us to spread our eggs around generously. I must recount one of those inane experiences that can happen only in high school. Some expert in adolescent behavior at my high school decided that students would be less likely to become teen parents if they realized how much responsibility it required. The best way to replicate parenthood, the experts reckoned, would be to have each student carry an egg around school. The egg represented a baby and was to be treated as such—handled delicately, never left out of sight, and so on. But this was high school. Eggs were dropped, crushed, left in gym lockers, hurled against the wall by bullies, exposed to secondhand smoke in the bathrooms, etc. The experience taught me nothing about parenthood; it did convince me forever that carrying eggs is a risky proposition.

The financial markets make it cheap and easy to put our eggs into many different baskets. With a $1,000 investment in a mutual fund, you can invest in five hundred or more companies. If you were forced to buy individual stocks from a broker, you could never afford so much diversity with a mere $1,000. For $10,000, you can diversify across a wide range of assets: big stocks, small stocks, international stocks, long-term bonds, short-term bonds, junk bonds, real estate. Some of those assets will perform well at the same time others are doing poorly, protecting you from Wall Street's equivalent of bullies hurling eggs against the wall. Indeed, one attraction of catastrophe bonds for investors is that their payout is determined by the frequency of natural disasters, which is not correlated with the performance of the stock market. For example, 2001 was a lousy year for stocks but a good year for hurricanes.

Speculation: Of course, once any financial product is created, it fulfills another basic human need: the urge to speculate, or bet on short-term price movements. One can use the futures markets to mitigate risk—or one can use the futures market to bet on the price of soybeans next year. One can use the bond markets to raise capital—or one can use it to bet on whether or not Alan Greenspan will cut interest rates next month. One can use the stock market to invest in companies and share their future profits—or one can buy a stock at 10:00 a.m., hoping to make a few bucks by noon. Financial products are to speculation what sporting events are to gambling. They facilitate it, even if that is not their primary purpose.

That's it. All the frantic activity on Wall Street or LaSalle Street (home of the futures exchanges in Chicago) fits into one or more of those buckets. The world of high finance is often described as a rich man's version of Las Vegas—risk, glamour, interesting personalities, and lots of money changing hands. Yet the analogy is terribly inappropriate. Everything that happens in Las Vegas is a zero-sum game. If the house wins a hand of blackjack, you lose. And the odds are stacked heavily in favor of the house. If you play blackjack long enough—at least without counting cards—it is a mathematical certainty that you will go broke. Las Vegas provides entertainment, but it does not serve any broader social purpose. Wall Street does. Most of what happens is a positive-sum game. Things get built; companies are launched; individuals and companies manage risk that might otherwise be devastating. Not every transaction is a winner, of course. Just as individuals make investments they later regret, the capital markets are perfectly capable of squandering huge amounts of capital; choose your favorite failed dot-com and think of that as an example. Billions of dollars of capital flowed into businesses that now have nothing to show for it. Meanwhile, some potentially profitable enterprises are starved for capital because they have insufficient collateral.

Economists worry, for example, that too little credit is available for poor families who would like to invest in human capital. A college degree is an excellent investment, but it is not something that can be repossessed in the event of default.

Still, the financial markets do for capital what other markets do for everything else: allocate it in a highly productive, albeit imperfect, way. Capital flows to where it can earn the highest return, which is not a bad place to have it flowing (as opposed to, say, into businesses run by top communist officials or friends of the king). As with the rest of the economy, government can be enemy or friend. Government can mess up the capital markets in the same ways it can mess up anything else—with overly burdensome taxes and regulations, by diverting capital into pet projects, by refusing to allow creative destruction to work its harshly efficient ways. Or government can make the financial markets work better: by minimizing fraud, forcing transparency on the system, creating and enforcing a regulatory framework, providing public goods that lower the cost of doing business, and so on. Once again, the wisdom lies in telling the difference.

All that is well and good. *But how does one get rich in the markets?* One of my colleagues at *The Economist* suggested that this book should be called *Are You Rich Enough?* His logic was that most people would answer no and rip the book off the shelves. Sadly, I'm not a big believer in surefire strategies to trade your way to riches. Just as miracle weight-loss programs violate nearly everything we know about health and nutrition, get-rich-quick schemes violate the most basic principles of economics.

Let me begin with an example. Suppose you are shopping for a home in the Lincoln Park neighborhood of Chicago. After many weeks of searching, you find that a three-story single-family brownstone will cost you somewhere in the range of $500,000. Some homes are listed for $450,000 but they need work; others are listed for $600,000 because they have extra amenities. Just when you begin to despair that you will have to spend $500,000 for a home, you find a brownstone listed for $250,000 that meets all of your specifications. When you investigate, you learn that this home is every bit as nice as the ones you've been looking at—same location, same size, same structural integrity. Still wary, you ask your real estate agent for her assessment. She assures you that this house is indeed a remarkable bargain and should be selling for $500,000. In her professional opinion, there is no doubt that you could buy this house for $250,000 and sell it only months later for $500,000 or more. Then you see the final piece of evidence. An article on page 3 of *Crain's Chicago Business* has a screaming headline: "Bargain of the Month: Lincoln Park Brownstone Listed for $250,000."

So you snap up the house for $250,000. Sure enough, six months later you sell it for $500,000—doubling your money.*

How many things are wrong with this story? Quite a few. A reasonable person might begin by asking some of the following questions:

1. If this house was really worth $500,000, who was the moron selling it for $250,000? Was this person not willing or able to do the three minutes of work necessary to determine that comparable houses in the neighborhood were selling for twice as much? If not, wasn't there a family member or a real estate agent—whose commission is based on the sale price—willing to point out this enormous discrepancy?

2. Maybe not. In that case, why hasn't my real estate agent bought this house for herself? If this house is a "sure thing" to double in price, why is she working for my 3 percent commission when $250,000 is staring her in the face?

3. Perhaps my real estate agent is a moron, too. In that case, where are all of the other buyers looking for bargains, especially after this house is featured in *Crain's Chicago Business*? If this brownstone is a tremendous bargain—and has been widely advertised as such—then presumably all kinds of people are going to want to buy it. A bidding war would result, with potential buyers offering larger and larger sums until the price reached its fair market value, which is around $500,000.

---

*Your actual return would be much higher, since much of the purchase would be financed. If you put $50,000 down, for example, you would have earned $250,000 on a $50,000 investment (minus the interest you paid to carry the mortgage during the period you owned the house).

In other words, there is virtually no chance that you will find a Lincoln Park brownstone (without some surprise lurking in the basement) for $250,000. Why? Because of the most basic idea in economics. You are trying to maximize your utility—and so is everyone else. In a world in which everyone is looking to make profitable investments, no one is going to leave $250,000 sitting on the table. *Yet people assume the stock market works like this all the time.* We believe that after reading about a "hot stock" in *Business Week*, or reading a Wall Street analyst's buy recommendation (offered to all the firm's clients), we can load up on stocks that will trounce the market average. But those supposed "hot stocks" are merely the Lincoln Park brownstone in different clothing. Here's why:

Let's start with a stunningly simple but often overlooked point: Every time you buy a stock (or any other asset), someone has to sell it to you. The guy who sells you this "hot stock" has decided that he would rather have cash. He has looked at the current "bargain price" and he wants out—right when you are getting in. Sure, he may need the money for something else, but he is still going to demand a fair market price, just as we would expect someone who has to move out of Lincoln Park to ask $500,000 for a brownstone, not $250,000. The stock market, as the name would suggest, is a market. The price of a stock at any given time is the price at which the number of buyers equals the number of sellers. Half of the investors trading your "hot stock" are trying to get rid of it.

Or maybe you know something that the sellers don't. Perhaps all the people unloading XYZ Corp. missed the *Wall Street Journal* article about XYZ's new blockbuster drug for male-pattern baldness. Okay, that might happen. But where are the world's other sophisticated buyers? This stock is a sure thing at $45, yet for some reason Warren Buffett, the traders at Morgan Stanley, and the top Fidelity portfolio managers are not snapping it up. (If they were, the stock would be bid up to a much higher price, just like the Lincoln Park brownstone.) Do you know something that no one else on Wall Street knows (bearing in mind that trading on any information not available to the public is against the law)?

Or maybe someone on Wall Street is pitching you this stock idea. America's brokerage houses employ a cadre of analysts who spend their days kicking the tires of corporate America. Is all that information wrong? No—though there are plenty of cases of incompetence and conflict of interest, the aggressive touting of overvalued Internet stocks being the most recent and egregious example. Analysts provide all kinds of legitimate information, just like your real estate agent. When you are shopping for a home, your agent can tell you about neighborhoods, schools, taxes, crime—the kinds of things that matter. Wall Street analysts do the same things for companies; they report on management, future products, the industry, the competition. But that does nothing to guarantee that you are going to earn an above-average return on the stock.

The problem is that everyone else has access to the same information. This is the essence of the efficient markets theory. The main premise of the theory is that asset prices already reflect all available information. Thus it is difficult, if not impossible, to choose stocks that will outperform the market with any degree of consistency. Why can't you buy a brownstone in Lincoln Park for $250,000? Because buyers and sellers recognize that such a home is worth much more. A share of XYZ Corp. is no different. Stock prices settle at a fair price given everything that we know or can reasonably predict; prices will rise or fall in the future only in response to unanticipated events—things that we cannot know in the present.

Picking stocks is a lot like trying to pick the shortest checkout line at the grocery store. Do some lines move faster than others? Absolutely, just as some stocks outperform others. Are there things that you can look for that signal how fast one line will move relative to another? Yes. You don't want to be behind the guy with two full shopping carts or the old woman clutching a fistful of coupons. So why is it that we seldom end up in the shortest line at the grocery store (and most professional stock pickers don't beat the market average)? Because everyone else is looking at the same things we are and acting accordingly. They can see the guy with two shopping carts, the cashier in training at register three, the coupon queen lined up at register six. Everybody at the checkout tries to pick the fastest line. Sometimes you will be right; sometimes you will be wrong. Over time they will average out, so that if you go to the grocery store often enough, you'll probably spend about the same amount of time waiting in line as everyone else.

Indeed, we can take the analogy one step further. Suppose that somewhere near the produce aisle you saw an old woman stuffing wads of coupons in her pockets. When you arrive at the checkout and see her in line, you wisely steer your cart somewhere else. As she gets out her coin purse and begins slowly handing coupons to the cashier, you smugly congratulate yourself. Moments later, however, you realize the guy ahead of you forgot to weigh his avocados. "Price check on avocados at register three!" your cashier barks repeatedly as you watch the coupon lady push her groceries out of the store. Who could have predicted that? No one, just as no one would have predicted that MicroStrategy, a high-flying software company, would restate its income on March 19, 2000, essentially wiping millions of dollars of earnings off its books. The stock fell $140 in one day, a 62 percent plunge. Did the investors and portfolio managers who bought MicroStrategy shares think this was going to happen? Of course not. *It's the things you can't predict that matter.* Indeed, the next time you are tempted to invest a large sum of money in a single stock, even that of a large and well-established firm, repeat these magic words: Enron, Enron, Enron.

Proponents of the efficient markets theory have advice for investors: Just pick a line and stand in it. If assets are priced efficiently, then a monkey throwing darts at the stock pages should choose a porfolio that will perform as well, on average, as the portfolios picked by the Wall Street stars. (Burton Malkiel has pointed out that since diversification is important, the monkey should actually throw a wet towel at the stock pages.) Indeed, investors now have access to their own monkey with a towel: index funds. Index funds are mutual funds that do not purport to pick winners. Instead, they buy and hold a predetermined basket of stocks, such as the S&P 500, the index that comprises America's largest five hundred companies. Since the S&P 500 is a broad market average, we would expect half of America's actively managed mutual funds to perform better, and half to perform worse. But that is before expenses. Fund managers charge fees for all the tire-kicking they do; they also incur costs as they trade aggressively. Index funds, like towel-throwing monkeys, are far cheaper to manage.

But that's all theory. What do the data show? It turns out that the monkey with a towel can be an investor's best friend. According to Morningstar, a firm that tracks mutual funds, roughly half the U.S. actively managed diversified funds beat the S&P 500 over the past year. Look what happens as the time frame gets longer: Only 30 percent of actively managed funds have performed better than the S&P 500 over the past five years, and only 15 percent of such funds have done so over the past twenty years. *In other words, 85 percent of the mutual funds that claim to have some special stock-picking ability did worse over two decades than a simple index fund, our modern equivalent of a monkey throwing a towel at the stock pages.*

If you had invested $10,000 in the average actively managed equity fund in 1973, when Malkiel's heretical book *A Random Walk down Wall Street* first came out, it would be worth $171,950 today (seven editions later). If you had invested the same amount of money in an S&P 500 index fund, it would now be worth $311,000.

Data notwithstanding, the efficient markets theory is obviously not the most popular idea on Wall Street. There is an old joke about two economists walking down the street. One of them sees a $100 bill lying in the street and points it out to his friend. "Is that a $100 bill lying in the gutter?" he asks.

"No," his friend replies. "If it were a $100 bill, someone would have picked it up already."

So they walk on by.

Academics, on the other hand, have generally embraced the idea of efficient markets. Still, some of the brightest minds in finance claim to have found fault with it. One fascinating field of study is behavioral economics, which marries psychology with economics. A cadre of economists have documented the ways in which human beings make flawed decisions. We are prone to herdlike behavior, we have too much confidence in our own abilities, we place too much weight on past trends when predicting the future, and so on. History is certainly littered with irrational speculative behavior, from the Dutch tulip craze to the NASDAQ bubble. The behavioral economists believe that by anticipating the flawed decisions that other investors are likely to make, we can beat the market. Richard Thaler, a University of Chicago economist, was even

willing to put his money where his theory was. He and some collabora-
tors created a mutual fund that would take advantage of our human
imperfections: the behavioral growth fund. I will even admit that after I
interviewed Mr. Thaler for Chicago public radio, I decided to toss aside
my strong belief in efficient markets and invest a small sum in his fund.
How has it done? The last time I checked, the behavioral growth fund
had lost 40 percent of its value in one year, compared to a 15 percent loss
for the S&P 500 over the same period. So much for that grapefruit and
ice cream.

The efficient markets theory is not dogma, though even its critics
usually concede that indexing is a very good strategy for small investors.
Andrew Lo of MIT and A. Craig MacKinlay of the Wharton School are
the authors of a book entitled *A Non-Random Walk down Wall Street* in
which they assert that financial experts with extraordinary resources,
such as supercomputers, can beat the market by finding and exploiting
pricing anomalies. A *Business Week* review of the book noted,
"Surprisingly, perhaps, Lo and MacKinlay actually agree with Malkiel's
advice to the average investor. If you don't have any special expertise or
the time and money to find expert help, they say, go ahead and purchase
index funds."[4] *And those are the guys who don't accept the efficient markets
hypothesis.* Indexing is to investing what regular exercise and a low-fat diet
are to losing weight: a very good starting point. The burden of proof
should fall on anyone who claims to have a better way.

As I've already noted, this chapter is not an investment guide. I'll leave
it to others to explain the pros and cons of college savings plans, munici-
pal bonds, variable annuities, and all the other modern investment options.
That said, basic economics can give us a sniff test. It provides us with a
basic set of rules to which any decent investment advice must conform:

Save. Invest. Repeat. Let's return to the most basic idea in this chapter:
Capital is scarce. This is the only reason that any kind of investing yields
returns. If you have spare capital, then someone will pay you to use it.
But you've got to have the spare capital first, and the only way to generate spare capital is to spend less than you earn—i.e., save. The more you
save, and the sooner you begin saving it, the more rent you can command

from the financial markets. Any good book on personal finance will daz-zle you with the virtues of compound interest. Suffice it here to note that Albert Einstein is said to have called it the greatest invention of all time.

The flip side, of course, is that if you are spending more cash than you earn, then you will have to "rent" the difference somewhere. And you will have to pay for that privilege. Paying the rent on capital is no different from paying the rent on anything else: It is an expense that crowds out other things you may want to consume later. The cost of liv-ing better in the present is living less well in the future. Conversely, the payoff for living frugally in the present is living better in the future. So for now, set aside questions about whether your 401(k) should be in stocks or bonds. The first step is far more simple: Save early, save often, and pay off the credit cards.

Take risk, earn reward. Okay, now we'll talk about whether your 401(k) should be in stocks or bonds. Suppose you have capital to rent, and you are deciding between two options: lending it to the federal government (a treasury bond), or lending it to your neighbor Lance, who has been tinkering in his basement for three years and claims to have invented an internal combustion engine that runs on sunflower seeds. Both the fed-eral government and your neighbor Lance are willing to pay you 6 per-cent interest on the loan. What to do? Unless Lance has photos of you in a compromising position, you should buy the government bond. The sunflower combustion engine is a risky proposition; the government bond is not. Lance may eventually attract the capital necessary to build his invention, but not by offering a 6 percent return. *Riskier investments must offer a higher expected return in order to attract capital.* That is not some arcane law of finance; it is simply markets at work. No rational person will invest money somewhere when he or she can earn the same expected return with less risk somewhere else.

The implication for investors is clear: You will be compensated for taking more risk. Thus, the more risky your portfolio, the higher your return—*on average.* Yes, it's that pesky concept of "average" again. If your portfolio is risky, it also means that some very bad things might happen. Nothing encapsulates this point better than a single 1998 headline in the

Wall Street Journal: "Bonds Let You Sleep at Night but at a Price."[5] The story examined stock and bond returns from 1945 to 1997. Over that period, a portfolio of 100 percent stocks earned an average annual return of 12.9 percent; a portfolio of 100 percent bonds earned a relatively meager 5.8 percent average annual return over the same period. So you might ask yourself, who are the chumps holding bonds? Not so fast. The same story then examined how the different portfolios performed in their worst years. The stock portfolio lost 26.5 percent of its value in its worst year; the bond portfolio never lost more than 5 percent of its value in a single bad year. Similarly, the stock portfolio had negative annual returns eight times between 1945 and 1997; the bond portfolio lost money only once. The bottom line: Risk is rewarded—if you have a tolerance for it.

Diversify. When I teach finance, I like to have my students flip coins. It is the best way to make certain points. Here is one of them: A well-diversified portfolio will significantly lower the risk of serious losses without lowering your expected return. Let's turn to the coins. Suppose the return on the $100,000 you have tucked away in a 401(k) depends on the flip of a coin: Heads, it quadruples in value; tails, you lose everything. The average outcome of this exercise is very good. (Your expected return is 100 percent.)* The problem, of course, is that the downside is unacceptably bad. You have a 50 percent chance of losing your whole nest egg. Try explaining that to a spouse.

So let's bring on some more coins. Suppose you spread the $100,000 in your 401(k) into ten different investments, each with the same payoff scheme: Heads, the investment quadruples in value; tails, it becomes worthless. Your expected return has not changed at all: On average, you will flip five heads and five tails. Five of your investments would quadruple in value, and five would become worthless. That works out to the same handsome 100 percent return. But look at what has happened to your downside risk. The only way you can lose your entire 401(k) is by flipping ten tails, which is highly unlikely. (The probability is less than one in a thousand.) Now imagine the same exercise if you buy several

---

*The expected return is .5($400,000) + .5($0) = $200,000, which is a 100 percent return on your $100,000 investment.

index funds that include thousands of stocks from around the world.[*] That many coins will never come up all tails.

Invest for the long run. Have you ever been in a casino when someone wins big? The casino operators are just as happy as everybody else. Why? Because they are going to make an extraordinary amount of money in the long run; this is just one minor hiccup along the way. The beauty of running a casino is that the numbers are stacked in your favor. If you are willing to wait long enough—and pose happily for photos as you give a giant check to the occasional big winner—then you will get rich.

Investing has the same benefits as running a casino: The odds are stacked in your favor if you are patient and willing to endure the occasional setback. Any reasonable investment portfolio must have a positive expected return. Remember, you've rented capital to assorted entities and you expect to get something back in return. Indeed, the riskier the ventures, the more you expect to get back, on average. So the longer you hold your (diversified) investments, the longer you have for probability to work its magic. Where will the Dow close tomorrow? I have no clue. Where will it be next year? I don't know. Where will it be in five years? Probably higher than it is today, but that's no sure thing. Where will it be in twenty-five years? Significantly higher than it is today; I'm nearly certain of it. The idiocy of day trading—buying a stock in hopes of selling it several hours later at a profit—is that it incurs all the costs of trading stocks (commissions and taxes, not to mention your time) without any of the benefits that come from holding equities for the long run.

So there you have it—the sniff test for personal investing. The next time an investment adviser comes to you promising a 20 or 40 percent return, you know that one of three things must be true: (1) This must be a very risky investment in order to justify such a high expected return; (2) your

---

[*] This exercise is somewhat oversimplified. The flips of a coin are independent while the performance of individual stocks are not. Some events, such as an interest rate hike, will affect the whole market. Thus, buying two stocks will not offer as much diversification as would splitting your portfolio between two flips of a coin. Nonetheless, the broader point is valid.

investment adviser has stumbled upon an opportunity still undiscovered by all the world's sophisticated investors, and he has been kind enough to share it with you; or (3) your investment adviser is incompetent and/or dishonest. All too often the answer is (3).

The fascinating thing about economics is that the fundamental ideas don't change. Monarchs in the Middle Ages needed to raise capital (usually to fight wars), just as biotech startups do today. I have no idea what the planet will look like in one hundred years. Perhaps we will be settling Mars or converting salt water into a clean, renewable source of energy. I do know that either of those undertakings would use the financial markets to raise capital and to mitigate risk. And I'm positive that Americans will not have become thin and healthy by eating only grapefruit and ice cream.

CHAPTER 8

The Power of Organized Interests:
What economics can tell us about politics

everal years ago I took a vacation with a group of friends. As the sole academic among the bunch, I was the object of mild curiosity. When I explained that I was studying public policy, one of my peers asked skeptically, "If people know so much about public policy, then why is everything so messed up?" On the one hand, the question was idiotic; it's a bit like asking, "If we know so much about medicine, why do people keep dying all the time?" One can always come up with clever rejoinders a decade later. (At the time, I mumbled something like "Well, it's complicated.") I might have pointed out that in the realm of public policy, as in medicine, we have achieved some pretty good wins. Americans are healthier, richer, better-educated, and less vulnerable to economic booms and busts than at any time in our history—the dot-com bubble notwithstanding.

Still, the question has stuck with me for years, in large part because it hints at an important point: Even when economists reach consensus on policies that would make us better off, those policies often run into a brick wall of political opposition. International trade is a perfect example. I am not aware of a single mainstream economist who believes that international trade is anything less than crucial to the well-being of rich and poor countries alike. There is just one small problem: It's an issue that literally causes riots in the streets. Even before the violent antiglobalization protests in places like Seattle and Genoa, agreements to expand trade, such as the North American Free Trade Agreement, caused ferocious political battles.

Meanwhile, pork-barrel legislation sails through Congress, lavishing money on small projects that cannot possibly be described as promoting the national interest. For nearly forty years, the federal budget included a cash payment to American mohair farmers. (Mohair comes from the Angora goat and is a wool substitute.) The mohair subsidy was created in 1955 at the behest of the armed forces to ensure that there would be sufficient yarn for military uniforms in the event of a war. I won't quibble with that. *But the military switched to synthetic fibers for its uniforms around 1960.* The government continued to give large cash payments to mohair farmers for another thirty-five years. Why?

It was not because the mohair farmers are enormously powerful, well funded, or politically sophisticated. They are not any of those things. In fact, the small number of mohair farmers was an advantage. What the mohair farmers had going for them was that they could get large payments from the government without taxpayers ever really noticing. Suppose there are a thousand mohair farmers, each of whom gets a check from the federal government for $100,000 every spring, just for being a mohair farmer. The farmers who get that subsidy care a lot about it— probably more than they care about any other government policy. Meanwhile, the rest of us, who pay mere pennies extra in taxes to preserve an unnecessary supply of mohair, don't care much about it at all. Any politician with a preference for job security can calculate that a vote for the mohair subsidy will earn the strong support of the mohair farmers while costing nothing among other voters. It's a political no-brainer.

The problem is that mohair farmers aren't the only group lining up to get a subsidy, or a tax break, or trade protection, or some other government policy that puts money in their pockets. Indeed, the most savvy politicians can trade favors with one another—if you support the mohair farmers in my district, then I'll support the Bingo Hall of Fame in your district. During my days as a speechwriter for the governor of Maine, we used to refer to the state budget as a Christmas tree. Every legislator could hang an ornament or two. I currently live in the Illinois Fifth

Congressional District, the seat held for decades by Dan Rostenkowski. We Chicagoans can drive around the city and literally point to the things that Rosty built. When the Museum of Science and Industry needed tens of millions of dollars to build an underground parking garage, Dan Rostenkowski found federal funds.[1] Should taxpayers in Seattle or rural Vermont have paid for a parking garage at a Chicago museum? Of course not. But when I took my daughters to the museum last weekend in a downpour, I was delighted to be able to park indoors. That helps to explain why Dan Rostenkowski, not long out of federal prison, can still command a standing ovation at political gatherings in Chicago.

The mohair subsidy is now gone. At some point it became the poster child for pork-barrel politics and was doomed by its sheer absurdity. But the process that generated three decades of cash payments for mohair farmers is alive and well. Let's talk about ethanol, a corn-based gasoline additive with putative environmental benefits. Gasoline blended with ethanol is taxed 5.4 cents less per gallon than pure gasoline, ostensibly because it burns more cleanly than pure gasoline and because it lowers our dependence on foreign oil. Of course, neither scientists nor environmentalists are convinced that ethanol is such a great thing. A 1997 study by the General Accounting Office, the nonpartisan research arm of Congress, found that ethanol had little effect on either the environment or our dependence on foreign oil. The ethanol subsidy had, however, cost the Treasury $7.1 billion in forgone tax revenues. Worse, ethanol may actually make some kinds of air pollution worse. It evaporates faster than pure gasoline, contributing to ozone problems in hot temperatures. A 1999 study by the National Academy of Sciences came to a similar conclusion.[2]

But to dwell on the science is to miss the point. As the *New York Times* noted in the throes of the 2000 presidential race, "Regardless of whether ethanol is a great fuel for cars, it certainly works wonders in Iowa campaigns."[3] The ethanol tax subsidy increases the demand for corn, which puts money in farmers' pockets. The National Corn Growers Association figures that the ethanol program adds 30 cents to the price of every bushel of corn sold. Bill Bradley knows that. He opposed the ethanol subsidy during his three terms as a senator from New Jersey (not a big corn-growing state). Indeed, some of his most important accomplishments as a senator involved purging the tax code of subsidies and loopholes that collectively do more harm than good. But when Bill Bradley arrived in Iowa as a Democratic presidential candidate, he "spoke to some farmers" and suddenly found it in his heart to support tax breaks for ethanol. In short, he realized that ethanol is crucial to Iowa voters, and Iowa is crucial to the presidential race. Every mainstream presidential candidate supported the ethanol subsidy except John McCain, who did not campaign in Iowa because he knew his ethanol stance would eliminate any chance of doing well there. (While Senator McCain's "straight talk" is admirable, let us remind ourselves that he is not currently president of the United States.) Just before the 2000 Iowa caucuses, the *New York Times* interviewed Iowa corn farmer Marvin Flier. "Sometimes I think [the candidates] just come out and pander to us," he said. Then he added, "Of course, that may not be the worst thing."

Ethanol is not a case of a powerful special interest pounding the rest of us into submission. Farmers are a scant 2 or 3 percent of the population; even fewer of them actually grow corn. If squeezing favors out of the political process were simply a matter of brute strength, then those of us who can't tell a heifer from a steer should be kicking the farmers around. Indeed, America's right-handed voters could band together and demand tax breaks at the expense of the lefties. And we could really have our way with those mohair farmers. But that's not what happens.

Economists have come up with a theory of political behavior that fits better with what we actually observe. *When it comes to interest group politics, it pays to be small.* Gary Becker, the same University of Chicago Nobel Prize winner who figured so prominently in our thinking about human capital, wrote a seminal paper in the early 1980s that nicely encapsulated what had become known as the economics of regulation. Building on work that went all the way back to Milton Friedman's doctoral dissertation, Becker theorized that, all else equal, small, well-organized groups are most successful in the political process. Why? Because the costs of whatever favors they wrangle out of the system are spread over a large, unorganized segment of the population.

Think about ethanol again. The benefits of that $7 billion tax subsidy are bestowed on a small group of farmers, making it quite lucrative for each one of them. Meanwhile, the costs are spread over the remaining 98 percent of us, putting ethanol somewhere below good oral hygiene on our list of everyday concerns. The opposite would be true with my plan to have left-handed voters pay subsidies to right-handed voters. There are roughly nine right-handed Americans for every lefty, so if every right-handed voter were to get some government benefit worth $100, then every left-handed voter would have to pay $900 to finance it. The lefties would be hopping mad about their $900 tax bills, probably to the point that it became their preeminent political concern, while the righties would be only modestly excited about their $100 subsidy. An adept politician would probably improve her career prospects by voting with the lefties.

Here is a curious finding that makes more sense in light of what we've just discussed. In countries where farmers make up a small fraction of the population, such as America and Europe, the government provides large subsidies for agriculture. But in countries where the farming population is relatively large, such as China and India, the subsidies go the other way. Farmers are forced to sell their crops at below-market prices so that urban dwellers can get basic food items cheaply. In the one case, farmers get political favors; in the other, they must pay for them. What makes these examples logically consistent is that in both cases the large group subsidizes the smaller group.

In politics, the tail can wag the dog. This can have profound effects on the economy.

Death by a thousand subsidies. The cost of Dan Rostenkowski's underground parking garage at the Museum of Science and Industry is insignificant in the face of our $10 trillion economy. So is the ethanol subsidy. So is the trade protection for sugar producers, and the tax break for pharmaceutical companies with operations in Puerto Rico, and the price supports for dairy farmers. But in total, these things—and the thousands of others like them—*are* significant. Little inefficiencies begin to disrupt the most basic function of a market economy: taking inputs and producing goods and services as efficiently as possible. If the government has to support the price of milk, the real problem is that there are too many dairy farmers. The best definition I've ever heard of a tax shelter is some kind of investment or behavior that would not make sense in the absence of tax considerations. And that is exactly the problem here: Governments should not be in the business of providing incentives for people to do things that would not otherwise make sense.

Chapter 3 outlined all the reasons why good government is not just important, but essential. Yet it is also true that when Congress turns its attention to a problem, a lot of ornaments end up on the Christmas tree. The late George Stigler, a University of Chicago economist who won the Nobel Prize in 1982, proposed and defended a counterintuitive notion: Firms and industries often benefit from regulation. In fact, they can use the political process to generate regulation that either helps them or hobbles their competitors.

Does that sound unlikely? Consider the case of teacher certification. Every state requires public school teachers to do or achieve certain things before becoming licensed. Most people consider that to be quite reasonable. In Illinois, the requirements for certification have risen steadily over time. Again, that seems reasonable given our strong emphasis on public school reform. But when one begins to scrutinize the politics of certification, things become murkier. The teachers' unions, one of the most potent political forces in America, always support reforms that require more rigorous training and testing for teachers. Read the fine print, though. Almost without exception, these laws exempt current teachers from whatever new requirement is being imposed. In other words, individuals who would like to become teachers have to take additional classes or pass new exams; existing teachers do not. That doesn't make much sense if certification laws are written for the benefit of students. If doing certain things is necessary in order to teach, then presumably anyone standing at the front of a classroom should have to do them.

Other aspects of certification law don't make much sense either. Private school teachers, many of whom have decades of experience, cannot teach in public schools without jumping through assorted hoops (including student teaching) that are almost certainly unnecessary. Nor can university professors. When Albert Einstein retired to Princeton, New Jersey, he was not legally qualified to teach high school physics. Meanwhile, researchers have found that certification requirements have virtually no correlation with performance in the classroom. Mr. Stigler would have argued that all of this is easy to explain. Just think about how the process benefits teachers, not students. Making it harder to become a teacher reduces the supply of new entrants into the profession, which is a good thing for those who are already there. Any barrier to entry looks attractive from the inside.

I have a personal interest in all kinds of occupational licensure (cases in which states require that individuals become licensed before practicing certain professions). My doctoral dissertation set out to explain a seemingly anomalous pattern in Illinois: The state requires barbers and manicurists to be licensed, but not electricians. A shoddy electrical job could burn down an entire neighborhood; a bad manicure or haircut seems relatively more benign. Yet the barbers and manicurists are the ones regulated by the state. The short explanation for the pattern is two words: interest groups. The best predictor of whether or not a profession is licensed in Illinois is the size and budget of its professional association. (Every profession is small relative to the state's total population, so all of these groups have the mohair advantage. The size and budget of the professional association reflects the extent to which members of the profession have organized to exploit it.) Remarkably, political organization is a better predictor of licensure than the danger members of the profession pose to the public (as measured by their liability premium). George Stigler was right: *Groups seek to get themselves licensed.*

Small, organized groups fly under the radar and prevail upon legislators to do things that do not necessarily make the rest of us better off. Economists, particularly those among the more free-market "Chicago school," are sometimes perceived to be hostile toward government. It would be more accurate to describe them as skeptical. The broader the scope of government, the more room there is for special interests to carve out deals for themselves that have nothing to do with the legitimate functions of government described in Chapter 3.

Tyranny of the status quo. If small groups can get what they want out of the legislative process, they can also stop what they don't want, or at least try. Joseph Schumpeter, who coined the term "creative destruction," described capitalism as a process of incessantly destroying the old structure and creating a new one. That may be good for the world; it is bad for the firms and industries that make up the "old structure." The individuals standing in capitalism's path of progress—or destruction, from their standpoint—will use every tool they have to avoid it, including politics. And why shouldn't they? The legislative process helps those who help themselves. Groups under siege from competition may seek trade protection, a government bailout, favorable tax considerations, limitations on a competing technology, or some other special treatment. With layoffs or bankruptcy looming, the plea to politicians for help can be quite compelling.

So what's the problem? The problem is that we don't get the benefits of the new economic structure if politicians decide to protect the old one. Roger Ferguson, Jr., vice chairman of the board of governors of the Federal Reserve, explains, "Policymakers who fail to appreciate the relationship between the relentless churning of the competitive environment and wealth creation will end up focusing their efforts on methods and skills that are in decline. In so doing, they establish policies that are aimed at protecting weak, outdated technologies, and in the end, they slow the economy's march forward."[4]

Both politics and compassion suggest that we ought to offer a hand to those mowed over by competition. If some kind of wrenching change generates progress, then the pie must get bigger. And if the pie gets bigger, then at least some of it ought to be offered to the losers—be it in the form of transition aid, job retraining, or whatever else will help those who have been knocked over to get back on their feet. One of the features that made the North America Free Trade Agreement more palatable was a provision that offered compensation to workers whose job losses could be tied to expanded trade with Mexico. Similarly, many states are using money from the massive legal settlement with the tobacco industry to compensate tobacco farmers whose livelihoods are threatened by declining tobacco use.

There is a crucial distinction, however, between using the political process to build a safety net for those harmed by creative destruction and using the political process to stop that creative destruction in the first place. Think about the telegraph and the Pony Express. It would have been one thing to help displaced Pony Express workers by retraining them as telegraph operators; it would have been quite another to help them by banning the telegraph. Sometimes the political process does the equivalent of the latter for reasons related to the mohair problem. The economic benefits of competition are huge but spread over a large group; the costs tend to be smaller but highly concentrated. As a result, the beneficiaries of creative destruction hardly notice; the losers chain themselves to their congressman's office door seeking protection, as any of us might if our livelihood or community were at risk.

Such is the case in the realm of international trade. Trade is good for consumers. We pay less for shoes, cars, electronics, food, and everything else that can be made better or more cheaply somewhere else in the world (or is made more cheaply in this country because of foreign competition). Our lives are made better in thousands of little ways that have a significant cumulative effect. Looking back on the Clinton presidency, former treasury secretary Robert Rubin reflected, "The economic benefits of the tariff reductions we negotiated over the last eight years represent the largest tax cut in the history of the world."[5]

Cheaper shoes here, a better television there—still probably not enough to get the average person to fly to Seattle and march *in favor* of the World Trade Organization (WTO). Meanwhile, the AFL-CIO and other unions did send some thirty thousand members to Seattle to protest against broadening the WTO. The flimsy pretext was that the union is concerned about wages and working conditions in the developing world. Nonsense. The AFL-CIO is worried about American jobs. More trade means cheaper goods for millions of American consumers *and* lost jobs and shuttered plants. That is something that will motivate workers to march in the streets, as it has been throughout history. The original Luddites were bands of English textile workers who destroyed textile-making machinery to protest the low wages and unemployment caused by mechanization. What if they had gotten their way?

Consider that at the beginning of the fifteenth century, China was far more technologically advanced than the West. China had a superior knowledge of science, farming, engineering, even veterinary medicine. The Chinese were casting iron in 200 B.C., some fifteen hundred years before the Europeans. Yet the Industrial Revolution took place in Europe while Chinese civilization languished. Why? One historical interpretation posits that the Chinese elites valued stability more than progress. As a result, leaders blocked the kinds of wrenching societal changes that made the Industrial Revolution possible. In the fifteenth century, for example, China's rulers banned long-sea-voyage trade ventures, choking off trade as well as the economic development, discovery, and social change that come with them.

We have designed some institutions to help the greater good prevail over narrow (if eminently understandable) interests. For example, the president will often seek "fast-track authority" from Congress when the administration is negotiating international trade agreements. Congress must still ratify whatever agreement is reached, but only with an up or down vote. The normal process by which legislators can add amendments is waived. The logic is that legislators are not allowed to eviscerate the agreement by exempting assorted industries; a trade agreement that offers protection to a few special interests in every district is no trade agreement at all. The fast-track process forces politicians who talk the talk of free trade to walk the walk, too.

The unfairly maligned World Trade Organization is really just an international version of the fast-track process. Negotiating to bring down trade barriers among many countries—each laden with domestic interest groups—is a monumental task. The WTO makes the process more politically manageable by defining the things that countries must do in order to join: open markets, eliminate subsidies, phase out tariffs, etc. That is the price of membership. Countries that are admitted gain access to the markets of all the existing members—a huge carrot that gives politicians an incentive to say no to the mohair farmers of the world.

Cut the Politicians a Break. In the fall of 2000, a promising political career was launched. I was elected president of the Seminary Townhouse

Association. (Perhaps "elected" is too strong a word; the outgoing president asked if I would do it, and I was too naive to say no.) At about that time, the Chicago Transit Authority (CTA) announced plans to expand an elevated train station very close to our homes. The proposed expansion would bring the station into compliance with the Americans with Disabilities Act and allow the CTA to accommodate more riders. It would also move the elevated train tracks (and all the accompanying noise) thirty feet closer to our homes. In short, this plan was good for Chicago public transportation and bad for our townhouse association. Under my excellent leadership, we wrote letters, we held meetings, we consulted architects, we presented alternative plans (some of which would have required condemning and demolishing homes elsewhere in the neighborhood). I can not so proudly report that Fullerton Avenue still does not have a new elevated train station.

Yes, ladies and gentlemen, we are the special interests. All of us. You may not raise Angora goats; you may not grow corn. But you are part of some group—probably many of them—that has unique interests: a profession, an ethnic group, a demographic group, a neighborhood, an industry, a part of the country. As the old saying puts it, "Where you stand depends on where you sit." It is facile to declare that politicians should just do the right thing. The hoary old cliché about tough decisions is true. Doing the right thing—making a decision that generates more benefits for the nation than costs—will not cause people to stand up and cheer. It is far more likely that the many people you have made better off will hardly notice while the small group you have harmed will pelt your car with tomatoes.

Would campaign finance reform change anything? At the margins, if that. Money is certainly one tool for grabbing a politician's attention, but there are others. If the dairy farmers (who benefit from federal price supports) can't give money, they will hire lobbyists, ring doorbells, hold meetings, write letters, threaten hunger strikes, and vote as a bloc. Campaign finance reform does not change the fact that the dairy farmers care deeply about their subsidy while the people who pay for it don't care much at all. The democratic process will always favor small, well-organized groups at the expense of large, diffuse groups.

Bob Kerrey, former Democratic senator from Nebraska, has said that he doesn't think campaign finance reform would change much at all. "The most important corruption that happens in politics doesn't go away even if you had full public financing of campaigns," he told *The New Yorker*. "And that is: I don't want to tell you something that's going to make you not like me. If I had a choice between getting a round of applause by delivering a twenty-six-second applause line and getting a round of boos by telling you the truth, I'd rather get the round of applause."[6]

So, if I were asked again why our growing knowledge of public policy does not always translate into a perfect world, this chapter would be my more complete answer.

CHAPTER 9

Keeping Score:
Is my economy bigger than your economy?

s I have mentioned, in the late 1980s I was a young speech-writer working for the governor of Maine. One of my primary responsibilities was finding jokes. "Funny jokes," he would admonish me. "Belly laughs, not chuckles." More than a decade later, one of those jokes stands out, not so much because it is funny now, but rather for what it tells us about what we were thinking then. Recall that George Bush, Sr., was president and Dan Quayle was vice president. New England was in the midst of an economic slump and Maine was particularly hard hit. Meanwhile, Japan appeared to be the world's economic powerhouse. The joke goes like this:

While vacationing at Kennebunkport, George Bush is hit on the head with one of his beloved horseshoes. He slips into a coma. Nine months later, he awakes and President Quayle is standing at his bedside. "Are we at peace?" Mr. Bush asks.

"Yes. The country is at peace," says President Quayle.

"What is the unemployment rate?" Mr. Bush asks.

"About 4 percent," says President Quayle.

"Inflation?" queries Mr. Bush.

"Under control," says President Quayle.

"Amazing," says Mr. Bush. "How much does a loaf of bread cost?"

President Quayle scratches his head nervously and says, "About 240 yen."

Believe it or not, that was good for a belly laugh. Some of the humor derived from the prospect of Dan Quayle as president, but mostly it was an outlet for anxiety over the popular notion that Japan was on the brink of world economic domination. Obviously times change. We now know that Japan went on to suffer from more than a decade of economic stagnation while the United States moved into what would become the longest economic expansion in the nation's history. The Nikkei Index, which reflects prices on the Japanese stock market, is lower today than it was when the governor of Maine was telling that joke.

Why is it that all economies, rich and poor, proceed in fits and starts, stumbling from growth to recession and back to growth again? America's long, robust growth of the 1990s ended with the retrenchment of 2001. During the boom, the labor market was so tight that fast-food restaurants were paying signing bonuses, college graduates were getting stock options worth millions, and anyone with a pulse was earning double-digit returns in the stock market. Then someone hit the reverse thrusters. The business section was soon full of stories about layoffs, bankruptcies, and plunging stock prices. We liked it better the first way. What happened?

To understand the cycle of recession and recovery—the "business cycle," as economists call it—we need to first learn the tools for measuring a modern economy. If the president really did wake up from a coma after suffering a horseshoe accident, it's a fair bet that he would ask for one number first: gross domestic product, or GDP. GDP represents the value of all the goods and services produced in an economy. Tally up the market price of all the goods we manufacture and all the services we provide, and you will get gross domestic product. When the headlines proclaim that the economy grew 2.3 percent in a particular year, we are talking about GDP growth. It means simply that we as a country produced 2.3 percent more goods and services than we did the year before. Similarly, if we say that public education promotes economic growth, we are saying that it raises GDP growth. Or if we were asked whether an African country is better off in 2002 than it was in 1990, our answer would begin (though certainly not end) with a description of what happened to GDP over the course of the decade.

Can we really gauge our collective well-being by the quantity of goods and services that we produce? Yes and no. We'll start with "yes," though we will come to "no" before the chapter is done. GDP is a decent measure of our well-being for the simple reason that what we can consume is constrained by what we can produce—either because we consume those goods directly or because we trade them away for goods produced somewhere else. A country with a GDP per capita of $1,000 cannot consume $20,000 per capita. Where exactly are the other $19,000 worth of goods and services going to come from? What we consume can deviate from what we produce for short stretches, just as family spending can deviate from family income for a while. In the long run, however, what a country produces and what it consumes are going to be nearly identical.

I must make two important qualifications. First, what we care about is *real* GDP, which means that the figure has been adjusted to account for inflation. In contrast, *nominal* figures have not been adjusted for inflation. If nominal GDP climbs 10 percent in 2002 but inflation is also 10 percent, then we haven't actually produced more of anything. We've just sold the same amount of stuff at higher prices, which has not made us any better off. Your salary has most likely gone up 10 percent but so has the price of everything you buy. It's the economic equivalent of swapping a $10 bill for ten $1 bills—it looks good in your wallet, but you're not any richer. We will explore inflation in greater depth in the next chapter. For now, suffice it to say that our standard of living depends on the quantity of goods and services we take home with us, not on the price that shows up at the register.

Second, we care about GDP *per capita*, which is a nation's GDP divided by its population. Again, this is necessary to prevent wildly misleading conclusions. India has a GDP of $427 billion while Israel has a GDP of $97 billion. Which is the richer country? Israel by far. India has nearly a billion people while Israel has only six million; GDP per capita in Israel is $16,180 compared to only $440 in India. Similarly, if a country's economy grows 3 percent in a given year but the population grows 5 percent, then GDP per capita will fall. The country is producing more goods and services, but not enough more to keep up with a population that is growing faster.

• • •

If we look at real GDP in America, it tells us several things. First, the American economy is massive by global standards. American GDP is roughly $10 trillion, or roughly the same as the fifteen countries in the European Union combined. The next-largest single economy is Japan, which has a GDP just over $4 trillion. On a per capita basis, we are rich, both by global standards and by our own historical standards. In 1998, America's GDP per capita was roughly $30,000, slightly less than Japan or Switzerland, but still nearly the highest in the world. Our real GDP per capita is also twice what it was in 1970 and three times what it was in 1950.

In other words, the average American is three times as rich as he or she would have been in 1950. How could that be? The answer is back in Chapter 5: We're more productive. The day is not any longer, but what we can get done in twenty-four hours has changed dramatically. The Federal Reserve Bank of Dallas came up with a novel way to express our economic progress in the twentieth century: Compare how long we have to work now in order to buy basic items with how long we had to work to buy the same items in 1900. As the officials at the Dallas Fed explain, "Making money takes time, so when we shop, we're really spending time. The real cost of living isn't measured in dollars and cents but in the hours and minutes we must work to live."[1]

So here goes: A pair of stockings cost 25 cents a century ago. Of course, the average wage at the time was 14.8 cents an hour, so the real cost of stockings in 1900 was one hour and forty-one minutes of work for the average American. If you walk into a department store today, stockings (pantyhose) are seemingly more expensive than they were in 1900—but they're not. The price has gone up, but our wages have gone up even faster. Stockings now cost around $4, while America's average wage is over $13 an hour. As a result, a pair of stockings costs the average worker only eighteen minutes of time, a stunning improvement from an hour and forty-one minutes.

The same is true for most goods. If your grandmother were to complain that a frying chicken costs more today than it did when she was growing up, she would be correct only in the most technical sense. The price of a three-pound chicken has indeed climbed from $1.23 in 1919 to $3.15 in 1997. But grandma really has nothing to complain about. The "work time" necessary to earn a chicken has dropped remarkably. In 1919, the average worker spent two hours and thirty-seven minutes to earn enough money to buy a chicken (and, I'm guessing, at least another forty-five minutes for the mashed potatoes). In short, you would work most of your morning just to earn lunch. How long does it take to "earn" a chicken these days? Fourteen minutes. Cut out one personal phone call and you've got Sunday dinner taken care of. Skip that *Survivor* chat room and you could probably feed the neighbors, too.

Do you remember the days when it was novel, perhaps even mildly impressive, to see someone speaking on a cellular phone in a restaurant? (Okay, it was a short stretch of time, but a cell phone did have a certain cachet in the mid-1980s.) No wonder; back then a cell phone "cost" about 456 hours of work for the average American. Two decades later, cell phones are just plain annoying, in large part because everyone has one. The reason everyone has one is that they now "cost" about nine hours of work for the average worker—98 percent less than they cost 20 years ago.

We take this material progress for granted; we shouldn't. A rapidly rising standard of living has not been the norm throughout history. Robert Lucas, Jr., winner of the Nobel Prize in 1995 for his numerous contributions to macroeconomics, has argued that even in the richest countries, the phenomenon of sustained growth in living standards is only a few centuries old. Other economists have concluded that the growth rate of GDP per capita in Europe between 500 and 1500 was essentially zero.[2] They don't call it the Dark Ages for nothing.

We should also make clear what it means for a country to be poor by global standards at the beginning of the twenty-first century. As I've noted, India has a per capita GDP of $440. But let's translate that into something that is more than just a number. Modern India has 500,000 cases of Hansen's disease, better known to the world as leprosy. Leprosy is a contagious disease that attacks the body's tissues and nerves, leaving horrible scars and limb deformities. The striking thing about Hansen's disease is that it is easily cured, and, if caught early, recovery is complete. How much does it cost to treat leprosy? One $3 dose of antibiotic will cure a mild case; a $20 regimen of three antibiotics will cure a more severe case. The World Health Organization even provides the drugs free, but India's health care infrastructure is not good enough to identify the afflicted and get them the medicine they need.[3]

So, half a million people in India are horribly disfigured by a disease that costs $3 to cure. That is what it means to have a per capita GDP of $440.

Having said all that, GDP is, like any other statistic, just one measure. Beauty pageants and golf notwithstanding, it is hard to collapse complex entities into a single number. The list of knocks against GDP as a measure of social progress is a long one. GDP does not count any economic activity that is not paid for, such as work done in the home. If you cook dinner, take care of the kids, and tidy up around the house, none of that counts toward the nation's official output. However, if you order out food, drop your kids off at a child care center, and hire a cleaning lady, all of that does. Nor does GDP account for environmental degradation; if a company clear-cuts a virgin forest to make paper, the value of the paper shows up in the GDP figures without any corresponding debit for the forest that is now gone. Indeed, there are no value judgments attached to GDP whatsoever. A dollar spent building a prison or cleaning up after a natural disaster counts, even though we would be better off if we did not need prisons or if there were no disaster to clean up after. GDP per capita takes no account of the distribution of income; it is a simple average that can mask enormous disparities between rich and poor.

The most effective knock against GDP may simply be that it is an imperfect measure of how well off we really consider ourselves to be. Economics has an overly tautological view of happiness: The things we do must make us happy; otherwise we would not do them. Similarly, growing richer must make us better off because we can do and have more of the things that we enjoy. Yet survey results tell us something different. Richer may not be happier. The period of rising real incomes from 1970 to 1999 coincided with a decrease in those who described themselves as "very happy" from 36 percent to 29 percent.[4] Economists are belatedly beginning to probe this phenomenon, albeit in their own perversely quantitative way. For example, David Blanchflower and Andrew Oswald, economists at Dartmouth and the University of Warwick, respectively, have found that a lasting marriage is worth $100,000 a year, since married people report being as happy, on average, as divorced (and not remarried) individuals who have incomes that are $100,000 higher. So, before you go to bed tonight, be sure to sure to tell your spouse that you would not give him or her up for anything less than $100,000 a year.

If GDP is a flawed measure of economic progress, why can't we come up with something better?

We can, argues Marc Miringhoff, a professor of social sciences at Fordham University, who believes that the nation should have a "social report card" that includes indicators such as the child poverty rate. Mr. Miringhoff told the *New York Times*, "If the country knows that interest rates are up by one-quarter of a percent, people need to know that we have a child poverty indicator that is the worst in the industrial world. When that hits a new low, bells ought to go off the way it does when Alan Greenspan slams the breaks on inflation."[5] He proposes a social health index that would combine sixteen social indicators, such as child poverty, infant mortality, crime, access to health care, and affordable housing. How do the last several decades look through this lens? Mr. Miringhoff's social health index plunged from 77 out of a possible 100 in 1973 to 38 in 1993 before bouncing back to 46 in 1997.

Conservative author and commentator William Bennett agrees with half of that analysis. We do need a measure of progress that is broader than GDP, he argues. But ditch all that liberal claptrap. Mr. Bennett's "index of leading cultural indicators" includes the kinds of things that he considers important: out-of-wedlock births, divorce rates, drug use, participation in church groups, and the level of trust in government. The United Nations has its own measure, too. The human development index combines measures of per capita income, life expectancy, literacy, and educational attainment. By this measure, the United States ranks second in the world, tied with Norway and behind Canada.

So you begin to see the problem. Any measure of economic progress depends on how you define progress. GDP just adds up the numbers. There is something to be said for that. All else equal, it is better for a nation to produce more goods and services than less. When GDP turns negative, the damage is real: jobs lost, businesses closed, productive capacity turned idle. But why should we ever have to deal with that anyway? Why should a modern economy switch from forward to reverse? If we can produce and consume $10 trillion worth of stuff, and put most Americans to work doing it, why should we toss a bunch of people out of work and produce 2 percent less the following year?

The best answer is that recessions are like wars: If we could prevent them, we would. Each one is just different enough from the last to make it hard to ward off. (Though presumably policymakers have prevented both wars and recessions on numerous occasions; it's only when they fail that we notice.) In general, recessions stem from some shock to the economy. That is, something bad happens. It may be the collapse of a stock market or property bubble (the United States in 1929 and Japan in 1989), a steep rise in the price of oil (the United States in 1973) or even a deliberate attempt by the Federal Reserve to slow down an overheated economy (the United States in 1990). In developing countries, the shock may come from a sudden fall in the price of a commodity on which the economy is heavily dependent. For example, Central America is currently reeling from low coffee prices, which have plunged from $150 per hundred pounds to $50 per hundred pounds.[6] Obviously there may be a combination of causes. The American slowdown that began in 2001 had its roots in the "tech wreck"—the overinvestment in technology that ultimately ended with the bursting of the Internet bubble. That trouble was compounded by the terrorist attacks of September 11 and their aftermath.

The most fascinating thing about recessions is how they spread. Take the coffee example. The *New York Times* reported in the fall of 2001:

> The collapse of the [coffee] market has set off a chain reaction that is felt throughout the region. Towns have been left to scrape by as tax receipts drop, forcing them to scale back services and lay off workers. Farms have scaled back or closed, leaving thousands of the area's most vulnerable people with no money to buy food or clothes or to pay their rent. Small growers, in debt to banks and coffee processors who lent them money to care for the crops and workers, have been idled, and some of them are facing the loss of their land.

Whether you live in Central America or Santa Monica, someone else's economic distress can become your problem very quickly. The terrorist attacks on the World Trade Center and the Pentagon are a sad example. In the aftermath of the terrorist hijackings, Americans sharply curtailed their travel, devastating the airline and travel industry. Almost immediately, the major airlines announced tens of thousands of layoffs. Boeing, anticipating fewer orders for new planes, announced thirty thousand layoffs of its own. But that only hints at the economic toll. Workers who lost jobs, and others who feared their jobs were at risk, began to spend less. Indeed, we all began to feel some trepidation about the future; we pared back our budgets as a result. Falling stock prices feed our spending anxiety. We check the stock tables and realize that we are less wealthy than we thought.

Here is the intriguing paradox: Our natural (and rational) reaction to precarious economic times is to become more cautious with our spending, which makes our collective situation worse. The loss of confidence caused by a shock to the economy may turn out to be worse than the shock itself. My thrift—a decision to curtail my advertising budget or buy a car next year instead of this year—may cost you your job, which will in turn hurt my business! Indeed, if we all believe that the economy is likely to get worse, then it will get worse. And if we all believe it will get better, then it will get better. Our behavior—to spend or not to spend—is conditioned on our expectations, and those expectations can quickly become self-fulfilling. Franklin Delano Roosevelt's admonition that we have "nothing to fear but fear itself" was both excellent leadership and good economics. Similarly, Rudy Giuliani's exhortation that New Yorkers should go out and do their holiday shopping in the weeks after the World Trade Center attack was not as wacky as it sounded. Spending can generate confidence that generates spending that causes a recovery.

This is not to suggest that recessions are entirely a figment of our collective imagination (though that is theoretically possible). There are often underlying issues that need to work themselves out. In the case of the "tech wreck," we massively overinvested in Internet businesses and related technology. As some firms go bust, and as other firms cut back their IT spending, resources are reallocated. Suddenly there are more U-hauls going out of Silicon Valley than in. Or, in the case of higher energy prices, we reorganize our economy to deal with a world in which oil is $30 a barrel instead of $10. Recessions may actually be good for long-term growth because they purge the economy of less productive ventures, just as a harsh winter may be good for the long-term health of a species (if not necessarily for those animals that freeze to death).

Recessions can spread quickly across international borders. If the U.S. economy weakens, then we buy fewer goods from abroad. Pretty soon Mexico, which sends more than 80 percent of its exports to the United States, is reeling. In business and sports, your competitor's misfortune is your gain. At the global level, the opposite is true. *If other powerful economies fall into recession, they stop buying our goods and services.* Think about it: If unemployment doubles in Japan or Germany, how exactly is that going to make you better off? One of the most serious threats to American economic growth at the moment is the lack of growth everywhere else. Since the world's largest economies, Japan, Europe, and America, are all on the brink of recession at the same time, there is no one left to spend the world back into good economic health.

The business cycle takes a human toll, as the layoffs splashed across the headlines attest. Policymakers are increasingly expected to smooth this business cycle; economists are supposed to tell them how to do it. Government has two tools at its disposal: fiscal policy and monetary policy. The objective of each is the same: to encourage consumers and businesses to begin spending and investing again so that the economy's capacity no longer sits idle.

Fiscal policy uses the government's capacity to tax and spend as a lever for prying the economy from reverse into forward. If nervous consumers won't spend, then the government will do it for them—and that can create a virtuous circle. While consumers are sitting at home with their wallets tucked firmly under the mattress, the government can start to build highways and bridges. Construction workers go back to work; their firms place orders for materials. Cement plants call idled workers back. As the world starts to look like a better place, we feel comfortable making major purchases again. The cycle we described earlier begins to work in reverse. The most famous fiscal stimulus was World War II, which gets much of the credit for spending the United States out of the Great Depression.

Or the government can stimulate the economy by cutting taxes. Consumers, finding more money in their paychecks at the end of the month, decide that they can afford to spend some of it. Again, this spending is supposed to break the back of the recession. Purchases generated by the tax cut put workers back on the job, which inspires more spending and confidence, and so on. The notion that the government can use fiscal policy—spending, tax cuts, or both—to "fine-tune" the economy was the central insight of John Maynard Keynes. There is nothing wrong with the idea. Most economists would concede that, in theory, government has the tools to smooth the business cycle. The problem is that fiscal policy is not made in theory; it's made in Congress. For fiscal policy to be a successful antidote to recession, three things must happen: (1) Congress and the president must agree to a plan that contains an appropriate remedy; (2) they must pass their plan in a timely manner; and (3) the prescribed remedy must kick in fast. The likelihood of nailing all three of these requirements is slim. *Remarkably, in most postwar recessions, Congress did not pass legislation in response to the downturn until after it had ended.* In one particularly egregious example, Congress was still passing legislation in May 1977 to deal with the recession that ended in March 1975.[7] More recently, consider a front-page headline in the *New York Times* on March 8, 2002: "Fed Chief Sees Decline Over; House Passes Recovery Bill." I'm not making this stuff up.

The second tool at the government's disposal is monetary policy, which has the potential to affect the economy faster than you can read this paragraph. The chairman of the Federal Reserve can raise or lower short-term interest rates with one phone call. No haggling with Congress; no waiting years for tax cuts. As a result, there is now a consensus among economists that normal business cycles are best managed with monetary policy. Thus, the whole next chapter is devoted to the mysterious workings of the Federal Reserve. For now, suffice it to say that cutting interest rates makes it cheaper for consumers to buy houses, cars, and other big-ticket items as well as for firms to invest in new plants and machinery. Cheap money from the Fed pries wallets open again.

An autoworker in Detroit, who has spent his career getting laid off for months at a time and then called back to work, is going to ask a simple question: Are we getting any better at all of this? Yes, we are. The United States has gone through eleven recessions since World War II.[8] The worst was during 1973–75 when GDP dropped 3.4 percent from peak to trough. That is not even the same order of magnitude as the Great Depression. From 1929 to 1933, real GDP fell by 30 percent while unemployment climbed from 3 percent to 25 percent. Prior to the Great Depression, the United States experienced ten depressions—each worse than anything we've had since.[9]

I conceded earlier in this chapter that GDP is not the only measure of economic progress. Our economy consists of hundreds of millions of people living in various states of happiness or unhappiness. Any president recovering from a horseshoe accident would demand a handful of other economic indicators, just as emergency room physicians ask for a patient's vital signs (or at least that is what they do on *ER*). If you were to take the vital signs of any economy on the planet, here are the economic indicators, along with GDP, that policymakers would ask for first.

Unemployment. My mother does not have a job; neither does either of my brothers. Yet only one of these family members is unemployed. The unemployment rate is the fraction of workers who would like to work but cannot find jobs. (My mother has no interest in working and one of my brothers is in graduate school.) America's unemployment rate fell below 4 percent during the peak of the boom in the 1990s; it has since climbed back over 5 percent.

Anyone who cares about unemployment should care about economic growth, too. The general rule of thumb, based on research done by economist Arthur Okun and known thereafter as Okun's law, is that GDP growth of 3 percent a year will leave the unemployment rate unchanged. Faster or slower growth will move the unemployment rate up or down by one half a percentage point for each percentage point change in GDP. Thus, GDP growth of 4 percent would lower unemployment by half a percentage point, and GDP growth of only 2 percent would cause unemployment to rise by half a percentage point. This relationship is not an iron law; rather, it describes the relationship in America between GDP growth and unemployment over the five-decade period studied by Mr. Okun, roughly 1930 to 1980.

Poverty. Even in the best of times, a drive through Chicago's housing projects is ample evidence that not everybody has been invited to the party. But how many Americans are poor? Indeed, what exactly constitutes "poor"? In the 1960s, the U.S. government created the poverty line as a (somewhat arbitrary) definition of the amount of income necessary to buy the basic necessities. Having been adjusted for inflation, the poverty level remains as the statistical threshold for who is poor in America and who is not. For example, the current poverty line for a single adult is $8,350; the poverty line for a family of two adults and two children is $17,050.

The poverty rate is simply the fraction of Americans whose incomes fall below the poverty line. Roughly 11 percent of Americans are poor, which is no better than we were doing in the 1970s. The poverty rate rose steadily throughout the 1980s and then drifted down in the 1990s. The overall poverty rate disguises some figures that would otherwise leap off the page: Roughly one in five American children is poor as are nearly 40 percent of black children. Our only resounding success is poverty among the elderly, which has fallen from 30 percent in the 1960s to below 10 percent, largely as the result of Social Security.

Income inequality. We care about the size of the pie; we also care about how it is sliced. Economists have a tool that collapses income inequality into a single number, the Gini index.* On this scale, a score of zero rep-

---

* To derive the Gini index, the personal incomes in a country are arranged in ascending order. A line, the Lorenz curve, plots the cumulative share of personal income against the cumulative share of population. Total equality would be a 45-degree line. The Gini coefficient is the ratio of the area between the diagonal and the Lorenz curve to the total area under the diagonal.

resents total equality—a state in which every worker earns exactly the same. At the other end, a score of 100 represents total inequality—a state in which all income is earned by one individual. The countries of the world can be arrayed along this continuum. In 2000, the United States had a Gini index of 41, compared to 33 for France, 25 for Sweden, and 60 for Brazil. By this measure, the United States has grown more unequal over the past several decades. America's Gini coefficient was 36.5 in 1980 and 37.9 in 1950.

Size of government. If we are going to complain about "big government," we ought to at least know how big that government is. One relatively simple measure of the size of government is the ratio of all government spending (local, state, and federal) to GDP. Government spending in America is roughly 30 percent of GDP, which is low by the standards of the developed world. Government spending in Britain is roughly 40 percent of GDP. In Japan, it is over 45 percent; in France and Sweden it is over 50 percent. On the other hand, America is the only developed country in which the government does not pay for the bulk of health care services. Our government is smaller, but we get less, too.

Budget deficit/surplus. Anyone who lived through the presidential election of 2000 heard plenty of talk about budget surpluses (after much talk in the 1980s and 1990s about budget deficits). The concept is simple enough; a budget deficit occurs when the government spends more than it collects in revenues and a surplus is the opposite. The more interesting question is whether either one of these things is good or bad. Unlike accountants, economists are not sticklers for balanced budgets. Rather, the prescription is more likely to be that governments should run modest surpluses in good times and modest deficits in tough times; the budget need only balance in the long run.

Here is why: If the economy slips into recession, then tax revenues will fall and spending on programs such as unemployment insurance will rise. This is likely to lead to a deficit; it is also likely to help the economy recover. Raising taxes or cutting spending during a recession will almost certainly make it worse. Herbert Hoover's insistence on balancing the budget in the face of the Great Depression is considered to be one of the great fiscal follies of all time. In good times, the opposite will be true. Tax revenues will rise and some kinds of spending will fall, leading to a surplus, as we saw in the late 1990s. (We also saw how quickly it disappeared when the economy turned south.) Anyway, there is nothing wrong with modest deficits and surpluses as long as they coincide with the business cycle.

Let me offer two caveats, however. First, if a government runs a deficit, then it must make up the difference by borrowing money. In the case of the United States, we issue treasury bonds. If a deficit becomes large enough, investors may begin to balk at the prospect of lending the government more money. For nations that are not particularly credit-worthy, such as Russia or Mexico, a large government deficit and a wary lending community can precipitate a financial crisis.

Second, there is a finite amount of capital in the world; the more the government borrows, the less that leaves for the rest of us. Large budget deficits can "crowd out" private investment by raising real interest rates. As America's large budget deficits began to disappear during the 1990s, one profoundly beneficial effect was a fall in long-term interest rates, making it cheaper for all of us to borrow.

Current account surplus/deficit. The U.S. current account deficit is somewhere in the range of $100 billion. Is it time to rush to the supermarket to stock up on canned goods and bottled water? Probably not. The current account balance, which can be in surplus or deficit, reflects the difference between the income that we earn from the rest of the world and the income that it earns from us. The bulk of that income comes from trade in goods and services. Thus, our balance of trade, which again can be in surplus or deficit, is the largest component of the current account. If we are running a trade deficit with the rest of the world, then we will almost always be running a current account deficit, too. (For the purists, the U.S. current account would also include dividends paid to Americans who own foreign stocks, remittances sent home by Americans working overseas, and other sources of income earned abroad.)

When the current account is in deficit, as ours is now, it is usually because a country is not exporting enough to "pay" for all of its imports.

In other words, if we export $50 billion of goods and import $100 billion, our trading partners are going to want something in exchange for that other $50 billion worth of stuff. We can pay them out of our savings, we can borrow from them to finance the gap, or we can sell them some of our assets, such as stocks and bonds. As a nation, we are consuming more than we are producing, and we have to pay for the difference somehow.

Oddly, this can be a good thing, a bad thing—or somewhere in between. For the first century of America's existence, we ran large current account deficits. We borrowed heavily from abroad so that we could import goods and services to build up our industrial capacity. That was a good thing. Indeed, a current account deficit can be a sign of strength as money pours into countries that show a promising potential for future growth. If, on the other hand, a country is simply importing more than it exports without making investments that will raise future output, then there is a problem, just as you might have a problem if you squandered $100,000 in student loans without getting a degree. You now have to pay back what you borrowed, plus interest, but you have done nothing to raise your future income. The only way to pay back your debt will be to cut back on your future consumption, which is a painful process. Countries that run large current account deficits are not necessarily in financial trouble; on the other hand, countries that have gotten themselves into financial trouble are usually running large current account deficits.

National savings. We all tuck money away for our individual needs: college, retirement, etc. Those private savings decisions, along with the government's decision to run a deficit or surplus, have a profound impact on our economy. The simple reason is that savings are necessary to finance investment, and investment is what makes us more productive as a society. If you put 10 percent of your income in the bank, then somewhere else in the country that money will end up building a plant or financing a college education. If Americans do not collectively put savings in the bank, then we must either forgo important investments or borrow from abroad. Again, that assumes that foreign investors are willing to lend at a reasonable rate, which may not be the case for an economy in a precarious state. Over time, countries' investment rates show a striking correlation with their domestic savings rates.

The U.S. savings rate tells a cautionary tale. It has fallen steadily from over 9 percent in the 1960s and 1970s to 6 percent in the 1980s to below 5 percent in the mid-1990s to roughly zero by the end of the 1990s.[10] We can and have borrowed from abroad to finance our investment—at a cost. Nobody lends money free, and borrowing from abroad means that we must pay some of our investment returns to our foreign lenders. Any country with significant exposure to foreign lenders must always worry that when times get tough, the herd of international investors will get spooked and flee with their capital.

Demographics. Americans are getting older, literally. As economist Paul Krugman has noted, the age distribution in America will eventually begin to look as it does in Florida. That is good for the companies that manufacture shuffleboard equipment. It is not so good for government finances. The bulk of government benefits, notably Social Security and Medicare, are bestowed on Americans who are retired. These programs are financed with payroll taxes imposed on younger Americans who are still working. If the ratio of young Americans to older Americans begins to change, then the financial health of programs like Social Security and Medicare begins to change, too.

Indeed, we can explain the importance of demographics *and* fix Social Security all in the next two paragraphs. Social Security is a "pay-as-you-go" program. When American workers pay into Social Security (that large FICA deduction on your paycheck), the money does not get invested somewhere so that you can draw on it twenty or thirty years later, as it would in a private pension fund. Rather, that money is used to pay current retirees. Straight from young Peter to old Paul. The program is one big pyramid scheme, and, like any good pyramid scheme, it works fine as long as there are enough workers on the bottom to continue paying the retirees at the top.

Therein lies the problem. Americans are having fewer children and living longer. That means that there are fewer workers to pay for every retiree—a lot fewer. In 1960, there were five workers for every retiree. Now there are three workers for every retiree. By 2032, there will be only two. Imagine Social Security (or Medicare) as a seesaw in which payments made by workers are on one side and benefits collected by retirees are on the other. The program is solvent as long as the seesaw balances. As the number of workers on one side shrinks while the number of retirees on the other side grows, the seesaw begins to tip. In theory, fixing the problem is easy. We can take more from current workers, either by increasing the payroll tax or by making them more productive and raising their incomes (so that the same tax generates more revenues). Or we can give less to retirees, either by cutting their benefits or by raising the retirement age. That is the very simple economic crux of the problem. Of course, if you think any of these solutions would be politically palatable, please go back and read Chapter 8 again.

I should comment on the Social Security Trust Fund—the money that Al Gore wanted to put in a "lockbox." For all the long-term challenges of Social Security, the system is currently taking in more than it pays out. The reason is that the baby boomers, the demographic equivalent of a pig in a python, are still working. When they begin to retire, the financial picture will change markedly. The surplus funds that we are taking in today are a down payment on what we will owe the baby boomers when they begin to collect benefits. Think of the money as sandbags that we can put on the side of the workers to help balance the seesaw twenty or thirty years from now. If we get rid of the sandbags now, it will be all the harder to balance the seesaw in the future.

Ronald Reagan described economists as individuals who see something work in practice and wonder if it might work in theory. His observation was no doubt inspired by a frustration that so much of what happens in the world economy still seems beyond our control, or even our understanding. At the end of the day, the world is still a fabulously complex and unpredictable place. In the wake of the World Trade Center attack, after Wall Street swooned and Americans began to fear a recession, one Wall Street economist wondered aloud, "Which economic forecast has this in it?"[11]

None. But we do know how to pick up the pieces better than we ever have in the past. Only hours after the attack, when Americans were still not sure where their president was, Alan Greenspan issued a simple but powerful statement that the Federal Reserve was open for business and would do whatever was necessary to prevent a wider economic calamity. A similarly adroit move in 1929 might have spared the United States from the Great Depression.

CHAPTER 10

The Federal Reserve:

Why that dollar in your pocket is more than just a piece of paper

Sometimes simple statements speak loudly. On September 11, 2001, hours after the terrorist attacks on the United States, the Federal Reserve issued the following statement: "The Federal Reserve System is open and operating. The discount window is available to meet liquidity needs."

Those terse and technical two sentences had a calming effect on global markets. The following Monday, as America's markets opened for their first trading sessions after the attack, the Federal Reserve cut interest rates by 0.5 percent, another act that moderated the financial and economic impact of the terrorist assaults.

How exactly does an inelegant two-sentence statement have such a profound effect on a $10 trillion economy—indeed, on the whole global economy? From where does the Federal Reserve, an institution that is not directly accountable to the voting public, derive such power? And how does that power affect the lives of everyday Americans? The answer to all those questions is the same: The Federal Reserve controls the money supply and therefore the credit tap for the economy. When that tap is open wide, interest rates fall and we spend more freely on things that required borrowed money—everything from new cars to new manufacturing plants. Thus, the Fed can use monetary policy to counteract economic downturns (or prevent them in the first place). And it can inject money into the financial system after sudden shocks, such as the 1987 stock market crash or the terrorist attacks of September 11, when consumers and firms might otherwise freeze in place and stop spending. Or the Fed can tighten the tap by raising interest rates. When the cost of borrowed funds goes up, our spending slows. It is an awesome power. Paul Krugman has written, "If you want a simple model for predicting the unemployment rate in the United States over the next few years, here it is: It will be what Greenspan wants it to be, plus or minus a random error reflecting the fact that he is not quite God."

God does not have to manage by committee; Alan Greenspan does. The Federal Reserve System is made up of twelve Reserve Banks spread across the country and a seven-person board of governors based in Washington. Alan Greenspan is chairman of the board of governors—he's the "Fed chairman." The Federal Reserve regulates commercial banks, supports the banking infrastructure, and generally makes the plumbing of the financial system work. Those jobs require competence, not genius or great foresight. Monetary policy, the Federal Reserve's other responsibility, is different. It might reasonably be described as the economic equivalent of brain surgery. Economists do not agree on how the Federal Reserve ought to manage our money supply. Nor do they even agree on exactly how or why changes in the money supply have the effects that they do. Yet economists do agree that effective monetary policy matters; the Fed must feed just the right amount of credit to the economy to keep it growing steadily. Getting it wrong can have disastrous consequences. Robert Mundell, winner of the 1999 Nobel Prize in Economics, has argued that bungled monetary policy in the 1920s and 1930s caused chronic deflation that destabilized the world. He has argued, "Had the price of gold been raised in the late 1920s, or, alternatively, had the major central banks pursued policies of price stability instead of adhering to the gold standard, there would have been no Great Depression, no Nazi revolution, and no World War II."[1]

The job would not appear to be that complicated. If the Fed can make the economy grow faster by lowering interest rates, then presumably lower is better. Indeed, why should there be any limit to the rate at which the economy can grow? If we begin to spend more freely when rates are cut from 7 percent to 5 percent, why stop there? There are still people without jobs and others without new cars; let's press on to 3 percent, or even 1 percent. New money for everyone! Sadly, there *are* limits to how fast any economy can grow. If low interest rates, or "easy money," causes consumers to demand 5 percent more new PT Cruisers than they purchased last year, then Chrysler must expand production by 5 percent. That means hiring more workers and buying more steel, glass, electrical components, etc. At some point, it becomes difficult or impossible for Chrysler to find these new inputs, particularly qualified workers. At that point, the company simply cannot make enough PT Cruisers to satisfy consumer demand; instead, the company begins to raise prices. Meanwhile, autoworkers recognize that Chrysler is desperate for labor, and the union demands higher wages.

The story does not stop there. The same thing would be happening throughout the economy, not just at Chrysler. If interest rates are exceptionally low, firms will borrow to invest in new computer systems and software; consumers will break out the VISA for big-screen televisions and Caribbean cruises—all up to a point. When the cruise ships are full and IBM is selling every computer it can produce, then those firms will raise their prices, too. (When demand exceeds supply, firms can charge more and still fill every boat or sell every computer.) In short, an "easy money" policy at the Fed can cause consumers to demand more than the economy can produce. The only way to ration that excess demand is with higher prices. The result is inflation.

The sticker price on the PT Cruiser goes up, and no one is better off for it. True, Chrysler is taking in more money, but it is also paying more to its suppliers and workers. Those workers are seeing higher wages, but they are also paying higher prices for their basic needs. Numbers are changing everywhere, but the productive capacity of our economy and the measure of our well-being, real GDP, has hit the wall. Once started, the inflationary cycle is hard to break. Firms and workers everywhere begin to expect continually rising prices (which, in turn, causes continually rising prices). Welcome to the 1970s.

The pace at which the economy can grow without causing inflation might reasonably be considered a "speed limit." After all, there are only

a handful of ways to increase the amount that we as a nation can produce. We can work longer hours. We can add new workers, through
falling unemployment or immigration (recognizing that the workers
available may not have the skills in demand). We can add machines and
other kinds of capital that help us to produce things. Or we can become
more productive—produce more with what we already have, perhaps
because of an innovation or a technological change. Each of these sources
of growth has natural constraints. Workers are scarce; capital is scarce;
technological change proceeds at a finite and unpredictable pace. In the
late 1990s, American autoworkers threatened to go on strike because
they were being forced to work too much overtime. Meanwhile, fast-food
restaurants were offering signing bonuses to new employees. We were at
the wall. Economists reckon that the speed limit of the American economy is somewhere in the range of 3 percent growth per year.

The phrase "somewhere in the range" gives you the first inkling of
how hard the Fed's job is. The Federal Reserve must strike a delicate balance. If the economy grows more slowly than it is capable of, then we are
wasting economic potential. Plants that make PT Cruisers sit idle; the
workers who might have jobs there are unemployed instead. An economy that has the capacity to grow at 3 percent instead limps along at 1.5
percent, or even slips into recession. Thus, the Fed must feed enough
credit to the economy to create jobs and prosperity but not so much that
the economy begins to overheat. William McChesney Martin, Jr.,
Federal Reserve chairman during the 1950s and 1960s, once noted that
the Fed's job is to take away the punch bowl just as the party gets going.

Or sometimes the Fed must rein in the party long after it has gone
out of control. The Federal Reserve has deliberately engineered a number of recessions in order to squeeze inflation out of the system. Most
notably, Fed chairman Paul Volcker was the ogre who ended the inflationary party of the 1970s. At that point, naked people were dancing
wildly on the tables. Inflation had climbed from 3 percent in 1972 to 13.5
percent in 1980. Mr. Volcker hit the monetary brakes, meaning that he
cranked up interest rates to slow the economy down. Short-term interest rates peaked at over 16 percent in 1981. The result was a painful
unwinding of the inflationary cycle. With interest rates in double digits,

there were plenty of unsold Chrysler K cars sitting on the lot. Dealers were forced to cut prices (or stop raising them). The auto companies idled plants and laid off workers. The autoworkers who still had jobs decided that it would be a bad time to ask for more money.

The same thing, of course, was going on in every other sector of the economy. Slowly, and at great human cost, the expectation that prices would steadily rise was purged from the system. The result was the recession of 1981–82, during which GDP shrank by 3 percent and unemployment climbed to nearly 10 percent. In the end, Mr. Volcker did clear the dancers off the tables. By 1983, inflation had fallen to 3 percent. Obviously it would have been easier and less painful if the party had never gone out of control in the first place.

Where does the Fed derive this extraordinary power over interest rates? After all, commercial banks are private entities. The Federal Reserve cannot force Citibank to raise or lower the rates it charges consumers for auto loans and home mortgages. Rather, the process is indirect. Recall from Chapter 7 that the interest rate is really just a rental rate for capital, or the "price of money." The Fed controls America's money supply. We'll get to the mechanics of that process in a moment. For now, recognize that money is no different from apartments: The greater the supply, the cheaper the rent. The Fed moves interest rates by making changes in the quantity of funds available to commercial banks. If banks are awash with money, then interest rates must be relatively low to attract borrowers for all the available funds. When capital is scarce, the opposite will be true. It's supply and demand—with the Fed controlling the supply.

These monetary decisions—the determination whether interest rates need to go up, down, or stay the same—are made by a committee within the Fed called the Federal Open Market Committee (FOMC), which consists of the board of governors, the president of the Federal Reserve Bank of New York, and the presidents of four other Federal Reserve Banks on a rotating basis. The Fed chairman is also the chairman of the FOMC. Alan Greenspan derives his power from the fact that he is sitting at the head of the table when the FOMC makes interest rate decisions.

If the FOMC wants to stimulate the economy by lowering the cost of borrowing, the committee has two primary tools at its disposal. The first is the discount rate, which is the interest rate at which commercial banks can borrow funds directly from the Federal Reserve. The relationship between the discount rate and the cost of borrowing at Citibank is straightforward; when the discount rate falls, banks can borrow more cheaply from the Fed and therefore lend more cheaply to their customers. There is one complication. Borrowing directly from the Fed carries a certain stigma; it implies that a bank was not able to raise funds privately. Thus, turning to the Fed for a loan is similar to borrowing from your parents after about age twenty-five: you'll get the money, but it's better to look somewhere else first.

Instead, banks generally borrow from other banks. The second important tool in the Fed's money supply kit is the federal funds rate, the rate that banks charge other banks for short-term loans. The Fed cannot stipulate the rate at which Wells Fargo lends money to Bank One. Rather, the FOMC sets a target for the federal funds rate, say 4.5 percent, and then manipulates the money supply to accomplish its objectives. If the supply of funds goes up, then banks will have to drop their prices—lower interest rates—in order to find borrowers for the new funds. One can think of the money supply as a furnace with the federal funds rate as its thermostat. If the FOMC cuts the target fed funds rate from 4.5 percent to 4.25 percent, then the Federal Reserve will pump money into the banking system until the rate Wells Fargo charges Bank One for an overnight loan falls to something very close to 4.25 percent.

All of which brings us to our final conundrum: How does the Federal Reserve inject money into a private banking system? Does Alan Greenspan print $100 million of new money, load it into a heavily armored truck, and drive it to a Citibank branch? Not exactly—though that image is not a bad way to understand what does happen.

Alan Greenspan and the FOMC do create new money. In the United States, they alone have that power. (The Treasury prints currency and mints coins to replace existing money.) And the Federal Reserve does deliver that new money to banks like Citibank. But the Fed does not give funds to the bank; it trades the new money for government bonds. In our metaphorical example, the Citibank branch manager meets Alan Greenspan's armored truck outside the bank, loads $100 million of new money into the bank's vault, and then hands the Fed chairman $100 million in government bonds from the bank's portfolio in return. Note that Citibank has not been made richer by the transaction. The bank has merely swapped $100 million of one kind of asset (bonds) for $100 million of a different kind of asset (cash, or, more accurately, its electronic equivalent).

Banks hold bonds for the same reason individual investors do; bonds are a safe place to park depositors' funds that are not being loaned out. To the economy, the fact that Citibank has swapped bonds for cash makes all the difference. When a bank has $100 million of deposits parked in bonds, those funds are not being loaned out. They are not financing houses, or businesses, or new plants. But after Alan Greenspan's metaphorical armored truck pulls away, Citibank is left holding funds that *can* be loaned out. That means new loans for all the kinds of things that generate economic activity. Indeed, money injected into the banking system has a cascading effect. A bank that swaps bonds for money from the Fed keeps some fraction of the funds in reserves, as required by law, and then loans out the rest. Whoever receives those loans will spend them somewhere, perhaps at a car dealership or a department store. That money eventually ends up in other banks, which will keep some funds in reserve and then make loans of their own. A move by the Fed to inject $100 million of new funds into the banking system may ultimately increase the money supply by ten times as much.

Of course, the Fed chairman does not actually drive a truck to a Citibank branch to swap cash for bonds. The FOMC can accomplish the same thing using the bond market (which works just like the stock market, except that bonds are bought and sold). Bond traders working on behalf of the Fed buy bonds from commercial banks and pay for them with newly created money—funds that simply did not exist twenty minutes earlier. (Presumably the banks selling their bonds will be those with the most opportunities to make new loans.) The Fed will continue to buy bonds with new money, a process called open market operations, until the target federal funds rate has been reached.

Obviously what the Fed giveth, the Fed can take away. The Federal Reserve can raise interest rates by doing the opposite of everything we've just discussed. The FOMC would vote to raise the discount rate and/or the target fed funds rate and issue an order to sell bonds from its portfolio to commercial banks. As banks give up lendable funds in exchange for bonds, the money supply shrinks. Money that might have been loaned out to consumers and businesses is parked in bonds instead. Interest rates go up, and anything purchased with borrowed capital becomes more expensive. The cumulative effect is slower economic growth.

The mechanics of the Fed's handiwork should not obscure the big picture. The Federal Reserve's mandate is to facilitate a sustainable pace of economic growth. But let's clarify how difficult that job really is. First, we are only guessing at the rate at which the economy can expand without igniting inflation. One debate among economists is over whether or not computers and other kinds of information technology have made Americans significantly more productive. If so, as Mr. Greenspan has suggested on several occasions, then the economy's potential growth rate may have gone up. If not, as other economists have argued convincingly, then the old speed limit still applies. Obviously it is hard to abide by a speed limit that is not clearly posted.

But that is only the first challenge. The Fed must also reckon what kind of impact a change in interest rates will have and how long it will take. Will a quarter-point rate cut cause twelve people to buy new PT Cruisers in Des Moines or 421? When? Next week or six months from now? Meanwhile, the Fed has the most control over short-term interest rates, which may or may not move in the same direction as long-term rates. Why can't Alan Greenspan work his magic on long-term rates, too? Because long-term rates do not depend on the money supply today; they depend on what the markets predict money supply (relative to demand) will be ten, twenty, or even thirty years from now. Alan Greenspan has no control over the money supply in 2015. As the recession of 2001 unfolded, the Fed cut the discount and fed fund rates aggressively, but long-term rates did not move much at all. Indeed, at times they were drifting up as the bond markets anticipated higher interest rates in the future. Meanwhile, fiscal policy—government decisions on taxes and spending—can counteract what the Fed is trying to accomplish with monetary policy.

So let's stick with our speed limit analogy and recap what exactly the Fed is charged with doing. The Fed must facilitate a rate of economic growth that is neither too fast nor too slow. Bear in mind: (1) We do not know the economy's exact speed limit. (2) Both the accelerator and the brake operate with a lag, meaning that neither works immediately when we press on it. Instead, we have to wait a while for a response—anywhere from a few weeks to a few years, but not with any predictable pattern. So an inexperienced driver might press progressively harder on the gas, wondering why nothing was happening (and enduring all kinds of public assaults on his pathetically slow driving), only to find the car screaming out of control nine months later. (3) Monetary and fiscal policy affect the economy independently, so while the Fed is gently tapping the brake, Congress and the president may be jumping up and down on the accelerator. (4) Last, there is the obstacle course of world events—a financial collapse here, a spike in the price of oil there. Bob Woodward's biography of Alan Greenspan was aptly titled *Maestro*.

It's a hard job. Still, that conclusion is a long way from Nobel laureate Robert Mundell's dire claim that bad monetary policy laid the groundwork for World War II. To understand why irresponsible monetary policy can have cataclysmic effects, we must first make a short digression on the nature of money. To economists, money is quite distinct from wealth. Wealth consists of all things that have value—houses, cars, commodities, human capital. Money, a tiny subset of that wealth, is merely a medium of exchange, something that facilitates trade and commerce. In theory, money is not even necessary. A simple economy could get along through barter alone. In a basic agricultural society, it's easy enough to swap five chickens for a new dress or to pay a schoolteacher with a goat and three sacks of rice. Barter works less well in a more advanced economy. The logistical challenges of using chickens to buy books at Amazon.com would be formidable.

In nearly every society, some kind of money has evolved to make trade easier. (The word "salary" comes from the wages paid to Roman soldiers, who were paid in sacks of *sal*—salt.) Any medium of exchange—whether it is a gold coin, a whale tooth, or an American dollar—serves the same basic purposes. First, it serves as a means of exchange, so that I might enjoy pork chops for dinner tonight even though the butcher has no interest in buying this book. Second, it serves as a unit of account, so that the cost of all kinds of goods and services can be measured and compared using one scale. (Imagine life without a unit of account: The Gap is selling bluejeans for three chickens a pair while Tommy Hilfiger has similar pants on sale for eleven beaver pelts. Which pants cost more?) Third, money must be portable and durable. Neither bowling balls nor rose petals would serve the purpose. Last, money must be relatively scarce so that it can serve as a store of value.

For much of American history, commerce was conducted with paper currency backed by precious metals. Prior to the twentieth century, private banks issued their own money. In 1913, the U.S. government banned private money and became the sole provider of currency. The basic idea did not change. Whether money was public or private, paper currency derived its value from the fact that it could be redeemed for a set quantity of gold or silver, either from a bank or from the government. Then something strange happened. In 1971, the United States permanently went off the gold standard. At that point, every paper dollar became redeemable for . . . nothing.

Examine that wad of $100 bills in your wallet. (If necessary, $1 bills can be substituted instead.) Those bills are just paper. You can't eat them, you can't drink them, you can't smoke them, and, most important, you can't take them to the government and demand anything in return. They have no inherent value. And that is true of nearly all the world's currencies. Left alone on a deserted island with $100 million, you would quickly perish. On the other hand, life would be good if you were rescued and could take the cash with you. Therein lies the value of modern currency: It has purchasing power. Dollars have value because people peddling real things—food, books, pedicures—will accept them. And people peddling real things will accept dollars because they are confident that other people peddling other real things will accept them, too. A dollar is a piece of paper whose value derives solely from our confidence that we will be able to use it to buy something we need in the future.

To give you some sense of how modern money is a confidence game, consider a bizarre phenomenon in India. Most Indians involved in commerce—shopkeepers, taxi drivers, etc.—will not accept a torn, crumpled, or overly soiled rupee note. Since other Indians know that many of their countrymen will not accept torn notes, they will not accept them either. Finally, when tourists arrive in the country, they quickly learn to accept only intact bills, lest they be stuck with the torn ones. The whole process is utterly irrational, since the Indian Central Bank considers any note with a serial number—torn, dirty, crumpled, or otherwise—to be legal tender. Any bank will exchange torn rupees for crisp new ones. That doesn't matter; rational people refuse legal tender because they believe that it might not be accepted by someone else. The whole bizarre phenomenon underscores the fact that our faith in paper currency is predicated on the faith that others place in the same paper.

Since paper currency has no inherent worth, its value depends on its purchasing power—something that can change gradually over time, or even stunningly fast. In the summer of 1997, I spent a few days driving across Iowa "taking the pulse of the American farmer" for *The Economist*. Somewhere outside of Des Moines, I began chatting with a corn, soybean, and cattle farmer. As he gave me a tour of his farm, he pointed to an old tractor parked outside the barn. "That tractor cost $7,500 new in 1970," he said. "Now look at this," he said angrily, pointing to a shiny new tractor right next to the old one. "Cost me $40,000. Can you explain that?"*

I could explain that, though that's not what I told the farmer, who was already suspicious of the fact that I was young, from the city, wearing a tie, and driving a Honda Civic. (The following year, when I was asked to write a similar story on Kentucky tobacco farmers, I had the good sense to rent a pickup truck.) My answer would have been one word: inflation. The new tractor probably wasn't any more expensive than the old tractor in real terms, meaning that he had to do the same

---

* I can't remember the exact numbers, but they were something along these lines.

amount of work, or less, in order to buy it. The sticker price on his tractor had gone up, but so had the prices at which he could sell his crops
and cattle.

Inflation means, quite simply, that average prices are rising. The
inflation rate, or the change in the consumer price index, is the government's attempt to reflect changing prices with a single number, say 4.2
percent. The method of determining this figure is surprisingly low-tech;
government officials periodically check the prices of thousands and thousands of goods—clothes, food, fuel, entertainment, housing—and then
compile them into a number that reflects how the prices of a basket of
goods purchased by the average consumer has changed. *The most instruc-
tive way to think about inflation is not that prices are going up, but rather that
the purchasing power of the dollar is going down.* A dollar buys less than it
used to. Therein lies the link between the Federal Reserve, or any central
bank, and economic devastation. A paper currency has value only because
it is scarce. The central bank controls that scarcity. Therefore a corrupt
or incompetent central bank can erode, or even completely destroy, the
value of our money.

In 1921, a German newspaper cost roughly a third of a mark; two
years later, a newspaper cost 70 million marks. It was not the newspaper
that changed during that spell; it was the German mark, which was rendered useless as the government printed new ones with reckless abandon.
Indeed, the mark lost so much value that it became cheaper for house-
holds to burn them than to use them to buy firewood. Inflation was so
bad in Latin America in the 1980s that there were countries whose largest
import became paper currency.[2] In the late 1990s, the Belarussian ruble
was known as the "bunny," not only for the hare engraved on the note
but also for the currency's remarkable ability to propagate. In August
1998, the Belarussian ruble lost 10 percent of its purchasing power in
one week.

Massive inflation distorts the economy massively. Workers rush to spend
their cash before it becomes worthless. A culture emerges in which workers rush out to spend their paychecks at lunch because prices will have
gone up by dinner. Fixed-rate loans become impossible because no finan-

cial institution will agree to be repaid a fixed quantity of money when that money is at risk of becoming worthless. Think about it: Anyone with a fixed-rate mortgage in Germany in 1921 could have paid off the whole loan in 1923 with fewer marks than it cost to buy a newspaper. Even today, it is not possible to get a thirty-year fixed mortgage in most of Latin America because of fears that inflation will come roaring back.

America has never suffered hyperinflation. We have had bouts of moderate inflation; the costs were smaller and more subtle but still significant. At the most basic level, inflation leads to misleading or inaccurate comparisons. Journalists rarely distinguish between real and nominal figures, as they ought to. Suppose that American incomes rose 5 percent last year. That is a meaningless figure until we know the inflation rate. If prices rose by 7 percent, then we have actually become worse off. Our paycheck may look bigger but it buys 2 percent fewer goods than it did last year. Hollywood is an egregious offender, proclaiming summer after summer that some mediocre film has set a new box office record. Comparing gross receipts in 2002 to gross receipts in 1970 or 1950 is a silly exercise unless they are adjusted for inflation. A ticket to *Gone with the Wind* cost 19 cents. A ticket to *Dude, Where's My Car* cost $10. Of course the gross receipts are going to look big by comparison.

Second, even moderate inflation has the potential to eat away at our wealth if we do not manage our assets properly. Any wealth held in cash will lose value over time. Even savings accounts and certificates of deposit, which are considered "safe" investments because the principal is insured, are vulnerable to the less obvious risk that their low interest rates may not keep up with inflation. It is a sad irony that unsophisticated investors eschew the "risky" stock market only to have their principal whittled away through the back door. Indeed, inflation can be particularly pernicious for individuals who are retired or otherwise living on fixed incomes. If that income is not indexed for inflation, then its purchasing power will gradually fade away. A monthly check that made for a comfortable living in 1985 becomes inadequate to buy the basic necessities in 2002.

Inflation also redistributes wealth arbitrarily. Suppose I borrow $1,000 from you and promise to pay back the loan, plus interest of $100, next year. That seems a fair arrangement for both of us. Now suppose that a wildly irresponsible central banker allows inflation to explode to 100 percent a year. The $1,100 that I pay back to you next year will be worth much less than either of us had expected; its purchasing power will be cut in half. In real terms, I will borrow $1,100 from you and pay back $550. Unexpected bouts of inflation are good for debtors and bad for lenders—a crucial point that we will come back to.

Inflation also distorts taxes. Take the capital gains tax, for example. Suppose you buy a stock and sell it a year later, earning a 10 percent return. If the inflation rate was also 10 percent over that period, then you have not actually made any money. Your return exactly offsets the fact that every dollar in your portfolio has lost 10 percent of its purchasing power—a point lost on Uncle Sam. You owe taxes on your 10 percent "gain." Taxes are unpleasant when you've made money; they really stink when you haven't.

Having said all that, moderate inflation, were it a constant or predictable rate, would have very little effect. Suppose, for example, that we knew the inflation rate would be 10 percent a year forever—no higher, no lower. We could deal with that easily. Any savings account would pay some real rate of interest plus 10 percent to compensate for inflation. Our salaries would go up 10 percent a year (plus, we would hope, some additional sum based on merit). All loan agreements would charge some real rental rate for capital plus a 10 percent annual premium to account for the fact that the dollars you are borrowing are not the same as the dollars you will be paying back. Government benefits would be indexed for inflation and so would taxes.

But inflation is not constant or predictable. Indeed, the aura of uncertainty is one of its most insidious costs. Individuals and firms are forced to guess about future prices when they make economic decisions. When the autoworkers and Ford negotiate a four-year contract, both sides must make some estimates about future inflation. A contract with annual raises of 4 percent is very generous when the inflation rate is 1 percent but a lousy deal for workers if the inflation rate climbs to 10 percent. Lenders must make a similar calculation. Lending someone money for thirty years at a fixed rate of interest carries a huge risk in an inflationary environment. So when lenders fear future inflation, they build in a buffer. The greater the fear of inflation, the bigger the buffer. On the other hand, if a central bank proves that it is serious about preventing inflation, then the buffer gets smaller. One of the most significant benefits of the persistent low inflation of the 1990s was that lenders became less fearful of future inflation. As a result, long-term interest rates dropped sharply, making homes and other big purchases more affordable. Robert Barro, a Harvard economist who has studied economic growth in nearly one hundred countries over several decades, has confirmed that significant inflation is associated with slower real GDP growth.

It seems obvious enough that governments and central banks would make fighting inflation a priority. Even if they made honest mistakes trying to drive their economies at the "speed limit," we would expect small bursts of inflation, not prolonged periods of rising prices, let alone hyperinflation. Yet that is not what we observe. Governments, rich and poor alike, have driven their economies not just faster than the speed limit, but at engine-smoking, wheels-screeching kinds of speeds. Why? Because shortsighted, corrupt, or desperate governments can buy themselves some time by stoking inflation. We spoke about the power of incentives all the way back in Chapter 2. Still, see if you can piece this puzzle together: (1) Governments often owe large debts, and troubled governments owe even more; (2) inflation is good for debtors because it erodes the value of the money they must pay back; (3) governments control the inflation rate. Add it up: Governments can cut their own debts by pulling the inflation rip cord.

Of course, this creates all kinds of victims. Those who lent the government money are paid back the face value of the debt but in a currency that has lost value. Meanwhile, those holding currency are punished because their money now buys much less. And last, even future citizens are punished because this government will find it difficult or impossible to borrow at reasonable interest rates again (though bankers do show an odd proclivity to make the same mistakes over and over again).

Governments can also benefit in the short run from what economists refer to as the "inflation tax." Suppose that you are running a government that is unable to raise taxes through conventional means, either because the infrastructure necessary to collect taxes does not exist or because your citizens cannot or will not pay more. Yet you have government workers, perhaps even a large army, who demand to be paid. Here is a very simple solution. Buy some beer, order a pizza (or whatever an appropriate national dish might be), and begin running the printing presses at the national mint. As soon as the ink is dry on your new pesos, or rubles, or dollars, use them to pay your government workers and soldiers. *Alas, you have taxed the people of your country—indirectly.* You have not physically taken money from their wallets; instead, you've done it by devaluing the money that stays in their wallets. The Continental Congress did it during the Revolutionary War; both sides did it during the Civil War; the German government did it between the wars; countries like Zimbabwe are doing it now.

A government does not have to be on the brink of catastrophe to play the inflation card. Even in present-day America, clever politicians can use moderate inflation to their benefit. One feature of irresponsible monetary policy—like a party headed out of control—is that it can be fun for a while. In the short run, easy money makes everyone feel richer. When consumers flock to the Chrysler dealer in Des Moines, his first reaction is that he is doing a really good job of selling cars. Or perhaps he thinks that Chrysler's new models are more attractive than the Fords and Toyotas. In either case, he raises prices, earns more income, and generally believes that his life is getting better. Only gradually does he realize that most other businesses are experiencing the same phenomenon. Since they are raising prices, too, his higher income will be lost to inflation.

By then, the politicians may have gotten what they wanted: reelection. A central bank that is not sufficiently insulated from politics can throw a wild party before the votes are cast. There will be lots of dancing on the tables; by the time voters become sick with an inflation-induced hangover, the election is over. Macroeconomic lore has it that Fed chairman Arthur Burns did such a favor for Richard Nixon in 1972 and that the Bush family is still angry with Alan Greenspan for not adding a little more alcohol to the punch before the 1992 election, when George H. W. Bush was turned out of office following a mild recession.

Political independence is crucial if monetary authorities are to do their jobs responsibly. Evidence shows that countries with independent central banks—those that can operate relatively free of political meddling—have lower average inflation rates over time. America's Federal Reserve is among those considered to be relatively independent. Members of its board of governors are appointed to fourteen-year terms by the president. That does not give them the same lifetime tenure as Supreme Court justices, but it does make it unlikely that any new president could pack the Federal Reserve with cronies. It is notable—and even a source of criticism—that the most important economic post in a democratic government is appointed, not elected. We designed it that way; we have made a democratic decision to create a relatively undemocratic institution. A central bank's effectiveness depends on its independence and credibility, almost to the point that a reputation can become self-fulfilling. If firms believe that a central bank will not tolerate inflation, then they will not feel compelled to raise prices. And if firms do not raise prices, then there will not be an inflation problem. Much of Alan Greenspan's reputation lies in his well-deserved inflation-fighting credentials. When presidential candidate John McCain was asked what he would do if Fed chairman Greenspan died before finishing his term, the senator replied, "I would prop him up and put a pair of dark glasses on him."

Fed officials are prickly about political meddling. In the spring of 1993, I had dinner with Paul Volcker, former chairman of the Federal Reserve. Mr. Volcker was teaching at Princeton, and he was kind enough to take his students to dinner. President Clinton had just given a major address to a joint session of Congress and Alan Greenspan had been seated next to Hillary Clinton. What I remember most about the dinner was Mr. Volcker grumbling that it was inappropriate for Alan Greenspan to have been seated next to the president's wife. He felt that it sent the wrong message about the Federal Reserve's independence from the executive branch. That is how seriously central bankers take their political independence.

Inflation is bad; deflation, or steadily falling prices, is much worse. Even modest deflation can be economically devastating, as Japan has learned over the past decade. It may seem counterintuitive that falling prices could make consumers worse off (especially if rising prices make them worse off, too), but deflation begets a dangerous economic cycle. To begin with, falling prices cause consumers to postpone purchases. Why buy a refrigerator today when it will cost less next week? Meanwhile, asset prices are falling, too, so consumers feel poorer and less inclined to spend. (Imagine if the value of your home fell year after year while your mortgage payments stayed the same.) As we know from the last chapter, when consumers stop spending, the economy stops growing. Firms respond to this slowdown by cutting prices further still. The result is an economic death spiral, as Paul Krugman has noted:

> Prices are falling because the economy is depressed; now we've just learned that the economy is depressed because prices are falling. That sets the stage for the return of another monster we haven't seen since the 1930s, a "deflationary spiral," in which falling prices and a slumping economy feed on each other, plunging the economy into the abyss.[3]

And monetary policy may not be able to help. In Japan, the central bank has already cut interest rates to zero, which means that they have no place left to go. (Interest rates can't be negative. Any bank that loaned out $100 and asked for only $98 back would be better off just keeping the $100 in the first place.) Yet the rental rate on capital—the real interest rate—might actually be quite high. Here is why. If prices are falling, then borrowing $100 today and paying back $100 next year is not costless. The $100 you pay back has *more* purchasing power than the $100 you borrowed, perhaps much more. The faster prices are falling, the higher your real cost of borrowing. Economists are increasingly convinced that what Japan needs is a stiff dose of inflation. Some officials have gone so far as to encourage the Bank of Japan to do "anything short of dropping bank notes out of helicopters."[4] To hark back to the politics of the macroeconomy, one theory for why Japanese officials have not done more to fight falling prices is that Japan's aging population, many of whom live on fixed incomes or savings, see deflation as a good thing despite its dire consequences for the economy as a whole.

The United States has had its own encounters with deflation. There is a consensus among economists that botched monetary policy was at the heart of the Great Depression. From 1929 to 1933, America's money supply fell by 28 percent.[5] The Fed did not deliberately turn off the credit tap; rather, it stood idly by as the money supply fell of its own volition. The process by which money is circulated throughout the economy had become unhitched. Because of widespread bank failures in 1930, both banks and individuals began to hoard cash. Money that was stuffed under a mattress or locked in a bank vault could not be loaned back into the economy. The Fed did nothing while America's credit dried up. It should have been doing just the opposite: pumping money into the system.

Monetary policy is tricky business. Done right, it facilitates economic growth and cushions the economy from shocks that might otherwise wreak havoc. Done wrong, it can cause pain and misery. In the 1990s, as the American economy roared through its longest expansion in economic history, Mr. Greenspan was given credit for his "Goldilocks" approach to monetary policy—doing everything just right. The twenty-first century has already presented a shocking array of new challenges, everything from war to global recession. A skilled hand on America's credit tap will matter all the more.

CHAPTER 11

Trade and Globalization:

The good news about Asian sweatshops

magine a spectacular invention: a machine that can convert corn into stereo equipment. When running at full capacity, this machine can turn fifty bushels of corn into a CD player. Or with one switch of the dial, it will convert fifteen hundred bushels of soybeans into a four-door sedan. But this machine is even more versatile than that; when properly programmed, it can turn Windows software into the finest French wines. Or a Boeing 747 into enough fresh fruits and vegetables to feed a city for months. Indeed, the most amazing thing about this invention is that it can be set up anywhere in the world and programmed to turn whatever is grown or produced there into things that are usually much harder to come by.

Remarkably, it works for poor countries, too. Developing nations can put the things they manage to produce—commodities, cheap textiles, basic manufactured goods—into the machine and obtain goods that might otherwise be denied them: food, medicine, more advanced manufactured goods. Obviously, poor countries that have access to this machine would grow faster than countries that did not. We would expect that making this machine accessible to poor countries would be part of our strategy for lifting billions of people around the globe out of dire poverty.

Amazingly, this invention already exists. It is called trade.

If I write books for a living and use my income to buy a car made in Detroit, there is nothing particularly controversial about the transaction. It makes me better off, and it makes the car company better off, too. That's Chapter 1 kind of stuff. A modern economy is built on trade. We pay others to do or make things that we can't—everything from manufacturing a car to removing an appendix. As significant, we pay people to do all kinds of things that we could do but choose not to, usually because we have something better to do with our time. We pay others to brew coffee, make sandwiches, change the oil, clean the house, even walk the dog. Starbucks, one of the great business success stories of the last decade, was not built on any great technological breakthrough. The company simply recognized that busy people will regularly pay several dollars for a cup of coffee rather than make their own or drink the lousy stuff that has been sitting around the office for several hours.

The easiest way to appreciate the gains from trade is to imagine life without it. You would wake up early in a small, drafty house that you had built yourself. You would put on clothes that you wove yourself after shearing the two sheep that graze in your backyard. Then you would pluck a few coffee beans off the scraggly tree that does not grow particularly well in Minneapolis—all the while hoping that your chicken had laid an egg overnight so that you might have something to eat for breakfast. The bottom line is that our standard of living is high because we are able to focus on the tasks that we do best and trade for everything else.

Why would these kinds of transactions be different if a product or service originated in Germany or India? They're not, really. We've crossed a political boundary, but the economics have not changed in any significant way. Individuals and firms do business with one another because it makes them both better off. That is true for a worker at a Nike factory in Vietnam, an autoworker in Detroit, a Frenchmen eating a McDonald's hamburger in Bordeaux, or an American drinking a fine Burgundy in Chicago. Any rational discussion of trade must begin with the idea that people in Chad or Togo or South Korea are no different from you or me; they do things that they hope will make their lives better. Trade is one of those things. Paul Krugman has noted, "You could say—and I would—that globalization, driven not by human goodness but

(A) Hairdresser tells you to invest in
media companies - hot stock - listen to her?
+ one page
(B) Read Chapter - Assessment of L-D approach
to crime?
+ two pages

half.com by ebay

Dear ghuddell,

I have enclosed this packing slip for your convenience.

Seller:	**kyotosan226**
Order Contents:	Culture Communication & Conflict (2000) ISBN-10: 0536613435 ; ISBN-13: 9780536613431 Price: $11.75 ▪ Condition: Very Good **Shipping Method**: Media Mail
Delivered to:	Alex Huddell 2043 W. Street Rd West Chester, PA 19382

I hope you enjoy this purchase. Your satisfaction is key to my success as a seller on both Half.com and eBay.
If you are happy with your experience I encourage you to leave positive feedback for me. This will help other buyers know I am a responsible and reliable seller. In order to leave feedback

this transaction and leave appropriate feedback. If you would like to buy more from me in the future, you can visit my Half.com shop at:

http://shops.half.ebay.com/ws/eBayISAPI.dll?HalfSearch&seller=kyotosan226

Remember, when you buy more than one item from me in the same order you save on shipping!

Thank you for your support,

kyotosan226

by the profit motive, has done far more good for far more people than all the foreign aid and soft loans ever provided by well-intentioned governments and international agencies." Then he adds wistfully, "But in saying this, I know from experience that I have guaranteed myself a barrage of hate mail."[1]

Such is the nature of "globalization," the term that has come to represent the increase in the international flow of goods and services. Americans and most others on the planet are more likely than ever to buy goods or services from another nation and to sell goods and services abroad in return. In the late 1980s, I was traveling through Asia while writing a series of articles for a daily newspaper in New Hampshire. In a relatively remote part of Bali, I was so surprised to find a Kentucky Fried Chicken that I wrote a story about it. "Colonel Sanders has succeeded in putting fast-food restaurants in the most remote areas of the world," I wrote. Had I realized that the idea of "cultural homogenization" would become a flashpoint for civil unrest a decade later, I might have become rich and famous as one of the earliest commentators on globalization. Instead, I merely noted, "In this relatively undisturbed environment, Kentucky Fried Chicken seems out of place."[2]

That KFC restaurant was more than the curiosity that I made it out to be. It was a tangible sign of what the statistics clearly show: The world is growing more economically interdependent. The world's exports as a share of global GDP have climbed from 8 percent in 1950 to over 26 percent today.[3] U.S. exports as a fraction of GDP grew from 5 percent to more than 10 percent over the same stretch. It is worth noting that the bulk of the American economy still consists of goods and services produced for domestic consumption. At the same time, because of the sheer size of that economy, America is the world's largest exporter. We export twice the value of goods and services that Japan does and roughly the same amount as the entire European Union. The United States has much to gain from an open, international trading system. Then again, so does the rest of the world.

I suppose that means I'll get hate mail, too. Nearly all theory and evidence suggest that the benefits of international trade far exceed the costs. The topic is worthy of an entire book; some good ones wade into everything from the administrative structure of the WTO to the fate of sea turtles caught in shrimp nets. Yet the basic ideas underlying the costs and benefits of globalization are simple and straightforward. Indeed, no modern issue has elicited so much sloppy thinking. The case for international trade is built on the most basic ideas in economics.

Trade makes us richer. Trade has the distinction of being one of the most important ideas in economics and also one of the least intuitive. Abraham Lincoln was once advised to buy cheap iron rails from Britain to finish the transcontinental railroad. He replied, "It seems to me that if we buy the rails from England, then we've got the rails and they've got the money. But if we build the rails here, we've got our rails and we've got our money."[4] To understand the benefits of trade, we must find the fallacy in Mr. Lincoln's economics. Let me paraphrase his point and see if the logical flaw becomes clear: If I buy meat from the butcher, then I get the meat and he gets my money. But if I raise a cow in my backyard for three years and slaughter it myself, then I've got the meat and I've got my money. Why don't I keep a cow in my backyard? Because it would be a tremendous waste of time—time that I could have used to do something else far more productive. *We trade with others because it frees up time and resources to do things that we are better at.*

Saudi Arabia can produce oil more cheaply than the United States can. In turn, the United States can produce corn and soybeans more cheaply than Saudi Arabia. The corn-for-oil trade is an example of absolute advantage. When different countries are better at producing different things, they can both consume more by specializing at what they do best and then trading. People in Seattle should not grow their own rice. Instead, they should build airplanes (Boeing), write software (Microsoft), and sell books (Amazon.com)—and leave the rice-growing to farmers in Thailand or Indonesia. Meanwhile, those farmers can enjoy the benefits of Microsoft Word even though they do not have the technology or skills necessary to produce such software. Countries, like individuals, have different natural advantages. It does not make any more sense for Saudi Arabia to grow vegetables that it does for Michael Jordan to do his own auto repairs.

Okay, but what about countries that don't do anything particularly well? After all, countries are poor because they are not productive. What can Bangladesh offer to the United States? A great deal, it turns out, because of a concept called comparative advantage. Workers in Bangladesh do not have to be better than American workers at producing anything for there to be gains from trade. Rather, they provide goods to us so that we can spend our time specializing at whatever we do best. Here is an example. Many engineers live in Seattle. These men and women have doctorates in mechanical engineering and probably know more about manufacturing shoes and shirts than nearly anyone in Bangladesh. So why would we buy imported shirts and shoes made by poorly educated workers in Bangladesh? Because our Seattle engineers also know how to design and manufacture commercial airplanes. Indeed, that is what they do *best*, meaning that making jets creates the most value for their time. Importing shirts from Bangladesh frees them up to do this, and the world is better off for it.

Productivity is what makes us rich. Specialization is what makes us productive. Trade allows us to specialize. Our Seattle engineers are more productive at making planes than they are at sewing shirts; *and* the textile workers in Bangladesh are more productive at making shirts and shoes than they are at whatever else they might do (or else they would not be willing to work in a textile factory). I am writing at the moment. My wife is running a software consulting firm. A wonderful woman named Clementine is looking after our daughters. We do not employ Clemen because she is better than we are at raising our children (though there are moments when I believe that to be true). We employ Clemen because she enables us to work during the day at the jobs we do well, and that is the best possible arrangement for our family—not to mention for Clemen, for the readers of this book, and for my wife's clients.

Trade makes the most efficient use of the world's scarce resources.

Trade creates losers. If trade transports the benefits of competition to the far corners of the earth, then the wreckage of creative destruction cannot be far behind. Try explaining the benefits of globalization to shoe workers in Maine who have lost jobs because their plant moved to

Vietnam. (Remember, I was the speechwriter for the governor of Maine; *I have tried to explain that*.) Trade, like technology, can destroy jobs, particularly low-skilled jobs. If a worker in Maine earns $14 an hour for something that can be done in Vietnam for $1 an hour, then he had better be fourteen times as productive. If not, a profit-maximizing firm will choose Vietnam. Poor countries lose jobs, too. Industries that have been shielded from international competition for decades, and have therefore adopted all the bad habits that come from not having to compete, can be crushed by ruthlessly efficient competition from abroad. How would you like to have been the producer of Thumbs-Up Cola in India when Coca-Cola entered the market in 1994?

In the long run, trade facilitates growth and a growing economy can absorb displaced workers. Exports rise and consumers are made richer by cheap imports; both of those things create demand for new workers elsewhere in the economy. Trade-related job losses in America tend to be small relative to the economy's capacity to produce new jobs. One post-NAFTA study concluded that an average of 37,000 jobs per year were lost from 1990 to 1997 because of free trade with Mexico, while over same period the economy was creating 200,000 jobs per month.[5] Still, "in the long run" is one of those heartless phrases—along with "transition costs" or "short-term displacement"—that overly minimize the human pain and disruption. Maine shoe workers are expected to pay their mortgages *in the short run*. The sad reality is that they may not be better off in the long run, either. Displaced workers often have a skills problem. (Far more workers are made redundant by new technology than by trade.) If an industry is concentrated in a geographic area, as they often are, laid-off workers may watch their communities and way of life fade away.

The *New York Times* documented the case of Newton Falls, a community in upstate New York that grew up around a paper mill that opened in 1894. A century later, that mill closed, in part because of growing foreign competition. It's not pretty:

> Since October—after a last-ditch effort to save the mill fell through—
> Newton Falls has edged closer to becoming a case study of doleful rural
> sociology: a dying town, where the few people left give mournful testa-

ment to having their community wind down like an untended clock, ticking inexorably toward a final tock.[6]

Yes, the economic gains from trade outweigh the losses, but the winners rarely write checks to the losers. And the losers often lose badly. What consolation is it to a Maine shoe worker that trade with Vietnam will make the country as a whole richer? *He's poorer and probably always will be.* Indeed, we're back to the same discussion about capitalism that we had at the beginning of the book and again in Chapter 8. Markets create a new, more efficient order by destroying the old one. There is nothing pleasant about that, particularly for individuals and firms equipped for the old order. International trade makes markets bigger, more competitive, and more disruptive. Mark Twain anticipated the fundamental dilemma: "I'm all for progress; it's change I don't like."

Marvin Zonis, an international consultant and a University of Chicago business school professor, has called the potential benefits of globalization "immense," particularly for the poorest of the poor. He has also noted, "Globalization disrupts everything, everywhere. It disrupts established patterns of life—between husband and wife, parents and children; between men and women, young and old; between boss and worker, governor and governed."[7] We can do things to soften those blows. We can retrain or even relocate workers. We can provide development assistance to communities harmed by the loss of a major industry. We can ensure that our schools teach the kinds of skills that make workers adaptable to whatever the economy may throw at them. In short, we can make sure that the winners do write checks (if indirectly) to the losers, sharing at least part of their gains. It's good politics and it's the right thing to do.

Protectionism saves jobs in the short run and slows economic growth in the long run. We can save the jobs of those Maine shoe workers. We can protect places like Newton Falls. We can make the steel mills in Gary, Indiana, profitable. We need only get rid of their foreign competition. We can erect trade barriers that stop the creative destruction at the border. So why don't we? The benefits of protectionism are obvious; we can point to the jobs that will be saved. Alas, the costs of protectionism are more subtle; it is difficult to point to jobs that are never created or higher incomes that are never earned.

To understand the costs of trade barriers, let's ponder a strange question: Would the United States be better off if we were to forbid trade across the Mississippi River? The logic of protectionism suggests that we would. For those of us on the east side of the Mississippi, new jobs would be created, since we would no longer have access to things like Boeing airplanes or Northern California wines. *But nearly every skilled worker east of the Mississippi is already working, and we are doing things that we are better at than making airplanes or wine.* Meanwhile, workers in the West, who are now very good at making airplanes or wine, would have to quit their jobs in order to make the goods normally produced in the East. They would not be as good at those jobs as the people who are doing them now. Preventing trade across the Mississippi would turn the specialization clock backward. We would be denied superior products and forced to do jobs that we're not particularly good at. In short, we would be poorer because we would be collectively less productive. This is why economists favor trade not just across the Mississippi, but also across the Atlantic and the Pacific. Global trade turns the specialization clock forward; protectionism stops that from happening.

Here is a related thought. America punishes rogue nations such as Iraq by imposing economic sanctions. In the case of severe sanctions, we forbid nearly all imports and exports. We cut off international trade *as a punishment.* Iraq is forbidden from trading what it does have, oil, for the things that it needs, which is basically everything else. (The sanctions have allowed some oil to be sold to import food and medicine.) The irony of the antiglobalization furor is that protesters are essentially demanding that we impose sanctions on the developing world. Is Iraq a thriving nation with safe workers and a clean environment? No. By all accounts, it is a poor country that has been made poorer. Depending on whom you believe, the sanctions are responsible for the deaths of somewhere between 100,000 and 500,000 children.[8] This seems an odd strategy for making the developing world better off. And it hurts us, too. What was one of the largest markets for Texas rice before the Gulf War? Iraq.

Trade lowers the cost of goods for consumers, which is the same as raising their incomes. Forget about shoe workers for a moment and think about shoes. Why does Nike make shoes in Vietnam? Because it is cheaper than making them in the United States, and that means less expensive shoes for the rest of us. One paradox of the trade debate is that individuals who claim to have the downtrodden at heart neglect the fact that cheap imports are good for low-income consumers (and for the rest of us). Cheaper goods have the same impact on our lives as higher incomes. We can afford to buy more. The same thing is true, obviously, in other countries.

Trade barriers are a tax—albeit a hidden tax. Suppose the U.S. government tacked a 30-cent tax on every gallon of orange juice sold in America. The conservative antigovernment forces would be up in arms. So would liberals, who generally take issue with taxes on food and clothing, since such taxes are regressive, meaning that they are most costly (as a percentage of income) for the disadvantaged. *Well, the government does add 30 cents to the cost of every gallon of orange juice, though not in a way that is nearly as transparent as a tax.* The American government slaps tariffs on Brazilian oranges and orange juice that can be as high as 63 percent. Parts of Brazil are nearly ideal for growing citrus, which is exactly what has American growers concerned. So the government protects them. Economists reckon that the tariffs on Brazilian oranges and juice limit the supply of imports and therefore add about 30 cents to the price of a gallon of orange juice. Most consumers have no idea that the government is taking money out of their pockets and sending it to orange growers in Florida.[9] That does not show up on the receipt.

Lowering trade barriers has the same impact on consumers as cutting taxes. The precursor to the World Trade Organization was the General Agreement on Tariffs and Trade (GATT). Following World War II, GATT was the mechanism by which countries negotiated to bring down global tariffs and open the way for more trade. In the eight rounds of GATT negotiations between 1948 and 1995, average tariffs in industrial countries fell from 40 percent to 4 percent. That is a massive reduction in the "tax" paid on all imported goods. It has also forced domestic producers to make their goods cheaper and better in order to stay competitive. If you walk into a car dealership today, you are better off than you were in 1970 for two reasons. First, there is a wider choice of excellent imports. Second, Detroit has responded by making better cars, too. The Honda Accord makes you better off, and so does the Ford Taurus that is better than it would have been.

Trade is good for poor countries, too. If we had patiently explained the benefits of trade to the protesters in Seattle or Washington or Davos or Genoa, then perhaps they would have laid down their Molotov cocktails. Okay, maybe not. The thrust of the antiglobalization protests has been that world trade is something imposed by rich countries on the developing world. If trade is mostly good for America, then it must be mostly bad for somewhere else. At this point in the book, we should recognize that zero-sum thinking is usually wrong when it comes to economics. So it is in this case. Representatives from developing nations were the ones who complained most bitterly about the disruption of the WTO talks in Seattle. Some believed that the Clinton administration secretly organized the protests to scuttle the talks and protect American interest groups, such as organized labor. Indeed, after the failure of the WTO talks in Seattle, UN chief Kofi Annan blamed the industrialized countries for erecting trade barriers that exclude developing nations from the benefits of global trade and called for a "Global New Deal."[10]

Trade gives poor countries access to markets in the developed world. That is where most of the world's consumers are (or at least the ones with money to spend). Consider the impact of the African Growth and Opportunity Act, a law passed in 2000 that allowed Africa's poorest countries to export textiles to the United States with little or no tariff. Within a year, Madagascar's textile exports to the United States were up 120 percent, Malawi's were up 1,000 percent, Nigeria's were up 1,000 percent, and South Africa's were up 47 percent. As one commentator noted, "Real jobs for real people."[11]

Trade paves the way for poor countries to get richer. Export industries often pay higher wages than jobs elsewhere in the economy. But that is only the beginning. New export jobs create more competition for workers, which raises wages everywhere else. Even rural incomes can go up; as workers leave rural areas for better opportunities, there are fewer mouths to be fed from what can be grown on the land they leave behind. Other important things are going on, too. Foreign companies introduce capital, technology, and new skills. Not only does that make export workers more productive; it spills over into other areas of the economy. Workers "learn by doing" and then take their knowledge with them.

In his excellent book *The Elusive Quest for Growth*, William Easterly tells the story of the advent of the Bangladeshi garment industry, an industry that was founded almost by accident. The Daewoo Corporation of South Korea was a major textile producer in the 1970s. America and Europe had slapped import quotas on South Korean textiles, so Daewoo, ever the profit-maximizing firm, skirted the trade restrictions by moving some operations to Bangladesh. In 1979, Daewoo signed a collaborative agreement to produce shirts with the Bangladeshi company Desh Garments. Most significant, Daewoo took 130 Desh workers to South Korea for training. In other words, Daewoo invested in the human capital of its Bangladeshi workers. The intriguing thing about human capital, as opposed to machines or financial capital, is that it can never be taken away. Once those Bangladeshi workers knew how to make shirts, they could never be forced to forget. And they didn't.

Daewoo later severed the relationship with its Bangladeshi partner, but the seeds for a booming export industry were already planted. Of the 130 workers trained by Daewoo, 115 left during the 1980s to start their own garment-exporting firms. Mr. Easterly argues convincingly that the Daewoo investment was an essential building block for what became a $3 billion garment export industry. Lest anyone believe that trade barriers are built to help the poorest of the poor, or that Republicans are more averse to protecting special interests than Democrats, it should be noted that the Reagan administration slapped import quotas on Bangladeshi textiles in the 1980s. I would be hard pressed to explain the economic rationale for limiting the export opportunities of a country that has a per capita GDP of $350.

Most famously, cheap exports were the path to prosperity for the Asian "tigers"—Singapore, South Korea, Hong Kong, and Taiwan (and for Japan before that). In contrast, India, which has remained strikingly insular, has been one of the world's great economic underachievers for decades. (Alas, Gandhi, like Lincoln, was a great leader and a bad economist; Gandhi proposed that the Indian flag have a spinning wheel on it to represent economic self-sufficiency.) China, too, has used exports as a launching pad for growth. Indeed, if China's thirty provinces were counted as individual countries, the twenty fastest-growing countries in the world between 1978 and 1995 would all have been Chinese. To put that development accomplishment in perspective, it took fifty-eight years for GDP per capita to double in Britain after the launch of the Industrial Revolution. In China, GDP per capita has been doubling every ten years. Nicholas Kristof and Sheryl WuDunn, Asian correspondents for the *New York Times* for over a decade, wrote recently:

> We and other journalists wrote about the problems of child labor and oppressive conditions in both China and South Korea. But, looking back, our worries were excessive. Those sweatshops tended to generate the wealth to solve the problems they created. If Americans had reacted to the horror stories in the 1980s by curbing imports of those sweatshop products, then neither southern China nor South Korea would have registered as much progress as they have today.[12]

China and Southeast Asia are not unique. The consultancy AT Kearney conducted a study of how globalization has affected thirty-four developed and developing countries. They found that the fastest-globalizing countries had rates of growth that were 30 to 50 percent higher over the past twenty years than countries less integrated into the world economy. Those countries also enjoyed greater political freedom and received higher scores on the UN Human Development Index. The authors reckon that some 1.4 billion people escaped absolute poverty as a result of the economic growth associated with globalization. There was bad news, too. Higher rates of globalization were associated with higher rates of income inequality, corruption, and environmental degradation. More on that later.

But there is an easier way to make the case for globalization. If not more trade and economic integration, then what instead? Those who oppose more global trade must answer one question, based on a point made by Harvard economist Jeffrey Sachs: Is there an example in modern history of a single country successfully developing without trading and integrating with the global economy?[13]

No, there is not.

Which is why Tom Friedman has suggested that the antiglobalization coalition ought to be known as "The Coalition to Keep the World's Poor People Poor."

Trade is based on voluntary exchange. Individuals do things that make themselves better off. That obvious point is often lost in the globalization debate. McDonald's does not build a restaurant in Bangkok and then force people at gunpoint to eat there. People eat there because they want to. And if they don't want to, they don't have to. And if no one eats there, the restaurant will lose money and close. Does McDonald's change local cultures? Yes. That was what caught my attention a decade ago when I wrote about Kentucky Fried Chicken arriving in Bali. I wrote, "Indonesians have their own version of fast food that is more practical than the Colonel's cardboard boxes and Styrofoam plates. A meal bought at a food stall is wrapped in a banana leaf and newspaper. The large green leaf retains heat, is impermeable to grease, and can be folded into a neat package."

By and large, the banana leaves of the world appear to be losing to cardboard. Not long ago I attended a business gathering with my wife in Puerta Vallarta, Mexico. Puerta Vallarta is a lovely city that spills down from the hills to the Pacific Ocean. The focal point of the city is a promenade that runs along the ocean. Near the middle of that promenade is a point that juts out into the ocean, and at the end of that point, on what I would reckon is one of the most valuable pieces of real estate in the city, is a Hooters restaurant. When our group spotted this infamous American export, one man grumbled, "That is just wrong."

A Hooters in all the world's great cities is probably not what Adam Smith had in mind. Marvin Zonis has noted, "Certain aspects of American popular culture—the depravity and the coarseness, the violence and the sexuality—are eminently worth resenting."[14] The threat of "cultural homogenization"—the worst of it coming from America—is a common knock against globalization. But it is an issue that leads us back to a crucial point from Chapter 1: who decides? I was not happy to see a Hooters in Puerta Vallarta, but, as I pointed out many pages ago, I don't run the world. More important, I don't live or vote in Puerta Vallarta. Neither do the rock-throwing thugs in Seattle and Genoa.

Are there legitimate reasons to limit the proliferation of fast-food restaurants and the like? Yes, they present classic externalities. Fast-food restaurants cause traffic and litter; they are ugly and can contribute to sprawl. (Before my valuable work opposing a new train station on Fullerton Avenue, I was part of a group trying to prevent a McDonald's from moving in across the street.) These are local decisions that ought to be made by the people affected—those who might eat in the safe, clean environment of a McDonald's restaurant as well as those who may have fast-food wrappers blown in their gutters. Free trade is consistent with one of our most fundamental liberal values: the right to make our own private decisions.

There is now a McDonald's in Moscow and a Starbucks in the Forbidden City in Beijing. Stalin never would have allowed the former; Mao would not have allowed the latter. Which is a point worth pondering.

The cultural homogenization argument may not be true anyway. Culture is transmitted in all directions. I can now rent Iranian movies at Blockbuster. National Public Radio recently ran a segment on craftsmen and artists in remote regions of the world who are selling their work via the Internet. One can log on to Novica.com and find a virtual global marketplace for arts and crafts. Katherine Ryan, who works for Novica, explained, "There's a community in Peru where most of the artists had gone to work in the coal mines. And now, because of the success of one artist in Novica, he has been able to hire many of his family members and neighbors back into the weaving business, and they're no longer coal miners. They're now doing what for many generations their family did, and that's weave incredible tapestries."[15] John Micklethwait and Adrian Wooldridge, authors of the globalization tract *A Future Perfect*, point out that in the realm of business, a previously obscure Finnish company like Nokia has been able to thump American behemoths like Motorola.

•　•　•

We're still just warming up when it comes to the side effects of global-ization. A Hooters in Puerta Vallarta is a mild headache relative to the horrors of Asian sweatshops. Yet the same principles apply. Nike does not use forced labor in its Vietnamese factories. Why are workers willing to accept a dollar or two a day? *Because it is better than any other option they have.* According to the Institute for International Economics, the aver-age wage paid by foreign companies in low-income countries is twice the average domestic manufacturing wage.

Nicholas Kristof and Sheryl WuDunn described a visit with a Mongkol Latlakorn, a Thai laborer whose fifteen-year-old daughter was working in a Bangkok factory making clothes for export to America.

> She is paid $2 a day for a nine-hour shift, six days a week. On several occasions, needles have gone through her hands, and managers have bandaged her up so that she could go back to work.
>
> "How terrible," we murmured sympathetically.
>
> Mongkol looked up, puzzled. "It's good pay," he said. "I hope she can keep that job. There's all this talk about factories closing now, and she said there are rumors that her factory might close. I hope that doesn't happen. I don't know what she would do then."[16]

The implicit message of the antiglobalization protests is that we in the developed world somehow know what is best for people in poor countries—where they ought to work and even what kind of restaurants they ought to eat in. As *The Economist* has noted, "The skeptics distrust governments, politicians, international bureaucrats and markets alike. So they end up appointing themselves as judges, overruling not just gov-ernments and markets but also the voluntary preferences of the workers most directly concerned. That seems a great deal to take on."[17]

The comparative advantage of workers in poor countries is cheap labor. That is all they have to offer. They are not more productive than American workers; they are not better educated; they do not have access to better technology. They are paid very little by Western standards because they accomplish very little by Western standards. If foreign companies are forced to raise wages significantly, then there is no longer any advantage to having plants in the developing world. Firms will replace workers with machines, or they will move someplace where higher productivity justifies higher wages. *If sweatshops paid decent wages by Western standards, they would not exist.* There is nothing pretty about people willing to work long hours in bad conditions for several dollars a day, but let's not confuse cause and effect. Sweatshops do not cause low wages in poor countries; rather, they pay low wages because those countries offer workers so few other alternatives. Protesters might as well hurl rocks and bottles at hospitals because so many sick people are suffering there.

Nor does it make sense that we can make sweatshop workers better off by refusing to buy the products that they make. Industrialization, however primitive, sets in motion a process that can make poor countries richer. Mr. Kristof and Ms. WuDunn arrived in Asia in the 1980s. "Like most Westerners, we arrived in the region outraged at sweatshops," they recalled fourteen years later. "In time, though, we came to accept the view supported by most Asians: that the campaign against sweatshops risks harming the very people it is intended to help. For beneath their grime, sweatshops are a clear sign of the industrial revolution that is beginning to reshape Asia." After describing the horrific conditions— workers denied bathroom breaks, exposed to dangerous chemicals, forced to work seven days a week—they conclude, "Asian workers would be aghast at the idea of American consumers boycotting certain toys or clothing in protest. The simplest way to help the poorest Asians would be to buy more from sweatshops, not less."[18]

You're not convinced? Paul Krugman offers a sad example of good intentions gone awry:

> In 1993, child workers in Bangladesh were found to be producing cloth-ing for Wal-Mart and Senator Tom Harkin proposed legislation ban-ning imports from countries employing underage workers. The direct result was that Bangladeshi textile factories stopped employing chil-dren. But did the children go back to school? Did they return to happy homes? Not according to Oxfam, which found that the displaced child

workers ended up in even worse jobs, or on the streets—and that a significant number were forced into prostitution.[19]

Oops.

Preferences change with income, particularly with regard to the environment. Poor people care about different things than rich people do. By global standards, poor does not mean settling for a Ford Fiesta when you really wanted the BMW. Poor is watching your children die of malaria because you could not afford a $5 mosquito net. For much of the world, $5 is five days of income. By those same standards, anyone reading this book is rich. The fastest way to end any meaningful discussion of globalization is to wave the environment card. But let's do a simple exercise to illustrate why it may be terribly wrong to impose our environmental preferences on the rest of the world. Here is the task: Ask four friends to name the world's most pressing environmental problem.

It's a fair bet that at least two of them will say global warming and none will mention clean water. *Yet inadequate access to safe drinking water— a problem easily cured by rising living standards—kills two million people a year and makes another half billion seriously ill.* Is global warming a serious problem? Yes. Would it be your primary concern if children in your town routinely died from diarrhea? No. The first fallacy related to trade and the environment is that poor countries should be held to the same environmental standards as the developed world. (The debate over workplace safety is nearly identical.) Producing things causes waste. I remember the first day of an environmental economics course when visiting professor Paul Portney, head of Resources for the Future, pointed out that the very act of staying alive requires that we produce waste. The challenge is to weigh the benefits of what we produce against the costs of producing it, including pollution. Someone living comfortably in Manhattan may view those costs and benefits differently from someone living on the brink of starvation in rural Nepal. Thus, trade decisions that affect the environment in Nepal ought to be made in Nepal, recognizing that environmental problems that cross political boundaries will be settled the same way they always are, which is through multilateral agreements and organizations.

The notion that economic development is inherently bad for the environment may be wrong anyway. In the short run, just about any economic activity generates waste. If we produce more, we will pollute more. Yet it is also true that as we get richer, we pay more attention to the environment. Here is another quiz. In what year did air quality in London (the city for which we have the best long-term pollution data) reach its worst level ever? To make it easier, let's narrow the choices: 1890; 1920; 1975; 2001. The answer is 1890. Indeed, the city's current air quality is better than at any time since 1585. (There is nothing particularly "clean" about cooking over an open fire.) Environmental quality is a luxury good in the technical sense of the word, which means that we place more value on it as we get richer. Therein lies one of the powerful benefits of globalization: Trade makes countries richer; richer countries care more about environmental quality and have more resources at their disposal to deal with pollution. Economists reckon that many kinds of pollution rise as a country gets richer (when every family buys a motorcycle) and then fall in the later stages of development (when we ban leaded gasoline and require more efficient engines).

Critics of trade have alleged that allowing individual countries to make their own environmental decisions will lead to a "race to the bottom" in which poor countries compete for business by despoiling their environments. It hasn't happened. The World Bank recently concluded after six years of study, "Pollution havens—developing countries that provide a permanent home to dirty industries—have failed to materialize. Instead, poorer nations and communities are acting to reduce pollution because they have decided that the benefits of abatement outweigh the costs."[20]

Poverty is a bitch. The principal of a high school near Chicago's Robert Taylor housing projects once told me that when I was writing a story on urban education. He was talking about the challenges of teaching kids who had grown up poor and deprived. He might as well have been talking about the state of the world. Many parts of the world—places we rarely think about, let alone visit—are desperately poor. We ought to make them richer; economics tells us that trade is an important way to do it. Paul Krugman has nicely summarized the anxiety over globalization with an old French saying: Anyone who is not a socialist before he is thirty has no heart; anyone who is still a socialist after he is thirty has no head. He writes:

> If you buy a product made in a third-world country, it was produced by workers who are paid incredibly little by Western standards and probably work under awful conditions. Anyone who is not bothered by those facts, at least some of the time, has no heart. But that doesn't mean the demonstrators are right. On the contrary, anyone who thinks that the answer to world poverty is simple outrage against global trade has no head—or chooses not to use it. The anti-globalization movement already has a remarkable track record of hurting the very people and causes it claims to champion.[21]

The trend toward more global trade is often described as an unstoppable force. It is not. We've been down this road before, only to have the world trading system torn apart by war and politics. One of the most rapid periods of globalization took place during the end of the nineteenth century and the beginning of the twentieth. John Micklethwait and Adrian Wooldridge, authors' of *A Future Perfect*, have noted, "Look back 100 years and you discover a world that by many economic measures was more global than it is today: where you could travel without a passport, where the gold standard was an international currency, and where technology (cars, trains, ships, and telephones) was making the world enormously smaller." Alas, they point out, "That grand illusion was shot to pieces on the playing fields of the Somme."[22]

Political boundaries still matter. Governments can slam the door on globalization, as they have before. That would be a shame for rich countries and poor countries alike.

CHAPTER 12

Development Economics:
The wealth and poverty of nations

L et us briefly contemplate the life of Nashon Zimba, a twenty-five-year-old man who lives with his wife and baby daughter in Malawi. There is no question that Mr. Zimba is a hardworking man. He built his own home, as *The Economist* describes:

> He digs up mud, shapes it into cuboids and then dries it in the sun to make bricks. He mixes his own cement, also from mud. He cuts branches to make beams, and thatches the roof with sisal or grass. His only industrial input is the metal blade on his axe. Working on his own, while at the same time growing food for his family, Mr. Zimba has erected a house that is dark, cramped, cold in the winter, steamy in summer and has running water only when tropical storms come through the roof.[1]

For all that work, Mr. Zimba is a poor man. His cash income in 2000 was roughly $40. He is hardly alone. Malawian GDP per capita is less than $200. The nation's entire annual economic output is $2 billion—or roughly an eighth the size of Vermont's economy. Lest anyone naively believe that there is something pleasantly simple about this existence, it should be pointed out that 30 percent of young children in Malawi are malnourished; more than two of every ten children will die before they reach their fifth birthday.

According to the UN's Food and Agriculture Organization, there are over 800 million people in the world who don't get enough to eat. The vast majority are in the developing world; roughly half are in India and China. How is that possible? At a time when we can split the atom, land on the moon, and decode the human genome, why do 2.8 billion people, or roughly half the world's population, live on less than $2 a day?[2]

The short answer is that their economies have failed them. At bottom, creating wealth is a process of taking inputs, including human talent, and producing things of value. Poor economies are not organized to do that. In his excellent book on economic development, *The Elusive Quest for Growth*, World Bank economist William Easterly describes a street scene in Lahore, Pakistan:

> People throng the markets in the old city, where the lanes are so narrow that the crowds swallow the car. People buying, people selling, people eating, people cooking. Every street, every lane crammed with shops, each shop crammed with people. This is a private economy with a lot of dynamism.[3]

It is also, he notes, a country that is largely illiterate, ill housed, and ill fed. The Pakistani government has built nuclear weapons but is unable to conduct an immunization program against measles. "Wonderful people," writes Mr. Easterly. "Terrible government." Every country has resources, if only the wits and hard work of the people who inhabit it. Most countries, including some of the poorest nations on earth, have far more resources than that.

Let me get the bad news out of the way: Economists do not have a recipe for making poor countries rich. True, there have been some fabulous success stories, such as the original Asian "tigers"—Hong Kong, Singapore, South Korea, and Taiwan—which saw their economies grow over 8 percent a year for nearly three decades. But we do not have a proven formula for growth that can be rolled out in country after country like some kind of development franchise. Even the tigers stumbled badly during the Asian financial crisis of 1997. On the other hand, we do have a good understanding of what makes rich countries rich. If we can catalog the kinds of policies that functional economies have in common, then we can turn our attention to Nobel laureate Douglass North's common-sense query "Why don't poor countries simply adopt policies that make for plenty?"[4]

The following is a sample of the kinds of policies and, in some cases, lucky geographical endowments that development economists have come to believe make the difference between the wealth and poverty of nations.

Effective government institutions. To grow and prosper, a country needs laws, law enforcement, courts, basic infrastructure, a government capable of collecting taxes—and a healthy respect among the citizenship for each of these things. These kinds of institutions are the tracks on which capitalism runs. They must be reasonably honest. Corruption is not merely an inconvenience, as it is sometimes treated; it is a cancer that misallocate resources, stifles innovation, and discourages foreign investment. While American attitudes toward government range from indifference to hostility, most other countries would love to have it so good, as *New York Times* foreign affairs columnist Tom Friedman has pointed out:

> I took part in a seminar two weeks ago at Nanjing University in China, and I can still hear a young Chinese graduate student pleading for an answer to her question: "How do we get rid of all our corruption?" Do you know what your average Chinese would give to have a capital like Washington today, with its reasonably honest and efficient bureaucracy? Do you know how unusual we are in the world that we don't have to pay off bureaucrats to get the simplest permit issued?[5]

The relationship between government institutions and economic growth prompted a clever and intriguing study. Daron Acemoglu and Simon Johnson, economists at the Massachusetts Institute of Technology, and James Robinson, an economist at the University of California, hypothesized that the economic success of developing countries that were formerly colonized has been affected by the quality of the institutions that their colonizers left behind.[6] The European powers adopted different colonization policies in different parts of the world, depending on how hospitable the area was to settlement. In places where Europeans could settle without serious hardship, such as the United States, the colonizers created institutions that have had a positive and long-lasting effect on economic growth. In places where Europeans could not easily settle because of a high mortality rate from disease, such as the Congo, the colonizers simply focused on taking as much wealth home as quickly as possible, creating what the authors refer to as "extractive states."

The study examined sixty-four ex-colonies and found that as much as three-quarters of the difference in their current wealth can be explained by differences in the quality of their government institutions. In turn, the quality of those government institutions is explained, at least in part, by the original settlement pattern. The legal origin of the colonizers—British, French, Belgian—had little influence (though the British come out looking good because they tended to colonize places more hospitable to settlement).

Basically, good governance matters. The World Bank rated 150 countries on six broad measures of governance, such as accountability, regulatory burden, rule of law, graft (corruption), etc. There was a clear and causal relationship between better governance and better development outcomes, such as higher per capita incomes, lower infant mortality, and higher literacy.[7] We don't have to love the Internal Revenue Service, but we ought to at least offer it some grudging respect.

Property rights. Private property may seem like a province of the rich; in fact, it can have a crucial impact on the poor. The developed world is full of examples of informal property rights—homes or businesses built on land that is communal or owned by the government and ignored (such as the shantytowns on the outskirts of many large cities). Families and entrepreneurs make significant investments in their "properties." But there is a crucial difference between those assets and their counterparts in the developed world: The owners have no legal title to the property. They cannot legally rent it, subdivide it, sell it, or pass it on to family. Perhaps most important, they cannot use it as collateral to raise capital.

Peruvian economist Hernando de Soto has argued convincingly that these kinds of informal property arrangements should not be ignored. He reckons that the total value of property held but not legally owned by poor people in the developing world is worth more than $9 trillion. That is a lot of collateral gone to waste, or "dead capital" as he calls it. To put that number in perspective, it is ninety-three times the amount of development assistance that the rich countries provided to the developing world over the past three decades.

The Economist tells a story of a Malawian couple who make a living slaughtering goats. Since business is good, they would like to expand. To do so, however, would require an investment of $250—or $50 more than the average annual income in Malawi. This couple "owns" a home worth more than that. Might they borrow against the value of their land and the bungalow they have built on it? No. The home is built on "customary" land that has no formal title. The couple has a contract signed by the local village chief, but it is not enforceable in a court of law. *The Economist* goes on to note:

> About two-thirds of the land in Malawi is owned this way. People usually till the land their parents tilled. If there is a dispute about boundaries, the village chief adjudicates. If a family offends gravely against the rules of the tribe, the chief can take their land away and give it to someone else.[8]

Those informal property rights are like barter—they work fine in a simple agrarian society, but are woefully inadequate for a more complex economy. It is bad enough that poor countries are poor; it is all the worse that their most valuable assets are rendered less productive than they might be.

No excessive regulation. Government has plenty to do—and even more that it should not do. Markets must do the heavy lifting. Let's talk about articles 575 and 615 of the Russian civil code. These regulations would be very important if you were a firm in Moscow doing something as simple as installing a vending machine. Article 575 forbids firms from giving anything away free; that includes the space that a firm "gives" to

Coca-Cola when a vending machine is installed. Meanwhile, article 615 forbids subletting property without the landlord's consent; the square meter taken up by the vending machine can be construed as a sublease. Meanwhile, the tax collector forbids commercial enterprises (e.g., vending machines) to operate without a cash register. And since selling soft drinks from a machine constitutes retail trade, there are assorted fire, health, and safety inspections.[9]

Excessive regulation goes hand in glove with corruption. Government bureaucrats throw up hurdles so that they can extort bribes from those who seek to get over or around them. Installing a vending machine in Moscow becomes much easier if you hire the right "security firm." What about opening a business elsewhere in the developed world? Again, Peruvian economist Hernando de Soto has done fascinating work. He and fellow team members documented their efforts to open a one-person clothing stall on the outskirts of Lima as a legally registered business. He and his researchers vowed that they would not pay bribes so that their efforts would reflect the full cost of complying with the law. (In the end, they were asked for bribes on ten occasions and paid them twice to prevent the project from stalling completely.) The team worked six hours a day for forty-two weeks in order to get eleven different permits from seven different government bodies. Their efforts, not including the time, cost $1,231, or thirty-one times the monthly minimum wage in Peru— all to open a one-person shop.[10]

Chapter 4 outlined all the reasons government should stick to the basics. Harvard economist Robert Barro's classic study of economic growth in roughly one hundred countries over three decades found that government consumption—total government spending excluding education and defense—was negatively correlated with per capita GDP growth. He concluded that such spending (and the required taxation) is not likely to increase productivity and will therefore do more harm than good. The Asian tigers, the all-star team in the economic development league, made their economic ascent with government spending in the range of 20 percent of GDP. Elsewhere in the world, high tax rates that are applied unevenly distort the economy and provide opportunities for graft and corruption. Many poor governments might actually collect more revenue if they implemented taxes that were low, simple, and easy to collect.

Human capital. Human capital is what makes individuals productive, and productivity is what determines our standard of living. As University of Chicago economist and Nobel laureate Gary Becker has pointed out, all countries that have had persistent growth in income have also had large increases in the education and training of their labor forces. (We have strong reasons to believe that the education causes the growth, not the other way around.) He has written, "These so-called Asian tigers grew rapidly by relying on a well-trained, educated, hard-working, and conscientious labor force."[11]

In poor countries, human capital does all the good things we would expect, and then some. Education can improve public health (which is, in turn, a form of human capital). Some of the most pernicious public health problems in the developing world have relatively simple fixes (boiling water, digging latrines, using condoms, etc.). Higher rates of education for women in developing countries are associated with lower rates of infant mortality. Meanwhile, human capital facilitates the adoption of superior technologies from developed countries. One cause for optimism in the development field has always been that poor countries should, in theory, be able to narrow the gap with richer nations by borrowing their innovations. Once a technology is invented, it can be shared with poor countries at virtually no cost. The people of Ghana need not invent the personal computer in order to benefit from its existence; they do need to know how to use it.

Now for more bad news. In Chapter 6, I described an economy in which skilled workers generate economic growth by creating new jobs or doing old jobs better. Skills are what matter—for individuals and for the economy as a whole. That is still true, but there is a glitch when we get to the developing world: Skilled workers usually need other skilled workers in order to succeed. Someone who is trained as a heart surgeon can succeed only if there are well-equipped hospitals, trained nurses, firms that sell drugs and medical supplies, and a population with sufficient resources to pay for heart surgery. Poor countries can become caught in a human capital trap; if there are few skilled workers, then there is less incentive for others to invest in acquiring skills. Those who do become skilled find that their talents are more valuable in a region or country with a higher proportion of skilled workers, creating the familiar "brain drain." As World Bank economist William Easterly has written, the result can be a vicious circle: "If a nation starts out skilled, it gets more skilled. If it starts out unskilled, it stays unskilled."[12]

As a side note, this phenomenon is relevant in rural America, too. Not long ago, I wrote a story for *The Economist* that we referred to internally as "The Incredible Shrinking Iowa."[13] As the working title would suggest, parts of Iowa, and other large swathes of the rural Midwest, are losing population relative to the rest of the country. Remarkably, forty-four of Iowa's ninety-nine counties had fewer people in 2000 than they had in 1900. Part of that depopulation stems from rising farm productivity; Iowa's farmers have literally grown themselves out of jobs. But something else is going on, too. Economists have found that individuals with similar skills and experience can earn significantly higher wages in urban areas than they can elsewhere. Why? One plausible explanation is that specialized skills are more valuable in metropolitan areas where there is a density of other workers with complementary skills. (Think Silicon Valley.)

Rural America has a mild case of something that deeply afflicts the developing world. Unlike technology or infrastructure or pharmaceuticals, we cannot export huge quantities of human capital to poor countries. We cannot airlift ten thousand university degrees to a small African nation. Yet as long as individuals in poor countries face limited opportunities, they will have a diminished incentive to invest in human capital.

How does a country break out of the trap? Remember that question when we come to the importance of trade.

Geography. Here is a remarkable figure: Only two of thirty countries classified by the World Bank as rich—Hong Kong and Singapore—lie between the Tropic of Cancer (which runs through Mexico across North Africa and through India) and the Tropic of Capricorn (which runs through Brazil and across the northern tip of South Africa and through

Australia). Geography may be a windfall that we in the developed world take for granted. Development expert Jeffrey Sachs has written a recent paper in which he posits that climate can explain much of the world's income distribution. He writes, "Given the varied political, economic, and social histories of regions around the world, it must be more than coincidence that almost all of the tropics remain underdeveloped at the start of the twenty-first century."[14] The United States and all of Europe lie outside the tropics; most of Central and South America, Africa, and Southeast Asia lie within.

Tropical weather is wonderful for vacation; why is it so bad for everything else? The answer, according to Mr. Sachs, is that high temperatures and heavy rainfall are bad for food production and conducive to the spread of disease. As a result, two of the major advances in rich countries, better food production and better health, cannot be replicated in the tropics. Why don't the residents of Chicago suffer from malaria? Because cold winters control mosquitoes—not because scientists have beaten the disease. So in the tropics, we find yet another poverty trap; most of the population is stuck in low-productivity farming. Their crops—and therefore their lives—are unlikely to get better in the face of poor soil, unreliable rainfall, and chronic pests.

Obviously countries cannot pick up and move to more favorable climates. Mr. Sachs proposes two solutions. First, we ought to encourage more technological innovation aimed at the unique ecology of the tropics. The sad fact is that scientists, like bank robbers, go where the money is. Pharmaceutical companies earn profits by developing blockbuster drugs for consumers in the developed world. Of the 1,233 new medicines granted patents between 1975 and 1997, only thirteen were for tropical diseases.[15] But even that overstates the attention paid to the region; nine of those drugs came from research done by the U.S. military for the Vietnam War or from research for the livestock and pet market.

How do we make private companies care as much about sleeping sickness (on which no major company is doing research) as they do about canine Alzheimer's (for which Pfizer already has a drug)? Change the incentives. One idea embraced by economists would be for a government or international agency to identify a disease in need of a cure and then offer a bounty to the firm that develops an acceptable treatment. Governments would inherit the patent and distribute the drug cheaply to those who need it. The pharmaceutical company would get what it needs to justify the research: a return on investment.

The other hope is that poor countries in the tropics can step out of the trap of subsistence agriculture by opening their economies to the rest of the world. Mr. Sachs notes, "If the country can escape to higher incomes via non-agricultural sectors (e.g. through a large expansion of manufactured exports), the burdens of the tropics can be lifted."[16] Which brings us once again to our old friend trade.

Openness to trade. We've had a whole chapter on the theoretical bene-fits of trade. Suffice it to say that those lessons have been lost on governments in many poor countries in recent decades. The fallacious logic of protectionism is alluring—the idea that keeping out foreign goods will make the country richer. Strategies such as "self-sufficiency" and "state leadership" were hallmarks of the postcolonial regimes, such as India and much of Africa. Trade barriers would "incubate" domestic industries so that they could grow strong enough to face international competition. Economics tells us that companies shielded from competition do not grow stronger; they grow fat and lazy. Politics tells us that once an industry is incubated, it will always be incubated. The result, in the words of one economist, has been a "largely self-imposed economic exile."[17]

At great cost, it turns out. The preponderance of evidence suggests that open economies grow faster than closed economies. In one of the most influential studies, Jeffrey Sachs and Andrew Warner, both researchers at Harvard's Center of International Development, compared the economic performance of closed economies, as defined by high tariffs and other restrictions on trade, to the performance of open economies. Among poor countries, the closed economies grew at .7 percent per capita annually during the 1970s and 1980s while the open economies grew at 4.5 percent annually. Most interesting, when a previously closed economy opened up, growth increased by more than a percentage point a year. To be fair, some prominent economists have taken issue with the study on the grounds (among other quibbles) that economies closed to trade often have a lot of other problems, too. Is it the lack of trade that makes these countries grow slowly, or is it general macroeconomic dysfunction? For that matter, does trade cause growth or is it something that just happens while economies are growing for other reasons? After all, the number of televisions sold rises sharply during extended spells of economic growth, but watching television does not make countries richer.

Conveniently for us, a recent paper in the *American Economic Review*, one of the most respected journals in the field, is entitled "Does Trade Cause Growth?" Yes, the authors answer. All else equal, countries that trade more have higher per capita incomes.[18] Jeffrey Frankel and David Romer, economists at Harvard and UC Berkeley respectively, conclude, "Our results bolster the case for the importance of trade and trade-promoting policies."

Researchers have plenty left to quibble about. That is what researchers do. In the meantime, we have strong theoretical reasons to believe that trade makes countries better off and solid empirical evidence that trade is one thing that has separated winners from losers in recent decades. The rich countries must do their part, too. Jeffrey Sachs, one of the leading thinkers in the development field, has called for a "New Compact for Africa." He writes, "The current pattern of rich countries—to provide financial aid to tropical Africa while blocking Africa's chances to export textiles, footwear, leather goods, and other labor-intensive products—may be worse than cynical. It may in fact fundamentally undermine Africa's chances for economic development."[19]

Responsible fiscal and monetary policy. Governments, like individuals, will get themselves in serious trouble if they consistently overspend on things that do not raise future productivity. At a minimum, large budget deficits require the government to borrow heavily, which takes capital out of the hands of private borrowers, who are likely to use it more efficiently. Chronic deficit spending can also signal other future problems: higher taxes (to pay back the debt), inflation (to erode the value of the debt), or even default (just giving up on the debt).

All of these problems are compounded if the government has borrowed heavily from abroad to finance its profligate spending. If foreign investors lose confidence and decide to take their money and go home—as skittish global investors are wont to do—then the capital that was financing the deficit dries up. In short, the music stops. The government is left on the brink of default, which we have seen in countries ranging from Mexico to Turkey.

On the monetary side, Chapter 10 made clear the dangers of letting the party get out of control. It happens often anyway. Argentina is the poster child for irresponsible monetary policy; from 1960 to 1994, the average Argentine inflation rate was 127 percent per year. To put that in perspective, an Argentine investor who had the equivalent $1 billion in savings in 1960 and kept all of it in Argentine pesos until 1994 would have been left with the equivalent spending power of one-thirteenth of a penny. World Bank economist William Easterly has noted, "Trying to have normal growth during high inflation is like trying to win an Olympic sprint hopping on one leg."

A digression on exchange rates. We need to make a short detour in order to understand yet one more way in which developing countries can mess themselves up. When countries begin trading with one another, currencies must be exchanged at some rate. If the American dollar is just a piece of paper, and the Japanese yen is just a piece of paper, too, then how much American paper should we swap for Japanese paper? All of this was much simpler in the days of the gold standard. Countries pegged their currencies to a fixed quantity of gold and therefore, implicitly, to each other. (It's like one of those third-grade word problems: If an ounce of gold is worth $35 in America and 350 francs in France, what is the exchange rate between the dollar and the franc?) The gold standard is history, and now the business of exchange rates is vastly more complicated. We do have a logical starting point, however. A Japanese yen has value because it can be used to purchase things; a dollar has value for the same reason. So, in theory, we ought to be willing to exchange $1 for however many yen would be required to purchase roughly the same amount of stuff. If some bundle of everyday goods costs $25 in the United States, and the same bundle of goods costs 350 rubles in Russia, then we would expect $25 to be worth roughly 350 rubles (and $1 should be worth roughly 14 rubles). This is the theory of purchasing power parity, or PPP.

Here is the twist: In the short run, exchange rates can deviate quite sharply from what PPP would predict. For our purposes, that makes two things important. First, governments have at least some control over their exchange rate; and second, that exchange rate can have a profound effect on the economy. Let's deal with the second point first. Imagine checking into your favorite hotel in Paris, only to discover that the rooms are nearly twice as expensive as they were when you last visited. When you protest to the manager, he replies that the room rates have not changed in several years. And he's telling the truth. What has changed is the exchange rate between the euro and the dollar. The dollar has "weakened" or "depreciated" against the euro, meaning that each of your dollars buys fewer euros than it did the last time you were in France. (The euro, on the other hand, has "appreciated.") To you, that makes the hotel more expensive. To someone visiting Paris from elsewhere in France, the hotel is the same price as it has always been. A change in the exchange rate can make foreign goods cheaper or more expensive, depending on the direction of the change.

That is the crucial point here. If the U.S. dollar is weak, meaning that it can be exchanged for fewer yen or euros than normal, then foreign goods become more expensive. What is true for the Paris hotel is also true for Gucci handbags and Toyota cars. But there is a flipside here: American goods start to look less expensive to the rest of the world. Suppose Ford decides to price the Taurus at $25,000 in the United States and at the local currency equivalent in other markets around the world. If the euro has grown stronger relative to the dollar, meaning that every euro buys more dollars than it used to, then the Taurus becomes cheaper for Parisian car buyers—and Ford still brings home $25,000. The good news for Ford does not end there. A weak dollar makes imports more expensive for Americans. At home, the sticker price jumps on every Toyota and Mercedes, making Fords cheaper by comparison. (Or Toyota and Mercedes can hold their prices down and take lower profits back to Japan and Germany.) Either way, Ford gets a competitive boost.

In general, a weak currency is good for exporters and punishing for importers. In 1992, when the dollar was relatively weak, a *New York Times* story began, "The declining dollar has turned the world's wealthiest economy into the Filene's basement of industrial countries."[20] A strong dollar has the opposite effect. In 2001, when the dollar was strong by historical standards, a *Wall Street Journal* headline proclaimed, "G.M. Official Says Dollar Is Too Strong for U.S. Companies." Stay with me here because exchange rates provide yet one more opportunity for bad governments to derail their economies.

Overvalued currencies. Government policies affect exchange rates. As economists like to put it, the most basic decision is "To float or not to float." "Floating" is just an insider's way of saying that the value of a currency is allowed to go up or down based on market forces. Floating currencies, such as the dollar or the euro or the yen, fluctuate by the second as they are traded on the foreign exchange market. Banks and brokerage houses buy and sell huge quantities of dollars every day at whatever rate is dictated by supply and demand. How many yen is a dollar worth at a given point in time? As many yen as someone is willing to trade for it. As a result, currency prices are volatile; you may well find that your dollars are worth more at the end of your French vacation than they were at the beginning. Swings in exchange rates can complicate life for firms trying to do international business. So far, that has proved to be a drawback of floating rates, though not a fatal flaw.

And then there are countries like Argentina, our inflation bad boy. Argentina is the monetary equivalent of someone who stands you up for three straight dates and then tries to tell you that the fourth time will be different. It won't be, and everyone knows it. So when Argentina finally got serious about fighting inflation, the central bank had to do something radical. It did. Basically, it hired the United States as a chaperon. At the end of 1990, Argentine inflation was more than 1,000 percent a year. In 1991, Argentina declared that it was relinquishing control over its own monetary policy. No more printing money. Instead, the government created a currency board with strict rules to ensure that henceforth every Argentine peso would be worth one U.S. dollar. To make that possible (and credible to the world), the currency board would guarantee that every peso in circulation would be backed by one U.S. dollar held in reserve. Thus, the currency board would be allowed to issue new pesos only if it had new dollars in its vaults to back them up. Moreover, every Argentine peso would be convertible on demand for one dollar. In effect, Argentina created a gold standard with the U.S. dollar as the gold.

It worked for a while. Inflation plummeted to double digits and then to single digits. Alas, there was a huge cost. Remember all those wonderful things Alan Greenspan can do to fine-tune the economy? The Argentine government could not do any of them; it abdicated control over the money supply in the name of fighting inflation. Nor did Argentina have any independent control over its exchange rate; the peso was fixed against the dollar. If the dollar was strong, the peso was strong. If the dollar was weak, the peso was weak.

The lack of control over the money supply and exchange rate ultimately took a steep toll. Beginning in the late 1990s, the Argentine economy slipped into a deep recession; authorities did not have the usual tools to fight it. Indeed, the currency board system makes any slump worse. As investors lose confidence in the economy, they demand dollars for their pesos—just as the government has promised they would be able to do. As the government hands over dollars to jittery investors, its reserves shrink, meaning that the supply of pesos in circulation must shrink as well (since every peso must be backed by a dollar in reserve). In short, the money supply shrinks, driving interest rates higher, exactly when it ought to be growing in order to reduce interest rates and stimulate the economy.

To make matters worse, the U.S. dollar was strong during America's economic boom, making the Argentine peso strong. That punished Argentine exporters and did further harm to the economy. In contrast, Brazil's currency, the real, fell more than 50 percent between 1999 and the end of 2001. To the rest of the world, Brazil had thrown a giant half-price sale and Argentina could do nothing but stand by and watch. As the Argentine economy limped along, economists debated the wisdom of the currency board. The proponents argued that it was an important source of macroeconomic stability; the skeptics said that it would cause more harm than good. In 1995, Maurice Obstfeld and Kenneth Rogoff, economists at Berkeley and Princeton respectively, published a paper warning that most attempts to maintain a fixed exchange rate, such as the Argentine currency board, were likely to end in failure.[21]

Time proved the skeptics right. In December 2001, the long-suffering Argentine economy unraveled completely. Street protests turned violent, the president resigned, and the government announced that it could no longer pay its debts, creating the largest sovereign default in history. (Ironically, Ken Rogoff had by then made his way from Princeton University to the International Monetary Fund, where, as chief economist, he had to deal with the economic wreckage that he had warned against years earlier.) The Argentine government scrapped its currency board and ended the guaranteed one-for-one exchange between the peso and the dollar. The peso immediatel plunged some 30 percent in value relative to the dollar.

The Argentine currency board experiment ended badly. Still, most economists would concede that the plan was conceived with noble intentions. It was a reasonable, if unsuccessful, effort to solve a serious macroeconomic problem—which is more than can be said for the exchange rate policies of many developing countries. The sad fact is that bad people can benefit from bad policies. Such is the case with the "overvalued" exchange rates maintained by corrupt regimes in many poor countries. An overvalued currency is one that is worth far more at the government's official exchange rate than purchasing power parity would suggest. For example, suppose that a can of Coca-Cola costs $1 in America and 50 nairas in Nigeria. We would reckon that the exchange rate is going to be somewhere in the range of $1 = 50 nairas. It is not uncommon, however, for governments to declare that the official exchange rate is something more like $1 = 25 nairas. In other words, the leaders are declaring that the naira is worth about twice as much as we would expect it to be worth based on what it can actually buy. Given a choice between one dollar and 25 nairas, most people would rather have the dollar. After all, a dollar buys one can of Coke while 25 nairas buys only half a can. Indeed, we would expect black market money changers to offer something closer to 50 nairas to the dollar.

But markets—what 50 nairas actually buys—don't matter in this case. The government chooses who gets foreign currency legally and at what exchange rate. In the process, they enrich themselves and crush their export industries. Here is what happens. Suppose a Nigerian exporter sells a product in the United States for $1,000. Based on purchasing power parity, he should be able to swap that $1,000 for roughly 50,000 nairas. Nope. Instead, he is forced by the government to convert the dollars into nairas at the official government exchange rate. Thus, he is paid 25,000 nairas—half of what is really due him. How many businesses can thrive when the government is essentially expropriating a large chunk of revenue? The government, on the other hand, is getting dollars on the cheap. They can use the dollars to buy luxury imports. Or they can sell them on the black market. Corrupt officials get rich buying dollars for 25 nairas and selling them for 50. Any official overvaluation (usually signaled by black market money changers) is a punishing tax on exporters—a tragic policy given the importance of exports in the development process.

Natural resources matter less than you would think. Israel, which has no oil to speak of, is a far richer country than nearly all of its Middle Eastern neighbors that have large petroleum reserves. Israeli GDP per capita is $16,000 compared to $7,000 for Saudi Arabia and $1,650 for Iran. Meanwhile, resource-poor countries like Japan and Switzerland have fared much better than resource-rich Russia.[22] Or consider oil-rich Angola. The country takes in some $3.5 billion a year from its oil industry.[23] What has happened to the people who might benefit from this treasure in the ground? Much of the oil money goes to fund a never-ending civil war that has ravaged the country. Angola has the world's highest rate of citizens maimed by land mines (1 out of 133). One-third of Angola's children die before age five; life expectancy is forty-two. Large swathes of the capital have no electricity, no running water, no sewers, and no garbage pickup.[24]

These are not anecdotal examples carefully picked to make a point. Economists believe that a rich endowment of natural resources may actually be a detriment to development. All else equal, it is great to discover the world's largest zinc deposit. *But all else is not equal.* Commodity-rich countries are changed by the experience in ways that can do more harm than good. One study of economic performance in ninety-seven countries over two decades found that growth was higher in countries that were less endowed with natural resources. Of the top eighteen fastest-growing nations, only two were rich in things that can be taken out of the ground. Why?

Mineral riches change an economy. First, they divert resources away from other industries, such as manufacturing and trade, that can be more beneficial to long-term growth. For example, the Asian tigers were resource-poor; their path to prosperity began with labor-intensive exports and progressed into more technology-intensive exports. The countries grew steadily richer in the process. Second, resource-rich economies become far more vulnerable to wild swings in the price of commodities. A country built on oil will have a rough stretch when the barrel price drops from $30 to $15. Meanwhile, demand for a nation's currency rises as the rest of the world begins to buy its diamonds or bauxite or oil or natural gas. That will cause the currency to appreciate, which, we now know, makes the country's other exports, such as manufactured goods, more expensive.

Economists started referring to the perverse effects of abundant natural resources as "Dutch disease" after observing the economic effects of an enormous North Sea natural gas discovery by the Netherlands in the 1950s. The spike in natural gas exports drove up the value of the Dutch guilder (as the rest of the world demanded more guilders in order to buy Dutch natural gas), making life more difficult for other exporters. The government also used the gas revenues to expand social spending, which raised employers' social security contributions and therefore their production costs. The Dutch had long been a nation of traders, with exports making up more than 50 percent of GDP. By the 1970s, other export industries, the traditional lifeblood of the economy, had grown far less competitive. One business publication noted, "Gas so distended and distorted the workings of the economy that it became a mixed blessing for a trading nation."[25]

Last, and perhaps most important, countries could use the revenues from natural resources to make themselves better off—but they don't. Money that might be spent on public investments with huge returns—education, public health, sanitation, immunizations, infrastructure—is more often squandered. After the World Bank helped to build an oil pipeline that originates in Chad and runs through Cameroon to the ocean, Chad's president, Idriss Déby, used the first $4.5 million installment of oil money to buy weapons for fighting rebels.[26]

Democracy. Does making the trains run on time matter more to the economic growth of poor countries than niceties like freedom of expression and political representation? No; the opposite is true. Democracy is a check against the most egregious economic policies, such as outright expropriation of wealth and property. Amartya Sen, an economist at Trinity College, Cambridge, was awarded the Nobel Prize in Economics in 1998 for several strands of work related to poverty and welfare, one of which is his study of famines. Mr. Sen's major finding is striking: The world's worst famines are not caused by crop failure; they are caused by faulty political systems that prevent the market from correcting itself. Relatively minor agricultural disturbances become catastrophes because imports are not allowed, or prices are not allowed to rise, or farmers are not allowed to grow alternative crops, or politics in some other way interferes with the market's normal ability to correct itself. He writes, "[Famines] have never materialized in any country that is independent, that goes to elections regularly, that has opposition parties to voice criticisms and that permits newspapers to report freely and question the wisdom of government policies without extensive censorship."[27] China had the largest recorded famine in history; thirty million people died as the result of the failed Great Leap Forward in 1958–61. India has not had a famine since independence in 1947.

Economist Robert Barro's seminal study of economic growth in some one hundred countries over many decades found that basic democracy is associated with higher economic growth. More advanced democracies, however, suffer slightly lower rates of growth. Such a finding is consistent with our understanding of how interest groups can promote policies that are not always good for the economy as a whole.

Experts could tick off many other things that matter in the development process: savings and investment rates, fertility rates, ethnic strife, colonial history, cultural factors, etc. All of which raises a question: If we have a decent idea of what constitutes good policy, why is the path out of poverty so steep and treacherous? The answer lies in the difference between describing why Michael Jordan is a great basketball player and actually playing like him. It is one thing to explain what makes rich countries work; it is quite another to develop a strategy for transforming the developing world. Consider one simple example: Building effective government institutions is easier when the population is literate and educated, yet decent public education requires effective government institutions. How do we solve that chicken-and-egg problem?

There is an old joke in development circles that says much about the failed strategies that have gone in and out of favor over the past half century:

> A peasant discovers that many of his chickens are dying, so he seeks advice from a priest. The priest recommends that the peasant say prayers for his chickens, but the chickens continue to die. The priest then recommends music for the chicken coop, but the deaths continue unabated. Pondering again, the priest recommends repainting the chicken coop in bright colors. Finally, all the chickens die. "What a shame," the priest tells the peasant, "I had so many more good ideas."[28]

The institution at the center of the global fight against poverty is the Washington-based World Bank. "The Bank," as it is known, was conceived after World War II at Bretton Woods, New Hampshire, at an international meeting of finance ministers. The goal of the meeting was to create a new international financial architecture. (The first $250 million loan was to France in 1947 for postwar reconstruction.) The Bank, which is owned by its 183 member countries, raises capital from its members and by borrowing in the capital markets. Those funds are loaned to developing nations for projects that are likely to promote economic development.

If the World Bank is the world's welfare agency, then its sister organization, the International Monetary Fund (IMF), is the fire department responsible for dousing international financial crises. The IMF was also conceived at Bretton Woods as a cooperative global institution. Members pay funds into the IMF; in exchange they can borrow in times of difficulty "on condition that they undertake economic reforms to eliminate these difficulties for their own good and that of the entire membership." When a country like Turkey or Argentina admits publicly that a financial crisis is imminent, one of the first calls will be to the IMF. No country is ever required to accept loans or advice from either the IMF or the World Bank. Both organizations derive power and influence from the carrots they wield.

Few institutions have attracted as much criticism as the World Bank and the IMF from such a broad swath of the political spectrum. *The Economist* once commented, "If the developing countries had a dollar for every proposal to change the 'international financial architecture,' the problem of third-world poverty would be solved."[29] Conservatives charge that the Bank and the IMF are bureaucratic organizations that squander money on projects that have failed to lead nations out of poverty. They also argue that IMF bailouts make financial crises more likely in the first place; investors make imprudent international loans because they believe the IMF will come to the rescue when a country gets into trouble. In 2000, the Republican-led Congress convened a commission that recommended shrinking and overhauling both the World Bank and the International Monetary Fund.[30]

At the other end of the political spectrum, the antiglobalization coalition accuses the World Bank and IMF of acting as capitalist lackeys, forcing globalization on the developing world and leaving poor countries saddled with large debts in the process. The organizations' meetings have become an occasion for violent protest. When the two institutions held their fall meeting in Prague in 2000, the local Kentucky Fried Chicken and Pizza Hut both ordered replacement glass ahead of time.

To be fair, the stumbling block to development has not always been bad advice from rich countries. The best ideas are quite simple, yet, as this chapter has pointed out, there are plenty of leaders in the developing world doing the economic equivalent of smoking, eating cheeseburgers, and driving without their seat belts. A study done by the

Harvard Institute for International Development of global growth patterns between 1965 and 1990 found that most of the difference between the huge success of East Asia and the relatively poor performance of South Asia, sub-Saharan Africa, and Latin America can be explained by government policy. In that respect, foreign aid presents the same kind of challenges as any other welfare policy. Poor countries, like poor people, often have very bad habits. Providing support can prolong behavior that needs to be changed. One recent study came to the unsurprising conclusion that foreign aid has a positive effect on growth when good policies are already in place and has little impact on growth when they are not. The authors recommended that aid be predicated on good policy, which would make the aid more effective and provide an incentive for governments to implement better policies.[31] (Similar criteria have been proposed for relieving the debts of heavily indebted poor countries.) Of course, turning our backs on the neediest cases (and denying bailouts to countries in crisis) is easier in theory than it is in practice.

Last, much of the world is poor because the rich countries have not tried very hard to make it otherwise. I realize that pointing out the failure of development aid and then arguing for more of it is like Yogi Berra criticizing a restaurant for having bad food *and* small portions. Still, things become better when there is an overwhelming political will to make them better; at present, solving the problems of the developing world is not a priority among the American public. Here is one example. AIDS is ravaging Africa. A recent study came to the stunning conclusion that 40 percent of adult deaths in South Africa in 2000 were caused by AIDS; the overall death rate for women in their twenties was higher than that for women in their sixties, something that researchers called "a unique phenomenon in biology."[32]

Harvard's Jeffrey Sachs argues that the world's rich countries should undertake a comprehensive program to fight AIDS in Africa. He reckons that America's share of such a program would cost about $10 a person—the price of a movie and popcorn, as he notes.[33] So far, the U.S. contributions to such efforts have been far smaller. Indeed, America's total foreign aid budget comes to one-tenth of 1 percent of GDP—a fraction of what we are capable of and a third of what the Europeans give. Mr. Sachs warned long before September 11 that we ought to invest in the developing world, "not only for humanitarian reasons, but also because even remote countries in turmoil become outposts of disorder for the rest of the world."[34]

Life in 2050:
Seven Questions

conomics can help us to understand and improve an imperfect world. In the end, though, it is just a set of tools. We must decide how to use them. Economics does not foreordain the future any more than the laws of physics made it inevitable that we would explore the moon. Physics made it possible; humans chose to do it—in large part by devoting resources that might have been spent elsewhere. John F. Kennedy did not alter the laws of physics when he declared that the United States would put a man on the moon; he merely set a goal that required good science to get there. Economics is no different. If we are to make the best use of these tools, we ought to think about where we are trying to go. We must decide what our priorities are, what trade-offs we are willing to make, what outcomes we are or are not willing to accept. To paraphrase economic historian and Nobel laureate Robert Fogel, we must first define the "good life" before economics can help us get there. Here are seven questions worth pondering about life in 2050, not for the sake of predicting the future, but because the decisions that we make now will affect how we live then.

How many minutes of work will a loaf of bread cost? It's the productivity question. From a material standpoint, it's pretty much all that matters. Nearly everything else we've discussed—institutions, property rights, investment, human capital—is a means toward this end (and other ends, too). If productivity grows at 1 percent a year over the next half century, our standard of living will be some 60 percent higher by 2050. If productivity grows at 2 percent a year, then our standard of living will nearly triple in the same time frame—assuming we continue to work as hard as we do now. Indeed, that leads to a subquestion that I find more interesting: How rich is rich enough?

Americans are richer than most of the developed world; we also work harder, take less vacation, and retire later. Will that change? There is something in labor economics called the "backward-bending labor supply curve." Thankfully, the idea is simpler and more interesting than the name would suggest. Economic theory predicts that as our wages go up, we will work longer hours—up to a point, and then we will begin to work less. Time becomes more important than money. Economists just aren't quite sure where that curve starts to bend backward, or how sharply it bends.

Productivity growth gives us choices. We can continue to work the same amount while producing more. Or we can produce the same amount by working less. Or we can strike some balance. Assuming Americans continue to grow steadily more productive, will we choose to work sixty hours a week in 2050 and live richly (in a material sense) as a result? Or will there come a time when we decide to work twenty-five hours a week and listen to classical music in the park for the balance? I had dinner not long ago with a portfolio manager for a large investment company who is convinced that Americans are going to wake up one day and decide that they work too hard. Ironically, he was not planning to work less hard himself; he was planning to invest in companies that make leisure goods.

How many people will be sleeping under Wacker Drive? This is the pie-slicing question. In 2000, I was assigned by *The Economist* to write a story on poverty in America. With the economy still booming, I sought some way to express the striking dichotomy between America's rich and poor. I found it right outside the front door of my office building:

A stroll down Wacker Drive, in Chicago, offers an instant snapshot of America's surging economy. Young professionals stride along, barking orders into mobile phones. Shoppers stream towards the smart shops on Michigan Avenue. Construction cranes tower over a massive new luxury condominium building going up on the horizon. All is bustle, glitter and boom.

But there is a less glamorous side to Wacker Drive, literally below the surface. Lower Wacker is the subterranean service road that runs directly beneath its sophisticated sister, allowing delivery trucks to make their way through the bowels of the city. It is also a favourite refuge for the city's homeless, many of whom sleep in cardboard encampments between the cement props. They are out of sight of all that gleams above, and largely out of mind. As Wacker Drive, so America.[1]

What are we willing to promise the most disadvantaged? The market economies of the developed world lie along a continuum, with America at one end and the relatively paternalistic European economies, such as France and Sweden, at the other. Europe offers the kinder, gentler version of a market economy—at some cost. In general, the European nations are more protective of workers and have a more substantial safety net. Generous benefits are mandated by law; health care is a birthright. This leads to a more compassionate society in many ways. European poverty rates, particularly for children, are far lower than those in the United States. Income inequality is lower, too.

It also leads to higher unemployment and a slower rate of innovation and job creation. Workers, bundled with lots of mandatory benefits, are expensive. Since employees cannot be fired easily, firms are slow to hire them in the first place. Meanwhile, generous unemployment and welfare benefits make workers slower to take jobs that might be offered. The result is what economists refer to as a "sclerotic" labor market. In recent years, European unemployment rates have been roughly twice as high as the American rate.

The American system is a richer, more dynamic, more entrepreneurial economy—and harsher and more unequal. It is conducive to creating a big pie in which the winners get huge slices. The European system is better at guaranteeing at least some pie for everybody. Capitalism comes in all kinds of flavors. Which one will we choose?

Will we use the market in imaginative ways to solve social problems? The easiest and most effective way to get something done is to give the people involved a reason to want it done. We all nod, as if this were the most obvious point in the world—and then we go out and design policies that do just the opposite. We have an entire public school system that does not reward teachers and principals when their students do well (or punish them when their students do poorly). We make it artificially cheap to travel by car, implicitly subsidizing everything from urban sprawl to global warming. We assess most of our taxes on productive activity, like work, savings, and investment, when we might raise revenue and conserve resources with more "green taxes."

If we get the incentives right, we can use markets to do all kinds of things. Consider the case of rare diseases. However bad it is to have a serious illness, it is worse to have a serious illness that is also rare. At one point, there were some five thousand diseases considered so rare that drug companies ignored them because they had no hope of recovering their research costs even if they found a cure.[2] In 1983, Congress passed the Orphan Drug Act, which provided incentives to make such work more profitable: research grants, tax credits, and exclusive rights to market and price drugs for rare diseases—so-called orphan drugs—for seven years. In the decade before the act, fewer than ten orphan drugs came to market. Since the act, roughly two hundred such drugs have come to market.

Or think about emissions trading, which is a powerful tool for dealing with global warming. The program works by putting a cap on the total emission of some pollutant, say CO_2, and then assigning companies (or even entire countries) a share of that total. Companies (or countries) that emit less than their quota can sell the balance on the emissions market. Companies that exceed their quota must go to that market to buy the right to emit more. Companies that conserve get a payoff. Indeed, the more they conserve (and the more cheaply they can find ways to do it), the more they get paid. Meanwhile, companies that pollute excessively suffer a comparative disadvantage; buying the right to emit beyond their quota becomes part of the cost of doing business.

Markets don't solve social problems on their own (or else they wouldn't be social problems). But if we design solutions with the proper incentives, it feels a lot more like rowing downstream.

Will we have strip malls in 2050? Nothing says that we must accept what the market tosses us. *New York Times* columnist Anthony Lewis recently paid homage to the beauty of Italy's Tuscany and Umbria regions: "The silvery olive groves, the fields of sunflowers, the vineyards, the stone houses and barns." He lamented that such small farms are not economical in a world of corporate agriculture but should be preserved anyway. He wrote, "Italy is evidence that there is more to life—a civilized life—than the unregulated competition of the market. There are values of humanity, culture, beauty, community that may require deviations from the cold logic of market theory."[3] There is nothing in economics that says he's wrong. We may well collectively decide that we would like to protect a way of life, or something that is aesthetically pleasing, even if it means higher taxes, more expensive food, or less economic growth. To an economist, and to Mr. Lewis, life is about maximizing utility, not income. Sometimes utility means preserving an olive grove or an old vineyard—just because we like the way it looks. As we grow wealthier, we are often more willing to put aesthetics above the pocketbook.

That point comes with several heavy doses of caution. First, we must always make explicit the costs of fiddling with markets, whatever those costs may be. Second, we should take care that these costs fall most heavily on those who enjoy the benefits. Last and most important, we should make sure that one group (such as those of us who think that strip malls are hideously ugly) does not use the political and regulatory process to impose its aesthetic preferences on another group (those who own strip malls and the people who enjoy cheap and convenient shopping there). That said, there is nothing to stop us from dreaming of a world without strip malls.

Will the federal government still be regulating the amount of pepperoni on a frozen pizza? The U.S. Department of Agriculture (USDA) currently requires every frozen meat pizza to contain at least 10 percent meat. That means approximately twenty slices of pepperoni on a twelve-inch pizza. (The USDA is considering a change that would reduce the required amount of meat by 40 percent—eight fewer pepperoni slices.)[4] Regulating pepperoni is stupid, but this question is not really about frozen pizza. It is about what government should and should not be doing. Economics can move us beyond the inane debate over "big government" versus "small government." Government has as much to do as ever—if not necessarily in the realm of frozen pizzas. The world is growing ever more complex and interdependent; our institutions must keep pace. What keeps world leaders awake at night: Global warming? Drugs? Terrorism? Trade? Financial crises? None of these problems can be addressed without government; *indeed, none can be managed successfully without cooperation among governments.*

Both extremes of the political spectrum have their heads in the sand on this one. The political right lives in perpetual fear of "world government." The political left sees a capitalist conspiracy in most international institutions. Governments aren't perfect; neither are international institutions. They're still necessary and will become even more so.

Do we really have monetary policy figured out? The Japanese economy, one of the largest and most productive in the world, has been stagnant for more than a decade. The Nikkei Index, Japan's equivalent of the S&P 500, is no higher today than it was in the late 1980s. This should give us pause. In the wake of September 11, *New York Times* economics columnist Paul Krugman wrote:

> I wish I could say with confidence that Japan's dismal experience is of no relevance to the United States. And certainly our nations are very different in many ways. But there is a distinct resemblance between what happened to Japan a decade ago and what was happening to the United States economy just a few weeks ago. Indeed, Japan's story reads all too much like a morality play designed for our edification.[5]

We have not conquered the business cycle (the economic ebb and flow that leads to periodic recessions). At best, we have tamed it. In the fifty years before the Great Depression, the economy was in recession roughly half the time. Since then, it has been in recession less than 20 percent of the time.[6] We have gained a better understanding of both fiscal and monetary policy; the economic ride has been smoother as a result.

Still, there is plenty to be humble about. Even now, we do not fully understand the Great Depression. How is it that a mature and productive economy could grind into reverse, erasing some 30 percent of our productive capacity and putting one in four Americans out of work? The Japanese economy—that miracle of the 1980s—remains stubbornly resistant to traditional monetary and fiscal fixes, prompting what the *Wall Street Journal* has called "one of the great economic debates of the age."[7] Could something similar happen here? Maybe.

In fifty years, will "African tigers" refer to wildlife or to development success stories? Here is an exercise: Find a young child, say age eight or nine, and try to explain to him or her why much of the world lives comfortably, even luxuriously, while millions of people elsewhere on the planet are starving to death and billions more are barely getting by. At some point, the explanation just starts to feel inadequate. Clearly we do not have a silver bullet for economic development. We don't have one for cancer either, but we haven't given up. Will the world be significantly less poor in 2050? That answer is not obvious. We can imagine an East Asian scenario, where countries transform themselves in a matter of decades. Or we can imagine a sub-Saharan Africa scenario, where countries stumble from decade to decade without any significant economic growth at all. One scenario will lift billions of people out of poverty and misery; the other won't.

When we ask whether poor countries will still be poor a half century from now, the question seems distant and abstract, almost as if the answer will be determined by some future alignment of the stars. But when we break that question into its component parts—when we ask about the things that we know will distinguish rich countries from poor countries—then global poverty seems more tractable. Will governments in developing countries create and sustain the kinds of institutions that support a market economy? Will they develop export industries that enable them to break out of the trap of subsistence agriculture—and will the U.S. open its huge market to those products? Will the rich countries use their technology and resources to fight the diseases that are ravaging the developing world, especially AIDS? Will the family of a baby girl born tomorrow in rural India have an incentive to invest in her human capital?

Those are just my questions. My hope is that by now you have more of your own. The remarkable thing about economics is that once you've been exposed to the big ideas, they begin to show up everywhere. The sad irony of Econ 101 is that students too often suffer through dull, esoteric lectures while economics is going on all around them. Economics offers insight into wealth, poverty, gender relations, the environment, discrimination, politics—just to name a few of the things we've touched upon. How could that possibly not be interesting?

Notes

Introduction

1. Thomas Friedman, "Senseless in Seattle," *New York Times*, December 1, 1999.
2. Claudia Goldin and Cecilia Rouse, "Orchestrating Impartiality: The Impact of 'Blind' Auditions on Female Musicians," *American Economic Review*, September 2000.

CHAPTER 1. THE POWER OF MARKETS

1. M. Douglas Ivester, Remarks to the Economic Club of Chicago, February 25, 1999.
2. Peter Passell. "Spending It: Every Second Counts Even More," *New York Times*, June 28, 1998, p. C9.
3. Stephen Moore and Julian Simon, *The Greatest Century That Ever Was: 25 Miraculous Trends of the Past 100 Years,* Cato Institute Policy Analysis, No. 364 (Washington, D.C.: Cato Institute, December 15, 1999).
4. Michael Grossman, "Health Economics," *NBER Reporter*, Winter 1998/99.
5. "America Then and Now: It's All in the Numbers," *New York Times*, December 31, 2000.
6. "Relieving O'Hare," *The Economist*, January 10, 1998.
7. June 21, 2001, p. A1.
8. Jaime Sneider, "Good Propaganda, Bad Economics," *New York Times*, May 16, 2000, p. A31.

CHAPTER 2. INCENTIVES MATTER

1. Costa Rican Embassy, Washington, D.C.
2. Ian Fisher, "Victims of War: The Jungle Gorillas, and Tourism," *New York Times*, March 31, 1999.
3. Daniel Yergin and Joseph Stanislaw, *The Commanding Heights* (New York: Simon & Schuster, 1998), pp. 216–17.
4. "Paying Teachers More," *The Economist*, August 24, 2000.
5. David Stout, "Child Safety Seats to Be Required for Commercial Planes," *New York Times*, December 16, 1999, p. A20.
6. Julia Preston, "Mexico's Political Inversion: The City That Can't Fix the Air," *New York Times*, February 4, 1996, Sect. 4, p. 4.
7. Ibid.
8. Donald C. Hambrick and Eric M. Jackson, "Outside Directors with a Stake: The Linchpin in Improving Governance," *California Management Review*, Summer 2000.
9. John Tierney, "A Tale of Two Fisheries," *New York Times Magazine*, August 27, 2000, p. 38.
10. Dirk Johnson, "Leaving the Farm for the Other Real World," *New York Times*, November 7, 1999, p. 3.
11. Virginia Postrel, "The U.S. Tax System Is Discouraging Married Women from Working," *New York Times*, November 2, 2000, p. C2.
12. Friedrich Schneider and Dominik H. Enste, "Shadow Economies: Size, Causes, and Consequences," *Journal of Economic Literature*, March 2000.

CHAPTER 3. GOVERNMENT AND THE ECONOMY

1. Donald G. McNeil, Jr., "A Fouled City Puts Its Foot Down, but Carefully," *New York Times*, November 9, 1999.
2. "Mum's the Word," *The Economist*, December 5, 1998.
3. "Czechs Puff Away to the Benefit of State Coffers," United Press International, July 17, 2001.
4. Robert Frank, "Feeling Crash-Resistant in an SUV," *New York Times*, May 16, 2000.
5. Keith Bradsher, "For the Megagrowth Family, Daimler to Offer a Bigger-Than-SUV," *New York Times*, February 21, 2001.
6. "Here's Hoping: A Survey of Nigeria," *The Economist*, January 15, 2000.
7. Blaine Harden, "Angolan Paradox: Oil Wealth Only Adds to Misery," *New York Times*, April 9, 2000.
8. Barbara Crossette, "U.N. Says Bad Government Is Often the Cause of Poverty," *New York Times*, April 5, 2000, p. A11.

9. John G. Fernald, "Roads to Prosperity? Assessing the Link Between Public Capital and Productivity," *American Economics Review*, vol. 89, no. 3 (June 1999), pp. 619–38.

10. Jerry L. Jordan, "How to Keep Growing 'New Economies,'" *Economic Commentary*, Federal Reserve Bank of Cleveland, August 15, 2000.

11. Barry Bearak, "In India, the Wheels of Justice Hardly Move," *New York Times*, June 1, 2000.

12. Thomas L. Friedman, "I Love D.C.," *New York Times*, November 7, 2000, p. A29.

13. Amartya Sen, *Development as Freedom* (New York: Alfred A. Knopf, 1999).

CHAPTER 4. GOVERNMENT AND THE ECONOMY II

1. John Markoff, "CIA Tries Foray into Capitalism," *New York Times*, September 29, 1999.

2. March 6, 2001.

3. Milton Friedman, *Capitalism and Freedom* (Chicago: University of Chicago Press, 1982).

4. Celia W. Dugger, "A Cruel Choice in New Delhi: Jobs vs. a Safer Environment," *New York Times*, November 24, 2000.

5. "A Useful Poison," *The Economist*, December 14, 2000.

6. Gary Becker and Guity Nashat Becker, *The Economics of Life* (New York: McGraw Hill, 1996).

7. Simeon Djankov, Rafael La Porta, Florencio Lopez-de-Silanes, and Andrei Shleifer, *The Regulation of Entry*, NBER Working Paper No. W7892 (National Bureau of Economic Research, September 2000).

8. Nicholas Lemann, "The Quiet Man: How Dick Cheney Rose to Power," *The New Yorker*, May 7, 2001.

9. Rebecca M. Blank, "Fighting Poverty: Lessons from Recent U.S. History," *Journal of Economic Perspectives*, vol. 14, no. 2 (Spring 2000).

10. Jerry L. Jordan, "How to Keep Growing 'New Economies,'" *Economic Commentary*, Federal Reserve Bank of Cleveland, August 15, 2000.

CHAPTER 5. ECONOMICS OF INFORMATION

1. Gary Becker, *The Economics of Discrimination* (Chicago: University of Chicago Press, 1971).

2. "Testing Times," *The Economist*, October 19, 2000.

3. "Outsourcing: Separate and Lift," *The Economist*, September 20, 1997.

4. Alan B. Krueger, "Children Smart Enough to Get into Elite Schools May Not Need to Bother," *New York Times*, April 27, 2000, p. C2.

5. All of the racial profiling examples come from a provocative article on the subject: Jeffrey Goldberg, "The Color of Suspicion," *New York Times Magazine*, June 20, 1999.

CHAPTER 6. PRODUCTIVITY AND HUMAN CAPITAL

1. Brier Dudley, "Gates Wants to Expand Mega-House," *Seattle Times*, February 28, 2001.
2. "The Rich Get Richer: A Survey of India's Economy," *The Economist*, June 2, 2001.
3. Evelyn Nieves, "Homeless Defy Cities' Drives to Move Them," *New York Times*, December 7, 1999.
4. "From Boots to Electronics: Shutting Military Bases," *The Economist*, June 21, 1997.
5. T. Paul Schultz, "Health and Schooling Investments in Africa," *Journal of Economic Perspectives*, vol. 13, no. 3 (Summer 1999), pp. 67–88.
6. Gary Becker, "Economic Evidence on the Value of Education," Remarks to executives of the Lotus Development Corporation, January 1999.
7. Gary S. Becker, Ryerson Lecture at the University of Chicago, as reprinted in Becker, *Human Capital* (Chicago: University of Chicago Press, 1993), p. 21.
8. Ibid., p. 23.
9. "Does Inequality Matter?" *The Economist*, June 16, 2001.
10. Ibid.
11. Dora Costa, "The Wage and the Length of the Work Day: From the 1890s to 1991," *Journal of Labor Economics*, January 2000.
12. All of the income inequality information, including the H. L. Mencken quotations, comes from Robert H. Frank, "Why Living in a Rich Society Makes Us Feel Poor," *New York Times Magazine*, October 15, 2000.
13. Philippe Aghion, Eve Caroli, and Cecilia Garcia-Penalosa, "Inequality and Economic Growth: The Perspective of the New Growth Theories," *Journal of Economic Literature*, vol. 37 (December 1999), pp. 1615–60.
14. Marvin Zonis, Remarks Presented at the University of Chicago Business Forecast Luncheon, December 6, 2000.

CHAPTER 7. FINANCIAL MARKETS

1. Johanna Berkman, "Harvard's Hoard," *New York Times Magazine*, June 24, 2001.
2. "Aon Profiting—So Far—from Customer Worry over Missing Big Mac," *Crain's Chicago Business*, July 31, 2000.
3. Joseph Treaster, "Even Nature Can Be Turned into a Security; High Yield and Big Risk with Catastrophe Bonds," *New York Times*, August 6, 1997.

4. Peter Coy, "Can You Really Beat the Market?" *BusinessWeek*, May 31, 1999.
5. Ruth Simon, "Bonds Let You Sleep at Night but at a Price," *Wall Street Journal*, September 8, 1998.

CHAPTER 8. THE POWER OF ORGANIZED INTERESTS

1. Robert Davis, "Museum Garage Is a Fine Cut; It May Be Pork, but City Hungry," *Chicago Tribune*, May 5, 1994.
2. Lizette Alvarez and David Barboza, "Support for Corn-Based Fuel Despite Critics," *New York Times*, July 23, 2001.
3. Nicholas Kristof, "Ethanol, for All Its Critics, Fuels Farmer Support and Iowa's Role in Presidential Races," *New York Times*, January 21, 2000.
4. Roger Ferguson Jr., "Economic Policy for Our Era: The Ohio Experience," *Economic Commentary*, Federal Reserve Bank of Cleveland, May 15, 2000.
5. Joe Klein, "Eight Years: Bill Clinton Looks Back on His Presidency," *The New Yorker*, October 16, 2000, p. 201.
6. Elizabeth Kolbert, "Back to School," *The New Yorker*, March 5, 2001.

CHAPTER 9. KEEPING SCORE

1. Michael Cox and Richard Alm, *Time Well Spent: The Declining Real Cost of Living in America*, Federal Reserve Bank of Dallas, 1997 Annual Report.
2. Oded Galor and David N. Weil, "Population, Technology, and Growth: From Malthusian Stagnation to the Demographic Transition and Beyond," *American Economic Review*, vol. 20, no. 4 (September 2000).
3. Miriam Jordan, "Brazil's Age-Old Endemic," *Wall Street Journal*, August 20, 2001.
4. David Leonhardt, "If Richer Isn't Happier, What Is?" *New York Times*, May 19, 2001.
5. Alexander Stille, "A Happiness Index with a Long Reach: Beyond GNP to Subtler Measures," *New York Times*, May 20, 2000, p. A17.
6. David Gonzalez, "A Coffee Crisis' Devastating Domino Effect in Nicaragua," *New York Times*, August 29, 2001.
7. Bruce Bartlett, "What Tax Cuts Can't Do," *New York Times*, December 20, 2000.
8. "What a Peculiar Cycle," *The Economist*, March 10, 2001.
9. James W. Paulsen, *Economic and Market Perspective*, Wells Capital Management, October 1999.
10. Jagadeesh Gokhale, "Are We Saving Enough?" *Economic Commentary*, Federal Reserve Bank of Cleveland, July 2000.
11. Danny Hakim, "Investors Seek a Refuge, and Experts Do, Too," *New York Times*, September 23, 2001.

CHAPTER 10. THE FEDERAL RESERVE

1. R.A. Mundell, "A Reconsideration of the Twentieth Century," *American Economic Review*, vol. 90, no. 3 (June 2000), pp. 327–40.
2. David Berreby, "All About Currency Printers: The Companies That Make Money from Making Money," *New York Times*, August 23, 1992.
3. Paul Krugman, "Fear Itself," *New York Times Magazine*, September 30, 2001.
4. Stephanie Strom, "Deflation Shackles Japan, Blocking Hope of Recovery," *New York Times*, March 12, 2001.
5. N. Gregory Mankiw, *Principles of Economics* (Fort Worth, Tex.: Dryden Press, 1998), p. 606.

CHAPTER 11. TRADE AND GLOBALIZATION

1. Paul Krugman, "The Magic Mountain," *New York Times*, January 23, 2001.
2. Charles Wheelan, "Fast Food, Balinese Style," *Valley News*, January 25, 1989, p. 18.
3. "The Battle in Seattle," *The Economist*, November 27, 1999.
4. "Economic Nationalism: Bashing Foreigners in Iowa," *The Economist*, September 21, 1991.
5. Mary E. Burfisher, Sherman Robinson, and Karen Thierfelder, "The Impact of NAFTA on the United States," *Journal of Economic Perspectives*, vol. 15, no. 1 (Winter 2001).
6. Dan Barry, "A Mill Closes, and a Hamlet Fades to Black," *New York Times*, February 16, 2001.
7. Marvin Zonis, "Globalization," *National Strategy Forum Review: Strategic Outlook 2001*, National Strategy Forum, Spring 2001.
8. David Cortright and George A. Lopez, eds., *The Sanctions Decade: Assessing UN Strategies in the 1990s* (Boulder, Colo.: Lynne Rienner, 2000).
9. Anthony DePalma and Simon Romero, "Orange Juice Tariff Hinders Trade Pact for U.S. and Brazil," *New York Times*, April 24, 2000, p. A1.
10. "UN Chief Blames Rich Nations for Failure of Trade Talks," *New York Times*, February 13, 2000, p. 12.
11. Thomas Friedman, "Protesting for Whom?" *New York Times*, April 24, 2001.
12. Nicholas D. Kristof and Sheryl WuDunn, "Two Cheers for Sweatshops," *New York Times Magazine*, September 24, 2000, pp. 70–71.
13. Thomas Friedman, "Parsing the Protests," *New York Times*, April 14, 2000, p. 31.
14. Zonis, "Globalization."
15. "Web Sites Provide Opportunity for Artisans Around the World to Sell Their Wares Thus Increasing Living Standards," National Public Radio, September 11, 2000.
16. Kristof and WuDunn, "Two Cheers for Sweatshops."
17. "A Survey of Globalization," *The Economist*, September 29, 2001.

18. Kristof and WuDunn, "Two Cheers for Sweatshops."
19. Paul Krugman, "Hearts and Heads," *New York Times*, April 22, 2001.
20. "Economic Man, Cleaner Planet," *The Economist*, September 29, 2001.
21. Krugman, "Hearts and Heads."
22. John Micklethwait and Adrian Wooldridge, "Why the Globalization Backlash Is Stupid," *Foreign Policy*, September/October 2001.

CHAPTER 12. DEVELOPMENT ECONOMICS

1. "No Title," *The Economist*, March 31, 2001.
2. *World Development Report 2000/2001: Attacking Poverty*, World Bank (New York: Oxford University Press, 2000).
3. William Easterly, *The Elusive Quest for Growth* (Cambridge, Mass.: MIT Press, 2001), p. 285.
4. *World Development Report 2002: Building Institutions for Markets*, World Bank Oxford University Press, p. 3.
5. Thomas L. Friedman, "I Love D.C.," *New York Times*, November 7, 2000, p. A29.
6. Daron Acemoglu, Simon Johnson, and James Robinson, *The Colonial Origins of Comparative Development: An Empirical Investigation*, NBER Working Paper No. W7771 (National Bureau of Economic Research, June 2000).
7. Daniel Kaufmann, Aart Kraay, and Pablo Zoido-Lobatón, *Governance Matters* (Washington, D.C.: World Bank, October 1999).
8. "No Title," *The Economist*, March 31, 2001.
9. "A Coke and a Frown," *The Economist*, October 7, 2000, p. 73.
10. "No Title," *The Economist*, March 31, 2001.
11. Gary S. Becker, *Human Capital*, p. 24.
12. Easterly, p. 160.
13. "Fare Thee Well, Iowa," *The Economist*, August 18, 2001.
14. Jeffrey Sachs, *Tropical Underdevelopment*, NBER Working Paper No. W8119 (National Bureau of Economic Research, February 2001).
15. Donald G. McNeil, "Drug Companies and Third World: A Case Study in Neglect," *New York Times*, May 21, 2000.
16. Jeffrey Sachs, "Nature, Nurture, and Growth," *The Economist*, June 14, 1997.
17. Jeffrey Sachs, "Growth in Africa: It Can Be Done," *The Economist*, June 29, 1996.
18. Jeffrey A. Frankel and David Romer, "Does Trade Cause Growth?" *American Economic Review*, vol. 89, no. 3 (June 1999), pp. 379–99.
19. Sachs, "Growth in Africa."
20. Sylvia Nasar, "Weak Dollar Makes U.S. World's Bargain Bazaar," *New York Times*, September 28, 1992.
21. Maurice Obstfeld and Kenneth Rogoff, "The Mirage of Fixed Exchange Rates," *Journal of Economic Perspectives*, vol. 9, no. 4 (Fall 1995), pp. 73–96.

22. Jeffrey D. Sachs and Andrew M. Warner, "The Big Push: Natural Resource Booms and Growth," *Journal of Development Economics*, June 1999, as cited in *Economic Intuition*, Montreal, Fall 1999.

23. "Tracking Angola's Oil Money," *The Economist*, January 15, 2000, p. 48.

24. Blaine Harden, "Angolan Paradox: Oil Wealth Only Adds to Misery," *New York Times*, April 9, 2000.

25. "Open to the Winds: A Nation of Traders," *The Economist*, September 12, 1987.

26. Norimitsu Onishi and Neela Banerjee, "Chad's Wait for Its Oil Riches May Be Long," *New York Times*, May 16, 2001.

27. Amartya Sen, *Development as Freedom* (New York: Alfred A. Knopf, 1999), p. 152.

28. Jeffrey Sachs, "Growth in Africa: It Can Be Done," *The Economist*, June 29, 1996.

29. "Reforming the Sisters," *The Economist*, February 15, 2001.

30. Joseph Kahn, "Report Seeks Big Changes in IMF and World Bank," *New York Times*, March 8, 2000.

31. Craig Burnside and David Dollar, "Aid, Policies, and Growth," *American Economic Review*, vol. 90, no. 4 (September 2000), pp. 847–68.

32. Rachel L. Swarns, "Study Says AIDS Is Now Chief Cause of Death in South Africa," *New York Times*, October 17, 2001.

33. Jeffrey Sachs, "The Best Possible Investment in Africa," *New York Times*, February 10, 2001.

34. "What's Good for the Poor Is Good for America," *The Economist*, July 14, 2001.

EPILOGUE. LIFE IN 2050

1. "Out of Sight, Out of Mind," *The Economist*, May 18, 2001.

2. Denise Grady, "In Quest to Cure Rare Diseases, Some Get Left Out," *New York Times*, November 16, 1999.

3. Anthony Lewis, "A Civilized Society," *New York Times*, September 8, 2001.

4. Lucio Guerrero, "The Meaty Issue: What Should Be on a Frozen Pizza," *Chicago Sun-Times*, November 8, 2001.

5. Paul Krugman, "Fear Itself," *New York Times Magazine*, September 30, 2001.

6. James W. Paulson, *Economic and Market Perspective*, Wells Capital Management, October 1999.

7. Phred Dvorak, " A Puzzle for Japan: Rock-Bottom Rates, but Few Borrowers," *Wall Street Journal*, October 25, 2001.

Index